'Soederberg should be thanked for revealing the elephant in the room – that corporations, along with their governance, power, ownership and management, are profoundly political, yet undemocratic. Through careful analysis, wide-ranging research and elegant writing she deconstructs comforting myths and shows us the true and unsettling politics and impacts of corporations in the world today. A must read – and also a good read – for anyone seeking true understanding of current economic, social and environmental upheavals.'

Joel Bakan, *Professor of Law, University of British Columbia, Canada, and author/filmmaker of* The Corporation

'In a capitalism deep into its second major crisis in 75 years, Soederberg's book is very welcome. It critically examines the real (as opposed to the ideologically glossed) mechanisms enabling the crisis-producing decisions of corporate boards of directors. She performs a valuable deconstruction of the mythologies of mainstream "corporate governance" literature.'

Richard D. Wolff, *Professor Emeritus of Economics, University of Massachusetts, Amherst and New School University*

'This book presents a much-needed and powerful critique of the "corporate governance doctrine" that was promoted both by the US state and by dominant capitalist interests in many societies to underpin the priority given to "shareholder value", to take advantage of workers' pension funds, and to direct labour and social movement challenges to corporate decisions into what Soederberg appropriately calls the "marketization of resistance". As empirically rich as it is theoretically strong, this is another important contribution by one of the most creative political economy scholars writing today.'

Leo Panitch, *Canada Research Chair in Comparative Political Economy and Distinguished Research Professor of Political Science, York University, Toronto*

Corporate Power and Ownership in Contemporary Capitalism

Despite the influence corporations wield over all aspects of everyday life, there has been a remarkable absence of critical inquiry into the social constitution of this power. In analysing the complex relationship between corporate power and the widespread phenomenon of share ownership, this book seeks to map and define the nature of resistance and domination in contemporary capitalism.

Drawing on a Marxist-informed framework, this book reconnects the social constitution of corporate power and changing forms of shareholder activism. In contrast to other texts that deal with corporate governance, this study examines a diverse and comprehensive set of themes, from socially responsible investing to labour-led shareholder activism and its limitations. Through this ambitious and critical study, author Susanne Soederberg demonstrates how the corporate governance doctrine represents an inherent feature of neoliberal rule, effectively disembedding and depoliticizing relations of domination and resistance from the wider power and paradoxes of capitalism.

Examining corporate governance and shareholder activism in a number of different contexts that include the United States and the global South, this important book will be of interest to students and scholars of international political economy, international relations and development studies. It will also be of relevance to a wider range of disciplines including finance, economics, and business and management studies.

Susanne Soederberg is a Canada Research Chair in Global Political Economy and an Associate Professor in the Departments of Global Development Studies and Political Studies at Queen's University, Canada. She is author of *The Politics of the New International Financial Architecture: Reimposing Neoliberal Domination in the Global South* (2004) and *Global Governance in Question: Empire, Class, and the New Common Sense in Managing North–South Relations* (2006).

RIPE series in global political economy

This series, published in association with the *Review of International Political Economy*, provides a forum for current and interdisciplinary debates in international political economy. The series aims to advance understanding of the key issues in the global political economy, and to present innovative analyses of emerging topics. The titles in the series focus on three broad themes:

* the structures, processes and actors of contemporary global transformations
* the changing forms taken by governance, at scales from the local and everyday to the global and systemic
* the inseparability of economic from political, social and cultural questions, including resistance, dissent and social movements.

The series comprises two strands:

The *RIPE Series in Global Political Economy* aims to address the needs of students and teachers, and the titles will be published in hardback and paperback. Titles include

The Industrial Vagina
The political economy of the global
sex trade
Sheila Jeffreys

Capital as Power
A study of order and creorder
Jonathan Nitzan and Shimshon Bichler

**The Global Political Economy
of Intellectual Property Rights,
Second Edition**
The new enclosures
Christopher May

**Corporate Power and Ownership in
Contemporary Capitalism**
The politics of resistance and
domination
Susanne Soederberg

Routledge/RIPE Studies in Global Political Economy is a forum for innovative
new research intended for a high-level specialist readership, and the titles will be
available in hardback only. Titles include:

* *Also available in paperback*

Corporate Power and Ownership in Contemporary Capitalism

The politics of resistance and domination

Susanne Soederberg

Routledge
Taylor & Francis Group

LONDON AND NEW YORK

First published 2010
by Routledge
2 Park Square, Milton Park, Abingdon, Oxon OX14 4RN

Simultaneously published in the USA and Canada
by Routledge
270 Madison Ave, New York, NY 10016

Routledge is an imprint of the Taylor & Francis Group, an informa business

© 2010 Susanne Soederberg

Typeset in Times New Roman by Wearset Ltd, Boldon, Tyne and Wear

British Library Cataloguing in Publication Data
A catalogue record for this book is available from the British Library

Library of Congress Cataloging in Publication Data
Soederberg, Susanne, 1966-
Corporate power and ownership in contemporary capitalism: the politics
of resistance and domination/Susanne Soederberg.
p. cm. – (RIPE series in global political economy)
Includes bibliographical references and index.
1. Corporate governance. 2. Corporations–Social aspects. 3. Stock
ownership–Social aspects. I. Title.
HD2741.S645 2009
338.6–dc22

2009008288

ISBN10: 0-415-46787-X (hbk)
ISBN10: 0-415-46788-8 (pbk)
ISBN10: 0-203-87169-3 (ebk)

ISBN13: 978-0-415-46787-2 (hbk)
ISBN13: 978-0-415-46788-9 (pbk)
ISBN13: 978-0-203-87169-0 (ebk)

To Sydney and Teivo

Contents

Illustrations

Figure

Tables

Acknowledgements

I would like to thank the many individuals who have helped – both indirectly and directly – in forging and clarifying my ideas and arguments in this book. I am particularly grateful to Ryan Foster and Erica Spink D'Souza for their excellent research assistance and to Victoria Henderson for her meticulous editorial skills. I am also indebted to the numerous individuals working in the corporate governance and socially responsible investing industry, as well as non-governmental organizations, pension funds and government officials in the US, Malaysia and the Philippines, who I have interviewed over the past several years. I would also like to acknowledge the generous financial support of the Social Sciences and Humanities Research Council of Canada and the Chancellor's Research Award at Queen's University.

I have developed the themes and questions examined in this book over the past several years. The book was put on hold twice due to two very welcome distractions – the birth of my daughter in June 2006 and my son in November 2007. My partner, Marcus Taylor, provided, as always, unwavering emotional and intellectual support and much needed humour during the demanding and difficult phases of early parenting.

Modified versions of Chapters 3 and 6 have appeared as the following articles, and I thank the publishers for their permission to reprint modified versions in this book: 'Deconstructing the Official Treatment for "Enronitis": The Sarbanes–Oxley Act and the Neoliberal Governance of Corporate America.' *Critical Sociology*, Vol. 34 (5), 2008, pp. 657–680; 'Socially Responsible Investing and the development agenda: Peering behind the veil of non-financial benchmarking.' *Third World Quarterly*, Vol. 28 (7), 2007, pp. 1219–1237; 'Socially Responsible Investing as a "New Conditionality"? Neoliberalism and the Case of CalPERS' Permissible Country Index.' *New Political Economy*, Vol. 12 (4), 2007, pp. 477–497; and 'Freedom, Ownership, and Social (In-)Security in the United States: Expanding Opportunities or Re-constructing Dependency?,' *Cultural Critique*, No. 65 (Fall), 2007, pp. 92 114. The author would also like to gratefully acknowledge the following for permission to reproduce copyright material: The Conference Board for Table 4.1; *Pensions & Investments* for data used in Table 5.1; Cornell University Press for data used in Table 5.2; the World Bank for the information appearing in Figure 6.1, and Wilshire Consulting for Table 6.1.

Susanne Soederberg, Kingston, Canada, January 2009

Abbreviations

AARP	American Association of Retired Persons
ABS	asset backed security
ADR	American depository receipts
AFL-CIO	American Federation of Labor and Congress of Industrial Organizations
AFSCME	American Federation of State, County, and Municipal Employees
AI	Amnesty International
AIG	American International Group Inc.
BR	Business Roundtable (US)
CalPERS	California Public Employee Retirement System
CBPP	Centre on Budget and Policy Priorities
CCSR	Corporation Committee on Shareholder Responsibility
CDOs	collateralized debt obligations
CEO	Chief Executive Officer
CII	Council of Institutional Investors
CIO	Chief Information Officer
DB plans	defined-benefit pension plans
DC plans	defined-contribution pension plans
EMH	efficient market hypothesis
ERISA	Employee Retirement Income Security Act
ESG	environmental, social and corporate governance
ETIs	economically targeted investments
FDI	foreign direct investment
HMC	Harvard Management Company
ICCR	Interfaith Centre for Corporate Responsibility
IFC	International Finance Corporation
IFIs	International Financial Institutions
ILO	International Labour Organization
IMF	International Monetary Fund
IRAs	Individual Retirement Accounts
IRRC	Investor Responsibility Research Centre
ISS	Institutional Shareholder Services
MCA	Millennium Challenge Account

NIFA	New International Financial Architecture
NYCERS	New York City Employees' Retirement System
NYSE	New York Stock Exchange
OECD	Organization for Economic Co-operation and Development
PBGC	Pension Benefit Guarantee Corporation
PCAOB	Public Company Accounting Oversight Board
PCI	Permissible Country Index
PSLRA	Private Securities Litigation Reform Act
SAPs	Structural Adjustment Programmes
SDTF	Sudan Divestment Task Force
SEC	Securities and Exchange Commission
SGRs	Second Generation Reforms
SIF	Social Investment Forum
SOX	Sarbanes–Oxley Act
SRI	socially responsible investment
SSA	Social Security Act
UNPRI	United Nations Principles for Responsible Investment
US	United States
WTO	World Trade Organization

Part I
Introduction

1 Repoliticizing corporate power and ownership in contemporary capitalism

Two spectacular, yet under-theorized, phenomena define the global economy over the past several decades: the first is the tremendous power that corporations wield over all aspects of everyday life; the second is the dramatic, albeit highly uneven, rise of mass ownership of these corporate behemoths. No longer the exclusive domain of family dynasties, tycoons and the super-rich, stock ownership in publicly traded corporations[1] has become increasingly widespread and dispersed (Blumberg, 1975). A key vehicle driving mass ownership has been the growing role of institutional investors, especially pension funds, in global financial markets. Take, for example, the pension market of countries in the Organization for Economic Co-operation and Development (OECD), which registered a staggering $24.6 trillion in 2006. Over half of this amount (66.1 per cent) was invested in two asset classes: company stocks; and government and corporate bonds (OECD, 2007). The increasing role of pension funds in corporations (both financial and non-financial) has meant that 'Main Street' savers have become increasingly dependent on, and therefore vigilant regarding, Wall Street (Clowes, 2000; Minns, 2001; Blackburn, 2002, 2006). Since the 1980s, pension funds have been actively attempting to influence company behaviour. Until now, the politics of resistance and domination vis-à-vis corporations have not been conceptualized as part and parcel of the power, paradoxes and struggles linked to the uneven and exploitative nature of capitalist society. This book attempts to reconnect these elements by mapping and analysing, on the one hand, the social constitution of corporate power in contemporary capitalism; and, on the other, the changing forms of, and limits to, shareholder activism.

Mainstream approaches, which have dominated the corporate governance literature, have opted to examine and explain shareholder activism in terms of a level playing field. Such perspectives are premised on the notion that key actors, such as management, creditors, the board of executives and so forth, are not only able to effectively express their concerns and discontent, but also to challenge certain practices and policies (e.g. excessive executive pay packages, discrimination policies, environmental disclosure, and a vast array of labour standards and human rights issues) pursued by corporate management. Seen from this perspective, resistance to corporate power is expressed in terms of shareholder activism, which takes the form of proxy voting, dialogue with management and, more rarely, divestment (Brancato, 1997; Monks and Minow, 2001; Tkac, 2006; see also Chapter 7). Resistance is framed by, and thereby limited to, a structured and sanitized exchange between those who own (shareholders or 'principals') and those who control (management and the board of directors or 'agents'). Moreover, the extent and content of the interaction between shareholders and management is legally prescribed by the rules of government bodies such as the Securities and Exchange Commission (SEC) in the United States (US). The main venue in which these allegedly democratic exchanges take place is corporate governance. While there is no consensus on the meaning of corporate governance, the dominant definition, used by practitioners and scholars alike, is rooted in economic discipline and based on agency theory (Fama, 1980). The primary concern of the latter is to align the interests of agents to ensure the company is run in an efficient and transparent manner so that it may deliver the highest possible returns for shareholders, i.e. the 'maximization of shareholder value' (Shleifer and Vishny, 1997; Jensen, 2000; Monks and Minow, 2001).

Since its emergence in the 1980s, corporate governance has assumed an almost cult-like status among scholars and practitioners. It stands both as the unity of institutions, processes and practices that shape the way shareholders, directors and management interrelate within the corporation, and as a framework for conceptualizing and legitimating these relationships. The most 'marketized' version of good corporate governance is the Anglo-American model, which accords primacy to shareholder activism and financial markets, among other things, and which has been heralded as one of the key pillars of a well-functioning and vibrant economy (Soederberg, 2004). Corporate governance has been the official treatment to perceived economic weaknesses ranging from the East Asian crisis and the subsequent construction of the New International Financial Architecture (NIFA) in 1999 (Chapter 6), to the Enron-style debacles of the early 2000s (Chapter 3). Because of its role and impact on the academic and policymaking circles and, more importantly, the everyday lives of people – with or without financial property – across the globe, I believe it is vital to challenge the idea of corporate governance as a given. We need to interrogate its political, social and ideological significance and meaning in the same way we have subjected other concepts that have entered and dominated our lexicon to rigorous appraisal and critique, such as globalization and global governance. The main objective of this study is to question and deconstruct the hegemonic position of corporate governance theory and practice so that its capitalist nature, paradoxes and relations of power may be exposed, scrutinized and, thereby, repoliticized.

Despite the attempt to couple mainstream corporate governance theories with plurality, democracy and the empowerment of shareholders, the fact remains that even the most active of shareholders – American institutional investors – have had a modest impact on management and management decisions over the past three decades. As I discuss later in the book, recent legal rulings have sought to either maintain or scale-back the formal powers of shareholders vis-à-vis management and the board of directors (see Chapters 3 and 4). This is not to suggest that there have not been important successes of shareholder activism over the past several decades. To the contrary, I believe activist owners have played, and continue to play, an important role in holding corporate power in check; indeed, several chapters of this book are devoted to exploring, albeit critically, the nature of shareholder activism. My point of contention, however, is that this form of resistance is limited and weakened within the corporate governance framework and its overriding goal of profit maximization (Glasbeek, 2002).

Mainstream approaches to corporate governance tend to explain away the impotence of shareholders to effectively and meaningfully influence the way in which corporations operate by suggesting it is a result of either the short-termism of the financial markets or weak corporate governance strategies (see Chapter 5). According to critical legal scholar Paddy Ireland, one of the main obstacles in identifying and explaining the relations of power and the politics of domination and resistance within the corporate governance framework is that it rests on neo-classical ideology about the nature of the markets. This view tends to flatten hierarchy and smooth over the paradoxical and exploitative elements within corporations, suggesting that corporations lack any built-in structure of authority and power (Ireland, 2001). In addition, corporate governance tends to ignore or gloss over issues of social justice by reducing and limiting shareholder activism to the tensions between agents and principals, as described in agency theory. Put another way, the framework of corporate governance transfigures political contestation by recasting the *form* of the struggle in terms of agents and principals and by refocusing the *content* of contestation around agent–principal realignment, thereby re-emphasizing the ultimate and singular motive of profit maximization.

Seen from the above angle, the hegemonic position of corporate governance in both the academy and policymaking circles – what I refer to as the 'corporate governance doctrine' – is constructed and reproduced by the US state and dominant interests in capitalist society. The danger of the corporate governance doctrine is that it depoliticizes power relations central to the workings of the corporation and obscures its impact on the wider social environment. Depoliticization of resistance occurs in at least two ways when framed within the bounds of corporate governance. On the one hand, resistance to current practices is recast in exclusionary terms of shareholder activism, i.e. those who do not directly own enough shares in a corporation cannot contest its policies, power or behaviour. On the other hand, resistance is subjected to a process of marketization, by which it is reduced to financial code and economic law. This tends to shift, and thus depoliticize, contestation of corporate power to the realm of the market, constructing what I term the 'marketization of resistance'. This is evident in the realm of socially responsible investment (SRI), where struggles for social justice in the areas of the environment, labour standards and human rights have been subsumed under dominant discourse to a risk or hazard that can be resolved only through, for example, cost-efficiency calculus and risk management strategies (see Chapters 6 and 7).

The remainder of this chapter has been organized into four sections. The first locates the present study within the wider literature. The second provides a stylized and mainstream account of the primary issues surrounding the corporate governance doctrine, as well as its origins. The third summarizes several premises that run through each chapter in the book and act as the analytical backbone of my main thesis. The fourth and final section lays out the structure of the book.

Situating the study

There have been significant contributions to the critical study of corporate governance, mass investment and corporate power across several disciplines, including: economic geography, critical legal scholarship, economic sociology and international political economy. However, these four areas of research have been subject to minimal cross-fertilization, which has resulted in a need for work that: (1) explores historically and comparatively the rise and impact of pension funds; (2) examines corporate power in the era of globalization; and (3) offers a critical approach to corporate governance. The literature has also remained silent on the capitalist nature of resistance and domination vis-à-vis corporate power in the mass investment culture. By 'capitalist nature' I am referring to the viewpoint that sees all social, political, economic and ideological phenomena shaped by, and in turn influence, the contradictions, dynamics and relations of power of capital accumulation. I elaborate on this in more detail below. For now, we look at each of the three relevant areas of study in turn.

First, there have been several influential and meticulous studies from a variety of ideological and disciplinary backgrounds that have examined and analysed comparatively the historical role and impact of pension funds with regard to global financial markets (Clowes, 2000; Minns, 2001; Blackburn, 2002; Clark, 2003). The studies have provided major contributions to the way in which we understand power relations and policy decisions affecting pension plans, corporations and the wider financial system, largely within the context of advanced industrialized countries in Western Europe and Anglo-American countries. This scholarship has been complemented by an impressive body of literature concerned with a rigorous and critical examination of the cultural dimensions of pension savings and investments in everyday life (e.g. narratives and performativity), and the important linkages between 'Main Street' and Wall Street, or what these scholars refer to as 'financialization' (Martin, 2002; Clark *et al.*, 2004; de Goede, 2004; Krippner, 2005; Aitken, 2007; Langley, 2008; Erturk *et al.*, 2008; Montgomerie, 2008).

Despite the insights offered by this rigorous research on pension plans and financialization, however, the debates have either under-represented or neglected three important areas of contemporary capitalism. First, the literature has neither explored within the wider context of capitalism the uneven power relations between pension funds and the corporations in which their assets are invested, nor has it engaged with the technical and economic assumptions of the corporate governance doctrine. Second, the scholarship on pension funds and financialization has largely neglected the impact of these institutional investors with regard to the global South. As noted earlier, US institutional investors have played a central role in global financial markets, including global development finance. It is critical, therefore, as part of our broader inquiry into the dynamics of corporate power, to explore how the geo-political power of ownership in the US affects the global South, both in terms of questions of development (Chapter 6) and social justice campaigns under the rubric of SRI (Chapter 7). Third, it is also essential to stress the role of the neoliberal state, not simply in policy formulation, but as a chief feature of, and perpetrator in, the creation and legitimation of market-rule over all aspects of life, including the privatization of pension savings and sanctioning of voluntary self-regulation norms, which presently guide the accumulation activities of financial markets and corporations in the US and elsewhere.

The second research area is comprised of critical, yet popular, investigations into corporate power. Naomi Klein (2000, 2007), David C. Korten (2001) and Joel Bakan (2004) have provided razor-sharp and prescient analyses of the global nature of corporate power that have reached and affected a wide and diverse audience. Curiously, aside from a few notable exceptions, the academic literature has not followed suit. Scholars have failed to deliver critical theorizations on the nature of, and limits to, contestation of pension funds and other institutional investors vis-à-vis corporations (Scott, 1997). There has also been virtual silence on the nature and dynamics of corporate power in neoliberal-led capitalism (Sklair, 2001; Parkinson *et al.*, 2001; Carroll, 2006). This neglect in the academic literature is extremely puzzling, as the past several decades have seen the rise and extension of corporate power over all areas of social and environmental life. Scholars, however, have chosen to focus largely on corporate activities in the era of globalization, ranging from production strategies (Gereffi and Korzeniewicz, 1993) and investment relations (Stopford *et al.*, 1991), to cultural features of advertising (Mazzarella, 2003), consumption patterns (Fine, 2002) or how voluntary, global standards should guide corporate behaviour in the areas of labour standards, the environment and human rights (Ruggie, 2004). The related area of global economic governance has explored the tensions and complementarities between public authority and private forms of governance represented by the involvement of corporations in international trade agreements (e.g. Cutler, 2003, 2006). While these approaches to the role of the corporation in globalization have provided important insights into the way in which corporate behemoths engage with and shape policy and processes, the discussions fail to tackle the underlying capitalist nature of the modern corporation and its connection to institutional investors, who, through various forms of shareholder activism, have not only sought to contest but also represent important features of corporate power.

The third research area that relates to the subject matter of the book is critical approaches to corporate governance. Over the past two decades, there have been a handful of critiques that insightfully examine various political and ideological features of corporate governance, including: the primacy of shareholder value and discipline of market forces (O'Sullivan, 2000), the role of neoliberalism and the rise of finance-led forms of capital accumulation (Aglietta and Rebérioux,

2005; van Apeldoorn and Horn, 2007; Overbeek *et al.* 2007), the role of classes (Scott, 1997), shareholder activism (Ireland, 1996; Clowes, 2000), shareholder ideology (Engelen, 2002) and discursive elements pertaining to governance and social responsibility in the era of neoliberalism (Erturk *et al.*, 2004). While these contributions throw critical light on the dominance of corporate governance, they do not grant sufficient attention to understanding the limits and nature of resistance in the form of shareholder activism (Chapters 4 and 5) as integral features of neoliberal-led capitalist restructuring and the relations of power and paradoxes therein (Chapters 2 and 3).

Another weakness of these critical approaches to corporate governance is the general tendency to focus on comparative analyses of corporate governance regimes, involving primarily the United Kingdom and Western Europe (cf. Scott, 1997). These contributions therefore fail to situate corporate governance vis-à-vis the geo-political significance of the US in global capitalism. There are three reasons why I have chosen to concentrate on the US context to study the nature of the relationship between ownership and corporate power. First, financial ownership in the US is the most decentralized and dispersed in the world (Cerny, 2008). The US share of pension fund assets in the OECD area, while down from a 2001 high of 68 per cent, still registered an impressive 60 per cent in 2006 (OECD, 2007). In 2005, American institutional investors, among which pension funds comprise the largest sector, owned a total of 67.9 per cent of shares in the top 1,000 corporations in the US (The Conference Board, 2007a: 5). Related to this, US institutional investors are widely regarded as the most active shareholders in the world (Blair, 1995). Second, as noted earlier in the chapter, Anglo-American forms of corporate governance are presented as the most efficient, market-based solutions and are, therefore, a paragon that other countries, especially those in the developing world, are strongly encouraged to emulate (Reed and Mukherjee, 2004; see Chapter 6). Third and finally, US corporations and institutional investors, especially pension funds, are among the largest in the world.[2] American pension funds also have a strong presence in emerging market economies (The Conference Board, 2007a), thus offering a window to the global reach and nature of corporate, including shareholder, power along North–South lines, and, more specifically, with regard to concerns of US imperialism (Harvey, 2003; Panitch and Gindin, 2004; Soederberg, 2006).

A brief history of corporate governance

The rise of the separation of ownership from control

The dominant narrative of the rise of corporate governance typically begins in the mid-1980s. Yet, one of the main concerns of the doctrine – the relationship between ownership and control – has a longer history. While corporations have an extensive historical lineage, it was the invention of securities, or, 'a transferable instrument evidencing ownership or creditorship, as a stock [share] or a bond', that would prove to be one of the most transformative features in the history of corporations, especially in terms of shaping the relations between those who own and those who control a publicly listed company (Braithwaite and Drahos, 2000: 143). Since being introduced in the seventeenth century, securities have enabled corporations to raise capital by selling shares to an expanded ownership base. Throughout the 1840s and 1850s, the steady replacement of family firms by large corporations financed by the pooled contributions of capital from thousands of shareholders and bondholders allowed for the creation of massive technological projects such as railroads, canals and mines in the US (ibid.; Mitchell, 2007). This ascent of the corporate form in the US was accompanied by the rise of investment banks and finance (Chandler, 1965). The period stretching from the mid-1890s to the 1920s, for instance, has often been referred to as the 'era of finance capital' (Fligstein, 1990; Hilferding, 1981).

As the nature of ownership began to change, many issues and questions about how, and in whose interests, these economic behemoths were managed began to emerge (Veblen, 1923). In what is considered a classic study into the nature of ownership and control in the US, especially within the corporate governance debates, Adolf Berle and Gardiner Means examined 200 of the largest US non-financial corporations in 1929. Their results revealed that the

> ever wider dispersion of stock ownership has brought about a fundamental change in the character of wealth – in the relation between the individual and his wealth, the value of that wealth and the nature of property itself. Dispersion in the ownership of separate enterprises appears to be inherent in the corporate system.
>
> (Berle and Means, 1932: 47)

In response to the changing nature of ownership and control in Corporate America, as well as the crisis of public confidence in corporations brought about by the 1929 stock market crash and subsequent Great Depression (Kindleberger, 2001), the US government created a framework that was almost entirely defined by two landmark statutes of the New Deal era: the Securities Act (1933) and the Securities and Exchange Act (1934). This regulatory environment, which laid the foundation for the modern-day understanding of the corporation and, by extension, the corporate governance doctrine, is believed to have its roots in American-style democracy. As Robert A.G. Monks and Nell Minow elaborate,

> Shareholders were seen as voters, boards of directors as elected representatives, proxy solicitations as election campaigns, corporate charters and bylaws as constitutions and amendments. Just as political democracy acted to guarantee the legitimacy of governmental or public power, the theory went, so corporate democracy would control – and therefore legitimate – the otherwise uncontrollable growth of power in the hands of private individuals. Underpinning that corporate democracy, as universal franchise underpinned its political counterpart, was the principle of one share, one vote.
>
> (Monks and Minow, 2001: 107)

Managerialism and shareholder passivity

The dissolution of stock ownership was believed to have watered down control of the capitalist classes and led to the rise of managerialism – an era of high merger activity and the ascendance of the so-called 'mega-corporation' (Chandler and Tedlow, 1985). From 1948 to 1972, for instance, the 200 largest corporations acquired 58.4 per cent of total assets in Corporate America, and, at the height of this movement, in 1967, mega-corporations were responsible for 69.9 per cent of all acquired assets (Blumberg, 1975: 50). Aside from the obvious effect of widespread acquisitions on the elimination of major firms from the economy, and thus reduction in competition and the resultant impact on price levels, this activity was also believed to heighten the control of management (cf. Baran and Sweezy, 1966). It should be noted that this concentration of corporate power was accompanied not only by the continued dispersal of stock ownership, but also the astronomical increase – both in size and concentration of ownership – in large financial institutions, especially investment companies, insurance companies and state and local government pension funds. Between 1952 and 1973, for instance, the number of Americans owning stock increased from about 6.5 million to about 31 million (Blumberg, 1975).

Despite the diffusion of ownership, shareholders rarely challenged management control over the major US corporations (Vogel, 1978; Brancato, 1997). A key explanation for shareholder passivity during this period is believed to be the nature of ownership. One of the basic rights of stock ownership is the right to transfer ownership to another party. In making transferability a priority, owners of common stock[3] were willing, for most of the twentieth century, to surrender other rights of ownership. The logic of this position runs something like this: for common stock to be freely transferable, shareholders had to have limited liability and shares had to trade at a fairly low rate. Both conditions loosened the connection between ownership and control. In order to have limited liability, for instance, shareholders had to give up control over all but the most basic corporate decisions. To keep trading prices low enough to ensure liquidity, shareholders had to allow their companies to issue millions of shares of stock, which makes it almost impossible for any one investor to hold a significant stake. This resulted in the in the so-called 'Wall Street Rule'. Recognizing that transferability was the only real right the shareholder had, investors would usually opt to vote with management or sell the shares (Monks and Minow, 2001: 99). According to the Wall Street Rule, shareholders could send a powerful message to a company's management by selling out, ideally in enough of a block to lower the share value just enough to make the corporation an attractive takeover target (ibid.: 99–100).

A poorly performing stock market in the 1970s – accompanied by structural problems of stagflation, high interest rates and sharp spikes in the price of oil – began to throw the Wall Street Rule into question, as managers were under increasing pressure from shareholders to perform well (Useem, 1984). Demands on management to ensure high returns for shareholders were complicated by worsening conditions in the American economy, which saw substantial trade and budget deficits for the first time, another round of mergers and acquisitions, and the subsequent rise of junk bonds in the 1980s.[4]

The rise of corporate governance and shareholder activism

According to mainstream accounts, several key events led to the rise of corporate governance as a guiding theory and practice. First, during the mid-1980s it became clear that US corporations were losing ground to their Japanese and German counterparts. This lack of competitiveness was blamed on, among other things, the inability of corporate management and their boards of directors to bring about higher productivity levels (Drucker, 1993). Second, the wave of hostile take-overs, leveraged buyouts and corporate restructurings in the 1980s, and again from 1993 to 1994, brought corporate governance issues such as the accountability of the board of directors to the forefront of public debates against the wider backdrop of a recessionary phase (Blair, 1995). The immense increase in compensation packages for corporate executives also drew public attention, especially in light of the fact that aggressive restructuring efforts, including substantial job losses, were not enough to reverse a steady decline in shareholder value (ibid.; Bogle, 2005). With the Enron-style debacles of the early 2000s, corporate governance rose, once again, to prominence, as the scandals and ensuing bankruptcies were largely blamed on weak corporate governance practices. The third, and related, development that is believed to have led to the pre-eminent position of corporate governance is the continual process of restructuring (layoffs, boardroom shake-ups, and so forth) to cut costs. Once renowned for providing secure, high-paying jobs with good benefits, large corporations in the US have been subject to radical forms of downsizing, to the point that large corporations have become riskier places to work at all levels in the organization (Blair, 1995; Lazonick and O'Sullivan, 2000; Monk and Minow, 2001).

A fourth major development that is considered to have led to the rise of corporate governance is the exponential growth of institutional investors and universal ownership, which in turn led to new expressions of shareholder activism. Although forms of shareholder activism may be traced to 1932,[5] the birth of what is generally regarded as the modern institutional investor movement in the US did not occur until the early 1980s (Brancato, 1997). One of the key actors driving this movement was pension funds (Clowes, 2000). The California Public Employee Retirement System (CalPERS), for example, is generally credited as a founder and lead-steer of shareholder activism, largely due to its heightened proxy voting activity at selected companies in the mid-1980s (Brancato, 1997; see also Chapter 6). The 1980s also saw the formation of several key organizations that would act as a conduit to bring together various institutional investors. In 1985, for example, the Council of Institutional Investors (CII) was established. Since its inception, the CII has lobbied for legislation and SEC rulings to strengthen the hand of shareholders – including institutional investors (Blair, 1995: 165).

As noted above, pension funds constitute the largest collection of investment capital in the world (Monks and Minow, 2001). Pension funds not only represent the fastest growing category of institutional investor, but also the type of institutional investor that 'tends to be the most "activist"' (The Conference Board, 2007a: 5). There are two key reasons for the activist status of pension funds. First, pension funds (private and public) are the least regulated of the major categories of institutional investors, including banks, insurance companies, mutual funds and investment companies (Blair, 1995). Second, the leading pension funds have become so large that their portfolios tend to mirror the whole economy. This has been captured by the term 'universal ownership' (Hawley and Williams, 2002). The pension funds cannot easily buy and sell large stakes in individual companies without affecting the share price because their holdings are big enough to move the market. More importantly, they are much less likely to be interested in engaging in 'zero-sum' (short-term) financial transactions and would, therefore, oppose transactions that do not create more value on one side than they destroy on the other (Blair, 1995: 168). The phrase, 'We own the economy now', uttered by former New York City finance commissioner Carol O'Cleireacain, captures this new sentiment among pension funds (Monks and Minow, 2001).

Repoliticizing corporate power and ownership: an alternative frame for understanding

In what follows, I elaborate briefly on the four interlocking premises upon which my central argument and analysis rests. The primary frame of reference of each premise is Marxism. Before turning to this discussion, a caveat is in order. I believe there has been a lot of misconception and misrepresentation of Marxist paradigms in many of the debates and approaches that relate to the present study. It is therefore important to stress that by insisting that all forms of social, economic and political life are shaped by the dynamic and paradoxical nature of capital accumulation, I am neither promoting an economistic nor a deterministic framework in understanding corporate power and ownership in contemporary capitalism. If we are to move beyond the neo-classical paradigm, which, as I suggested earlier, is intrinsic to the corporate governance doctrine, we must come to grips with the material basis of human agency and how the latter shapes, and in turn is influenced by, the processes and internal contradictions, frequently erupting as crises, in the accumulation of capital (Harvey, 2001). It is through the acknowledgement of the material conditions of our social existence in a capitalist system, including the central role of the state, that we can understand more fully the paradoxes, the nature of power and the politics of domination and resistance inherent in the corporate governance doctrine. We are now ready to turn to the four related premises that comprise the alternative framework of the book.

The first premise is that the corporation is a social relation of capitalism. A recurring problem in mainstream debates about ownership and control is that the corporation is conceptualized as either an instrument of managerial rule (Berle and Means, 1932), or, in the case of the corporate governance doctrine, as an autonomous, economic and legal entity (Blair, 1995; Jensen, 2000). These perspectives fail to grasp that corporations represent *historical social relations*, which cannot be understood without reference to class and state relations and the underlying contradictions that define capitalist development. Corporate power, including the relations of domination and contestation, cannot be separated from the wider struggles and contradictions of capitalism. This implies that the relationship between ownership and control not only reflects the underlying configurations of social power found in a given, historically specific phase of capitalist development, such as the current era of neoliberalism, but that these configurations are also highly dynamic and contradictory. In other words, the birth of the modern corporation had its roots in the constraints and contradictions of capital accumulation. In order to 'overcome the limits to capital accumulation', Marx argued that capitalists sought 'to concentrate the entire production of the branch of industry in question into one big joint-stock company (or, corporation) with a unified management' (Marx, 1991: 569).

Seen from the above angle, the corporation is a vehicle for capital accumulation, and this sets defining parameters for its operations regardless of its ownership patterns (ibid.). As Marx argued, the capitalist *content* of the corporation, despite its change in *form*, that is to say, the shift to ownership in the form of shares from individual property, 'remains trapped within capitalist barriers; instead of overcoming the opposition between the character of wealth as something social, and private wealth, this transformation only develops this opposition in new form' (ibid.: 571). The corporation, therefore, is as much a capitalist organization when it is owned and controlled by one person or family as when it is owned by a large number of shareholders in the *form* of a publicly listed company. It follows from this that while management may, indeed, hold disproportionate amounts of social power in relation to shareholders, or specific shareholder groups, the source of this power lies deeper than the bounds of the corporate governance doctrine. Instead, this power is created and socially reproduced by the state through legal and ideological means, and serves the interests of dominant classes in capitalist society. This is discussed in more detail in Chapters 3, 4 and 5.

The second premise is that the credit system represents a central and explicit link between corporations and capital accumulation. The need to constantly expand and restructure corporate activities creates a continuous need for corporations to access credit, e.g. through such means as issuing more shares. The role of credit is therefore not only a key feature of the financial system, but also integrally related to the expansion of the modern corporation. Marx viewed credit as 'the principal lever of overproduction and speculation' (ibid.: 572; Harvey, 2003). As such, the credit system is a product of capitalism, or, more specifically, the relations of power therein, as it endeavours to deal with capitalism's internal contradictions (Harvey, 1999). It is worth emphasizing that credit, like money, is a relationship imbued with power, exploitation and contradictions.

The origins of the corporation, for instance, are intimately tied to the expansion of credit. For Marx, the transformation of the corporation from the purview of the state to the realm of the market, and the ensuing separation of ownership from control, is a reaction to the limits posed by the accumulation of capital. A significant barrier to amassing more credit through wider participation of society in the stock markets was personal liability, i.e. regardless of the level of investment an individual placed in a company, he or she was personally liable without limit (Bakan, 2004). By the middle of the nineteenth century, business leaders and politicians pressured the government to amend the law to limit the liability of shareholders to the amounts they had invested in a corporation. By the latter half of the nineteenth century, limited liability was, with the aid of the state, entrenched. Joel Bakan rightfully points out that, aside from the economic motivation behind the expansion of the pool of potential investors, ending class conflict by co-opting workers into this new social institution of capitalism represented another justification. Citing an 1851 document issued by the Select Committee on Partnership in England that shares striking similarities to the rhetoric of President G.W. Bush's 'Ownership Society' (discussed in Chapter 2), Bakan notes that the utility of limited liability was also disciplinary and ideological in nature, as it allowed those of moderate means to take shares in investment with their richer neighbours. According to the Select Committee, this move would in turn 'preserve the order and respect for the laws of property' (ibid.: 11–12).

The third premise is that the contradictions of shareholder activism must not be understood solely within the narrow confines of the corporate governance doctrine, but instead within the configurations of power that have emerged historically from the interactions between the credit system and corporations. Questions of ownership and control are integral to the social relations of credit and, as such, the power relations implicit within corporate governance are shaped by what I refer to as the 'corporate–financial nexus', i.e. the unequal interdependency that binds together investors, Corporate America and the financial system. The mounting presence of institutional investors as owners of Corporate America has led to a significant interdependency between social security capital and publicly traded corporations, thus affecting the relationship between ownership and control. The rising number of workers (skilled and unskilled) has become increasingly reliant on the economic performance of public corporations – both inside and outside the US. Richard Minns captures this relationship between 'Main Street' and Wall Street with the term 'social security capital' (Minns, 2001). For Minns, social security capital describes all deferred wages or salaries that enter the credit system in the form of company stocks and bonds (ibid.). Institutional investors have, therefore, a vested interest in ensuring that corporations are managed to reflect their interests, whether these are defined in financial or societal terms, or both. At the same time, major corporations in the US have become more dependent on institutional investors – most of which deal with the savings of tens of millions of Americans (Chapter 5). Social security capital has become an important source of capital for corporations, as an increasing number of people are encouraged, in one way or another, to save privately for their retirement (ibid.; Martin, 2002; Langley, 2008; see also Chapter 2).

A chief contradiction underpinning the corporate–financial nexus is as follows: on the one hand, owners of social security capital have a strong stake in the preservation of the system that exploits them because the destruction of that system entails the destruction of their savings. This system entails the relations of domination and control in capitalist society. On the other hand, to the degree that pension savings represent a significant source of capital for corporations, holders of social security capital have begun to acquire a new status as share-holders with emerging forms of power over corporate management, i.e. as shareholder activists (Harvey, 1999: 263). At its most fundamental level, this contradiction underpins some of the key struggles of domination and resistance in corporations. It also lies at the heart of the changing *form* of the corporate governance doctrine. Corporate governance, for instance, has been constantly evolving in scope since it emerged on the business scene in the 1980s. Over the past decade, proponents have sought to widen the parameters of corporate governance to include key societal concerns such as human rights and environmental issues, or what is popularly referred to as SRI, which we discuss in Chapters 6 and 7.

Reflecting the unequal and exploitative relations of capitalist society, the corporate–financial nexus is asymmetrical as this interdependency has greatly bene-fited, and continues to benefit, Corporate America and the wider financial interests. As will become evident throughout the book, the beneficiaries of pension plans or social security capital, for instance, are not granted the same amount of welfare and protection as corporations and financial players. With each subsequent crisis, such as the mergers and acquisitions wave in the 1980s and 1990s and the Enron-style debacles in the early 2000s, beneficiaries of pension plans lost hundreds of millions of dollars. Many 'beneficiaries' were thrown into economic insecurity and even poverty. According to the OECD, for example, the 2008 financial crisis drained retirement funds worldwide by $4 tril-lion (*Pensions & Investments*, 2008a). While trillions of dollars were allocated to the financial corporations (banks, insurance companies and so forth) that helped precipitate the so-called 'First World Debt Crisis' of 2008, no bailout was offered to assist people on 'Main Street', whose standard of living was dramati-cally reduced as a result of the financial turmoil. These ongoing and increasingly protracted and widespread crises over the past three decades also reveal the underlying instability of the corporate–financial nexus.

The fourth and final premise upon which the argument and analysis of this book rests is that the capitalist state, especially with respect to its neoliberal form and functions, plays a central role in mediating, naturalizing, depoliticizing and disciplining the struggles that emerge from the corporate–financial nexus. As we discuss in Chapter 3, the state, like the corporation, is neither an instrument of class rule nor an autonomous actor, but instead represents a complex and highly contradictory social relation. One of the key functions of the state is to uphold the principles of freedom, private property and equality that are necessary for capital accumulation, while at the same time attempting to resolve conflicts emerging from the latter (Holloway and Picciottio, 1991; Hirsch, 1995). Unlike mainstream understandings of the state, which equate it with legislative, executive and judicial functions, our alternative framework entails a broader understanding of the capitalist state. For instance, while the capitalist state is comprised of various institutions and functions to create and uphold laws and policies, it is also characterized by coercive (e.g. the legitimate monopoly over violence) and ideological features that represent dominant groups and aid in reproducing the status quo through disciplinary and depoliticizing strategies linked to market rule, including the promotion of the corporate governance doctrine (Gramsci, 1992; Gill, 1995).

We examine more closely the connection between the neoliberal state and the construction of mass investment in Chapter 2, and the neoliberal state and the corporate governance doctrine in Chapter 3. For now, it is useful to define what is meant by the term 'neoliberalism'. In the context of this book, neoliberalism is understood as an ideology and a set of policies that emerged, in varying degrees and forms, in many countries in the Third World (Taylor, 2006) and in the advanced industrial countries in the 1970s and 1980s (Cerny, 2008). Neoliberal ideology and corresponding policies are premised on a belief in minimum state intervention in the marketplace, the competitive and rational features of which are considered by its promoters to be far more efficient in allocating resources than the government is. Key distinguishing features of neoliberalism are privatization, deregulation and liberalization – all of which are, according to neoliberal ideologues, aimed at 'freeing' the market from unnecessary government intervention (Piven and Cloward, 1997; Pollin, 2003). As moments of political domination, neoliberal ideology and policy formation are themselves attempts to overcome the manifestations of the underlying crisis of capital accumulation. In terms of the corporate–financial nexus, neoliberal policies have assisted the state in reorganizing capitalist social relations by, for example, deregulating financial markets (Chapter 3); encouraging middle- and working-class Americans to invest their pension savings in US corporations and, therefore, assisting in the social construction and reproduction of the corporate–financial nexus (Chapter 2); engaging in 'corporate welfare' (e.g. low corporate taxation rates or tax holidays); privatizing social welfare provisions; supporting the bid by employers to disempower unions (Chapter 5); and so forth.

The hegemonic status of neoliberalism is not, however, a static and cohesive force (Gramsci, 1992). The notion of a classless society, which lies at the heart of this perspective, is exemplified in the mantra of British Prime Minister Tony Blair (1997–2007), that 'we are all middle class now' (*International Herald Tribune*, 2007a). Moreover, because the hegemony of neoliberalism is not self-reproducing, it must be renegotiated and relegitimized as a world-view on a constant basis. As such, neoliberalism is neither rigid nor static, but is continually transforming itself. The rise of neoliberalism and, by extension, the corporate governance doctrine, derives neither from some functional external force nor from a natural evolution of the market, but through complex social struggles and contradictions that emerge within and are subsequently shaped by, as well as shape, the structures and processes of capitalist accumulation (Taylor, 2006; Harvey, 2005).

Having laid out the analytical backbone of our inquiry, it is helpful, once again, to restate the central thesis of book. The hegemonic position of corporate governance has an ideological, political and materialist basis in the neoliberal-led restructuring of capitalist society. Specifically, the dominance of corporate governance as the primary way to frame, explain and resolve conflict between shareholders and management serves to naturalize and reproduce market rule, excluding other voices that contest corporate power. Corporate governance is not only an integral feature of neoliberal domination (or market rule), but also assists in blurring and distorting struggles aimed at challenging corporate power by depoliticizing and marketizing resistance, which in turn reifies the corporation as a legal and economic entity or 'thing', as opposed to a social relation of capitalism. Furthermore, and in contrast to mainstream accounts, corporate governance is a political strategy that emerged both as a reaction to, and an attempt to naturalize and thus reproduce, the ever-deepening, asymmetrical and paradoxical interdependency captured by the term 'corporate–financial nexus'.

Structure of the book

The following chapters have been written and organized in a way that will help us to understand, critique and move beyond the corporate governance doctrine in order to expose the doctrine's underlying power relations, which are rooted, not in a sanitized and apolitical market, but in capitalist society itself. The next three chapters are concerned with elaborating on the corporate–financial nexus by charting: the construction of mass investment in the US, especially as it pertains to old-age savings (Chapter 2); the naturalization of the corporate governance doctrine and the neoliberal assumptions therein (Chapter 3); and the myth of corporate democracy (Chapter 4). More specifically, Chapter 2 examines neoliberal restructuring strategy and its effects on the ongoing attempts at widening and deepening the exposure of Americans' old-age provisions to the financial system and, in effect, corporations. This chapter investigates the capitalist nature and implications of the 'Ownership Society', the ideological battering ram on which the state and others have drawn in order to socialize savers to rely on – and trust – the stock markets to augment their retirement savings. This discussion not only reveals the ideology, policies and paradoxes involved in the construction and normalization of social security capital within the wider corporate–financial nexus, but also the disciplinary features of the wider context of neoliberal-led capitalism. Chapter 3 discusses the political and ideological dimensions of the key regulatory response to the raft of scandals and bankruptcies that beset Corporate America in the early 2000s, namely, the Sarbanes–Oxley Act (SOX). The primary aim of this discussion is to transcend the rhetoric of the SOX, including its insistence on protecting shareholder interests, by exposing the Act's core neoliberal assumptions – all of which are rooted in the corporate governance doctrine. When viewed through a critical lens, it becomes clear that the SOX, despite claims by its architects that it is one of the most far-reaching reforms since the New Deal (1933–1938), reproduces the existing relations of power within corporations and the financial system. In the wake of the SOX, the George W. Bush administration (2001–2009) attempted to introduce another major reform to the New Deal compromise: the privatization of Social Security. Chapter 4 explores a key theme in the post-SOX era, namely the case of the equal access proposal. The latter was a shareholder initiative demanding the (equal) right to nominate directors for corporate board elections. In exploring the debates and struggles around equal access, which the *Financial Times* has suggested is the most important corporate governance issue in the new millennium, this chapter critically assesses a basic assumption underpinning the corporate governance doctrine, corporate democracy, by tracing its origins to the separation of ownership and control.

The next three chapters of the book chart how shareholder activism seeks to challenge corporate power, while at the same time constituting and reproducing this power due to the depoliticizing and marketizing effects of the corporate governance doctrine. More specifically, Chapter 5 explores one of the most significant attempts to contest corporate power in neoliberalism via labour-led shareholder activism. Trade unions have become one of the most important actors in corporate governance reforms over the past two decades. Proponents of this so-called 'new activism' suggest that workers will secure greater prosperity by ensuring that management adheres to good corporate governance principles than by resorting to old bargaining tactics such as strikes. The new activism supporters concede, however, that despite the in-roads made by trade unions, workers still do not exercise control over their social security capital. By drawing on the theoretical insights from the first four chapters, Chapter 5 provides a more complete explanation to this problem by identifying some of the deeper causes of the limits plaguing the new activism. These limits are rooted in the contradictions and power relations of capitalist society in general and the corporate–financial nexus in particular.

Chapter 6 establishes and analyses the link between the Permissible Country Index (PCI), the benchmarking strategy of one of the largest public pension funds in the US, and the emergence of an entrepreneurial development initiative crafted by a World Bank institution, the International Financial Corporation (IFC). This investigation shifts the focus of analysis to the global stage in order to capture and explain the significance of the disciplinary power linked to shareholder activism and, by extension, social security capital, especially with regard to the ability of major US institutional investors to construct and reproduce the meaning of a preferred investment site in the global South, and, more broadly, to define the manner in which 'development' is construed, naturalized and reproduced within neoliberal-led capitalism. A related issue explored in this chapter is how, why and in whose interest the corporate governance doctrine has become transformed in order to embrace non-economic criteria such as political freedom and labour standards in the global South.

Drawing on the conceptual and contextual framework laid out in the previous chapter, Chapter 7 examines the social and political meaning of SRI and the tendency toward the marketization of social justice. The significance of this discussion is twofold. First, SRI is quickly becoming merged with traditional corporate governance doctrine. The PCI discussed in Chapter 6 is a case in point, as is the United Nations Principles for Responsible Investment, in which some of the world's largest and most powerful institutional investors are committed to ensuring that the companies in which they hold shares adhere to proper environmental, social and governance factors so as to reduce risk and increase value. Second, SRI has become one of the foremost and, according to some observers, most effective forms of activism for influencing corporate behaviour and policy. This chapter explores the processes and effects of the marketization of social justice by drawing on the case of the Sudan divestment campaign. The latter represents one of the most popular cases of SRI in the US since the South African boycott in the 1980s. Indeed, many have referred to the campaign as 'the next big movement'. Given these characteristics, the Sudan embargo is a useful case study to understand more fully and critically the politics and limitations of SRI strategies. At the end of this final chapter, I summarize the central argument of the book and highlight its implications for social change in contemporary capitalism.

Part II

Power and paradoxes of corporate power and mass investment

2 Repoliticizing the Ownership Society and the marketization of security

Since the 1980s, a growing number of middle-class Americans have become increasingly reliant on the stock market to augment and protect their old-age pension savings. This phenomenon is not a natural progression of market forces; but instead, as we will see below, has been constructed and legitimated historically in a complex and often contradictory manner by powerful political and economic interests. Through its bid to partially privatize the Social Security programme, for example, the Bush II administration has sought to widen the scope of the so-called 'Main Street America' investor base to include lower-income Americans, who represent the majority of the population (Mishel *et al.*, 2007). The administration has proposed accomplishing this goal by creating tax-free retirement accounts for lower-income individuals, supplementing existing private accounts and establishing government matching of personal contributions to those accounts. The amount of the match would depend on the income of the family and how much family members save. The establishment of voluntary personal retirement accounts would pertain to all workers under the age of 55. Proponents of the plan believe it is not only more efficient in terms of costs to taxpayers, but also that it is more socially just than the existing, state-managed system (*New York Times*, 2006a).

The Social Security programme was designed to advance the 'economic security of the nation's people'.[1] In its efforts to persuade Americans that privatizing Social Security is a viable, indeed desirable, strategy to save the programme, the Bush II administration leaned heavily on the conceptual battering ram of the 'Ownership Society'. The Ownership Society embodies all of the virtues of a fully privatized society. According to its supporters, the Ownership Society will help create conditions that empower individuals

> by freeing them from dependence on government handouts and making them owners instead, in control of their own lives and destinies. In the Ownership Society, patients control their own health care, parents control their own children's education, and workers control their retirement savings.
>
> (Boaz, 2004)

Or, as President George W. Bush put it:

If you own something, you have a vital stake in the future of our country. The more ownership there is in America, the more vitality there is in America, and the more people have a vital stake in the future of this country.

(White House, 2005a)

The Ownership Society aims to take what is considered an unproductive and costly state-sponsored mechanism for the social protection and management of old-age pensions, and replace it with a more efficient, market-based retirement policy.

Until now, the Ownership Society and its connection to the neoliberal state, as well as the construction and naturalization of a mass investment culture, have been under-theorized.[2] One reason for this oversight is the fact that economic analyses have dominated, and prevailed, within the debates. While these discussions have been useful in highlighting and explaining the technicalities around the benefits and costs of privatizing the old-age pension system in the US, they have failed to grapple with the role played by the relations of power that underpin the Ownership Society. Another reason for this neglect is that most scholars have dismissed the Ownership Society as insignificant due to the fact that the Bush II administration's attempt to partially privatize Social Security was unsuccessful – largely as a result of political opposition to the campaign from both Democrats and Republicans.

Notwithstanding the above points, there are at least two closely related reasons why it is important to engage critically with the rhetoric, politics and relations of power tied to the Ownership Society. First, when viewed in a broader and historical perspective, it becomes clear that the phenomenon of the Ownership Society is not exclusive to the Bush II administration and its wider neoconservative base; it also mirrors the dominant ideological and policy perspective of *many* powerful interests that benefit from the creation and naturalization of a mass investment culture. Second, it is useful to recognize that Bush's project is more than simply an exceptional, neoconservative exercise in rhetoric or the establishment of a utopian vision. As the following analysis reveals, the underlying premise of the Ownership Society not only represents a heightened expression of the ongoing privatization of Social Security that has occurred in the US since the early 1980s, following the lead of the Reagan and Clinton administrations. It also reveals the inner nature of the marketization of old-age savings, which figures within the pattern of neoliberal restructuring of American society.[3] Focusing on both points permits a fuller understanding of the corporate–financial nexus, which was discussed in Chapter 1.

The main argument of this chapter has two interlocking parts. First, I suggest that the ideology of the Ownership Society not only naturalizes, but also reproduces the dominance of market rule in the US. As we will see, the Ownership Society seeks to legitimize the general trend towards privatizing pension savings, while at the same time expanding the investor base to include working-class Americans. This political strategy further supports the ongoing expansion of what Richard Minns refers to as 'social security capital'. To recap briefly, this term refers to all deferred wages or salaries that enter the credit system in the form of company stocks and bonds. As explained in Chapter 1, social security capital is a product of the ongoing neoliberal-led restructuring of capitalist society, which is neither a natural phenomenon nor the extension of a self-expanding market, but which emerges through the contradictions and struggles of capitalist society.

Second, and building on Minns' insight, I argue that the social reproduction of neoliberalism involves two further and interrelated developments. On the one hand, by representing workers as investors and thereby shifting the realm of responsibility for old-age security from the state to the marketplace, the powerful class interests in the American state are seeking to depoliticize and naturalize social security capital by reducing it to a question of individual responsibility through market interactions. Economic opportunism, 'choice', and 'freedom' have replaced social rights and public safety nets in the ideology of the Ownership Society. A reality is therefore constructed in which workers are led to believe and trust in the impersonal financial system and, by extension, the economic performance of publicly listed corporations, to deliver sufficient material benefits in their old age. On the other hand, through its attempt to merge the interests of 'Main Street' and Wall Street, the supporters of the Ownership Society reinforce a culture of dependency, which is captured in the corporate–financial nexus.

Before continuing this discussion, it is important to provide a few critical notes with regard to the notion of 'Main Street', which invokes a classless and homogenous – with regard to both race and ethnicity – image of US society. 'Main Street' is not a neutral term, but instead one that represents an ideologically driven concept that serves to declass (and 'white-wash') US society, as it perpetuates the belief that the majority of Americans are middle-income earners. This term acts to depoliticize the declining fortunes of skilled and unskilled workers caused by, among other things, the stifling of wages and salaries vis-à-vis higher productivity rates and the ongoing privatization of social services – both of which have led to greater levels of indebtedness, and thus poverty rates, along gender, racial, ethnic and ageist lines (Piven and Cloward, 1997). According to James Cypher,

> the bottom 60 percent of US households earned only 95 cents in 2004 for every dollar they made in 1979. A quarter century of falling incomes for the vast majority, even though average household income rose by 27 percent in real terms.
>
> (Cypher, 2007; see also Duménil and Lévy, 2004)

The asymmetrical dependency of 'Main Street' on Wall Street – the corporate–financial nexus – has led to greater economic insecurity and inequality. It has also disempowered and disciplined labour by exposing workers' savings to the growing volatility and instability of deregulated stock markets and publicly listed corporations (Moody, 2007). In addition, this dependency facilitates the normalization of forms of economic exploitation that manifest themselves in stagnant wages vis-à-vis increasing levels of productivity, exclusion from decision making over the disposition of surplus produced by labour, the rising gap between executive pay and workers' wages, and so forth (Brennan, 2005; Cypher, 2007; Mishel *et al.*, 2007).

The argument in this chapter is developed in five sections. In the first section, I outline the main premises of the Ownership Society, as espoused by President George W. Bush and one of the initiative's staunchest supporters, the libertarian Cato Institute. This discussion sets the stage for three subsequent sections, which aim to peel back the material, cultural and ideological layers of the Ownership Society to reveal its connective tissue to the larger metaphorical organ, namely the neoliberal heart of capitalist society. Specifically, the second section briefly explores the changing nature of pension provision in the US, from the New Deal of the 1930s to the rise of neoliberalism in the early 1980s, and the subsequent attempts to privatize pensions under the Reagan and Clinton administrations. Drawing on this discussion, the third section examines the public and private motivations behind further privatization of social security capital by looking at how the so-called 'demographic argument' manifests in both policy and corporate discourse. This section captures an important dimension of a culture of dependency in the neoliberal era by explaining how the nature of money assists in the ability of the state and capitalists to portray the Ownership Society as a democratic initiative, despite growing socio-economic inequalities. The fourth section foreshadows the consequences of partial privatization of Social Security by examining the track record of private pension plans, such as the '401(k)'[4] plan in the US, upon which voluntary and private individual accounts are to be based. The fifth section summarizes the argument and draws conclusions regarding attempts to widen the securitization of pension savings.

The content of the Ownership Society: expanding new opportunities through the stock market

A free society is of necessity an ownership society.

(Palmer, 2004)

During his State of the Union Address in 2005, George W. Bush described the Social Security system as 'headed for bankruptcy' and outlined a proposal based on its partial privatization. The centrepiece of this new proposal was the Ownership Society, supported by powerful financial and corporate interests, the majority of younger voters[5] and conservative think tanks such as the Heritage Foundation, the American Enterprise Institute and the Cato Institute. Through its formidable presence in Washington and its central role in disseminating what it packages as 'market liberal' research, the Cato Institute has kept the libertarian dream of Social Security privatization alive over the past several decades. It should also be highlighted that, by 2005, powerful business groups such as the

Business Roundtable and the National Association of Manufacturers, and political groups like Progress for America, were donating millions of dollars to the campaign to abolish the existing Social Security system.

The main premises of the Ownership Society complement the Cato Institute's preference for the privatization of Social Security in the same way that the Bush II administration's mantra seeks to convince 'Main Street', along with policymakers, that the government should not be responsible for ensuring workers' financial security in their old age. Similarly, the rhetoric of the Ownership Society aims to encourage workers to become more proactive and to individually create the conditions for their own security by learning to embrace the rationality of the marketplace. According to President George W. Bush:

> In America's ideal of freedom, citizens find the dignity and security of economic independence, instead of labouring on the edge of subsistence.... We will widen the ownership of homes and businesses, retirement savings and health insurance – preparing our people for the challenges of life in a free society. By making every citizen an agent of his or her own destiny, we will give our fellow Americans greater freedom from want and fear, and make our society more prosperous and just and equal. In America's ideal of freedom, the public interest depends on private character – on integrity, and tolerance toward others, and the rule of conscience in our own lives. Self-government relies, in the end, on the governing of the self.
>
> (White House, 2005a)

President Bush clearly emphasizes Lockean ideas of society, most notably a possessive individualism and the pursuit of happiness through private enterprise. As Cato Institute analyst Tom Palmer notes, in an Ownership Society:

> Owners have the right to benefit from wise use of their property and therefore incentives to take care of it. Similarly, they bear the consequences of unwise management. Not only are they more likely to care for what they own, but a system of property requires people to treat others with respect, as well. Owners have the right to exclude others from the use of what belongs to them, meaning that others must seek their consent before taking action that affects their rights. Each owner must respect the rights of others and concern himself with their interests. *Property makes people – including lawmakers – respectful of others*.
>
> (Palmer, 2004, my emphasis)

The basic premise of the Ownership Society is that there is an underlying equality of private-property owning individuals, which in effect denies that there are unequal and exploitative relations of social classes rooted in the capitalist mode of production and exchange. The ideology of the Ownership Society thus acts to depoliticize the struggles involved in the marketization of social programmes in the US. At the same time, it seeks to recreate the basic conditions necessary for the reproduction and expansion of capitalism, such as private property. By positing a connection between citizenship, freedom and the market, the rhetoric of the Ownership Society aims to construct a version of reality in which the market is a neutral space for social interaction, wherein the interests of individuals and market actors are fundamentally similar, as if there were only *one* class and *one* society (Gramsci, 1992). This rhetoric reflects Adam Smith's theory that, through the market, the self-interested interactions of individuals serve both their personal wants and the common good (Smith, 1904). It follows from this line of reasoning that by trusting the marketplace, individuals will gain more access to, and have greater choice of, goods and services. In keeping with the neoliberal spirit, the ideology of the Ownership Society treats the government as an unsuitable provider in terms of ensuring adequate market access and choices to its citizens. The market, not the state, is the only logical domain that will grant individuals enough freedom to control their own lives and destinies (Boaz, 2004).

According to its proponents, the Ownership Society will create responsible and independent individuals, transforming them into active participants in the market through private property. David Boaz, Executive Vice President of the Cato Institute, points out that the US enjoys the most widespread property ownership in its history. According to data from 2004, 68.6 per cent of American households own their own homes, while an even greater number of Americans own a share of productive businesses through stocks or mutual funds. In fact, about 50 per cent of American households are considered 'stockholding' in some form (ibid.). Boaz goes on to note that

> this also means that about half of Americans are not benefiting as owners from the growth of the American economy (though of course they still benefit as wage-earners and consumers). *In general, those are the Americans below the average income.* The best thing we could do to create an ownership society in America is to give more Americans an opportunity to invest in stocks, bonds, and mutual funds so that they too can become capitalists. And the way to do that is obvious.
>
> (ibid., my emphasis)

The solution offered in response to the above problem is that there should be a mechanism in place to compel US workers to invest the money that is presently transferred automatically via payroll taxes to the Social Security system. As Boaz suggests, this money is neither invested in real assets, nor does it belong to the wage earner. To empower individuals, this line of reasoning goes, the government should persuade workers that they can and should assume control over their 'private property' (old-age savings). According to the rhetoric of the Ownership Society, this could be accomplished by allowing workers to invest their Social Security taxes in private retirement accounts organized around a defined contribution scheme. The advantage of this approach, for both Boaz and the Bush II administration, is that 'instead of hoping someday to receive a meagre retirement income from a Social Security system that is headed for bankruptcy, American workers would own their own assets in accounts that couldn't be reduced by Congress' (ibid.).

Various groups and organizations have contested the dismantling of Social Security, however. Opponents include: trade unions, such as the Teamsters and the American Federation of Labor and Congress of Industrialized Organizations (AFL-CIO); key public pension funds, such as New York City Employees' Retirement System (NYCERS); and tens of millions of seniors, soon-to-be seniors and their umbrella organization, the American Association of Retired Persons (AARP). A top lobbyist for the AFL-CIO warned the country's largest brokerage firms against supporting the Bush II administration's initiative while they manage workers' funds (Entine, 2005). These firms – including State Street, J.P. Morgan Chase & Co., Morgan Stanley, Merrill Lynch & Co., Barclays Global Investors, Wachovia, Charles Schwab, and others – stand to be the primary beneficiaries of Social Security privatization.

As mentioned in the introduction to this chapter, the movement in favour of the Ownership Society and the ensuing struggle over privatizing Social Security did not emerge in isolation, but instead has deep roots in the ongoing privatization of the pension system in the US. In turn, this is tied to class-led efforts to restructure capitalist relations, with the result of increasing class-based forms of domination and exploitation.

Social Security and limited ownership: a brief history

An overview of pensions and the Social Security system

Pension plans were established in the US by private enterprises after the Civil War (*c.*1865). The main motivation for creating pension plans, even as far back as the nineteenth century, was 'to promote loyalty to the corporation' (the worker would be less likely to quit his job if it meant sacrificing his retirement benefits) (Carnoy and Shearer, 1980: 96). Employers viewed pensions as a gift bestowed on workers for their loyalty and service. This claim evolved by the 1930s, as more and more workers began to view pensions as a 'right'; that is, as part of the wage structure. As deferred wages, pensions were not subject to taxation at the time of contribution, but income taxes had to be paid when employees received their pension benefits. The provision of pension plans was, however, viewed as the responsibility of the government. As Martin Carnoy and Derek Shearer point out, 'only in the post-war period were private employers pushed to provide retirement benefits' through labour action (ibid.: 102). It would be wrong, however, to assume that workers have either ownership or control over their pension benefits (cf. Drucker, 1976), as '[t]he worker cannot borrow the money, trade it, use it as collateral, or do any of the other things that ownership entails' (Carnoy and Shearer, 1980: 104). In terms of control, most workers have no influence over how the funds are utilized. Writing in the 1950s, Paul Harbrecht notes that financial control has been delegated by the employers to the bank trustees, which exercise considerable power in the capital markets as a result. The employer controls the day-to-day operation of the plan itself, in many cases in accordance with a basic agreement arrived at with the union. It is the employer who, either unilaterally or in conjunction with a union, fixes the amount of pensions and usually alone determines how a plan is to be financed. The employee himself, without his union, has little or nothing to say about the pension plan, which, ultimately, is financed out of his earnings.[6]

(ibid.: 105)

In the late 1970s, *Pensions & Investments* magazine echoed the above concern about the powerlessness of workers with regard to their pension savings:

Forced savings ... [are what make] pension funds such a plus [for capitalists]; that, along with the virtual guarantee that the individual beneficiary will have no say in how the funds are used. In a sense, this new form of social capital is even better than taxes as a source of revenue. With taxes there is some accountability built into the system itself. *In the final analysis, the private exploitation of pension capital represents 'investment without representation.'*

(Rifkin and Barber, 1978: 96, my emphasis)

In the wake of economic and social devastation brought about during the Great Depression and the Second World War, the US government needed to intervene in mounting class tensions by devising a series of safety nets that took form in President Roosevelt's New Deal. An integral part of the attempt to appease struggles and enter into a compromise with union demands was the creation of the Social Security Act (SSA) in 1935. The SSA represented a savings programme that ensured universal benefits for the retired and unemployed, and thereby allowed elderly Americans to begin receiving benefits. The 2005 tax rate (also known as the payroll tax) was 12.4 per cent, split on a 50–50 basis between employee and employer and used to meet Social Security entitlements. As Robin Blackburn observes, 'The integrity of the programme is linked to a public perception that those who pay into this programme of "social insurance" are acquiring rights and claims which the government is bound to uphold' (Blackburn, 2002: 353). The popularity of Social Security resides in the fact that it provides 'non-means-tested' assistance to millions of Americans; that is, it does not involve humiliating rituals of certifying need, including investigation and surveillance, defining features of means-tested programmes (Piven, 2004: 83).

Despite its meagre payouts, Social Security is still considered a safety net for millions of low-income Americans. It must be kept in mind, however, that like all welfare programmes, Social Security is not only about meeting a need; it is also about controlling behaviour, or, more to the point, disciplining the labour market (Dean, 1990; Moody, 1988, 1997, 2007; Piven and Cloward, 1997;

Minns, 2001; Pollin, 2003). Social programmes, according to Frances Fox Piven, 'are being refashioned to make long hours of low-wage the only option available to many. Even the vein of meanness contributes to this logic, for it heaps insult on those who turn to government support' (Piven, 2004: 75).

Reconfiguring Social Security: from social right to individual duty

Before continuing with our discussion of the key attacks to Social Security during the era of neoliberalism, it is important to situate these policy choices within the wider historical context of crisis-led forms of capital accumulation. One of the hallmark features of capital accumulation has been the dominant role of largely deregulated financial markets and the impulse toward short-term and speculative investing patterns, which, since the early 1970s, has affected all areas of economic activity, including production (Harvey, 2003). It is against this backdrop that the following three main attempts to privatize Social Security must be understood.

The first endeavour to reform Social Security occurred during the initial years of the Reagan administration (1981–1989). Despite the privatizing impulse of the more conservative elements of this administration – characterized by slash-and-burn cost-cutting strategies that resulted in the sell-off of public assets – caution was shown with respect to reducing welfare services for the poor. In 1983 President Reagan dealt with the 'funding issue' by signing into law several amendments to the Social Security system, such as a substantial rise in the payroll tax, adding additional employees to the system, increasing the full-benefit retirement age and allowing up to one-half of the value of the Social Security benefit to count as potentially taxable income (Minns, 2001; Blackburn, 2002). At the same time, the administration encouraged private retirement savings through more market-linked, 'defined-contribution' plans (DC plans), such as Individual Retirement Accounts (IRAs)[7] and 401(k) plans (Blair, 1995: 161). In these plans, contributions to an employee's individual account, together with market rates of return on these contributions, determine the benefits. The introduction of the Thrift Savings Plan in 1986 was an attempt to encourage a shift toward the DC plans and away from the more costly (for employers), but more secure (for employees), 'defined-benefit' plans (DB plans). DB plans refer to pension benefit entitlements determined by a formula that takes into account an employee's years of service for the employer and, in most cases, wages or salaries (Bodie *et al.*, 1988). The shift from DB to DC plans in the public service, for example, was encouraged by offering federal employees the same type of savings and tax benefits as many private corporations offered their employees under 401(k) plans.

It is important to understand why DB plans are generally considered by workers to provide more economic security than their DC counterparts, as this sheds light on the disciplinary nature of the latter's market-oriented schemes. The American Federation of State, County, and Municipal Employees (AFSCME), a subsidiary of the AFL-CIO, lists several benefits of DB plans versus DC plans. Unlike proponents of the privatization of pension plans in the form of 401(k)s, the AFSCME does not subscribe to the assumption that markets are able to provide stable returns on workers' retirement investments (deferred wages). According to the union, DB plans are better for employees for some of the following reasons: (1) DB plans provide guaranteed income security to workers for their retirement, no matter what happens in the stock market, how long an employee lives after retirement, or whether he or she becomes disabled; (2) DB retirement benefits are not dependent on employees' ability to save; and (3) DB plans provide cost-of-living adjustments and pension formulas tied to the highest-paid years, which protects employees from inflation (AFSCME, 1997). As will be illustrated below in presenting some of the problems of 401(k) plans, this is not an unreasonable stance.

The second major attempt to reform the Social Security system occurred during the Clinton administration (1993–2001). Unlike the Reagan administration, Clinton's presidency saw spectacular economic growth, largely fuelled by unanticipated developments in the stock market and by the tech bubble. Under these fortuitous circumstances, the tension between privatization and increased taxation assumed a different expression. President Clinton's strategy for improving public finances was launched under the banner 'Save Social Security First'. While this campaign defended Social Security benefits, Clinton was not interested in increasing the terms for old-age pensions, especially for lower-income Americans. Like the voluntary individual accounts proposed by the Bush II administration, Clinton's strategy for 'saving' Social Security was also market-based. In his 1999 State of the Union Address, Clinton suggested the allocation of 62 per cent of the budget surplus to Social Security over the next 15 years. Clinton also proposed the investment of $700 billion of a new trust fund in the stock market in order to obtain a higher rate of return.

Clinton's attempt to push Social Security into the realm of the marketplace was met with political opposition from, among others, the AARP, labour groups, including the AFL-CIO and major public pension funds, such as the NYCERS. Other events also played a role in undermining the administration's bid to further 'securitize' pension savings. The Mexican Peso Crash of 1994–1995, for example, saw many middle-class Americans lose their pension savings. The tumult in Mexico marked the first of a series of major financial crises in the global South, including the East Asian crisis in 1997, followed by the downfall of the Russian and Brazilian economies.[8] These events, which negatively impacted savers in the US (and elsewhere), sank investor confidence levels in financial markets to a new low and threatened the ideological appeal of free market liberalization (Soederberg, 2004).

By 2001, the year that George W. Bush assumed power, the economic climate in the US had changed dramatically. The stock market boom came to a screeching halt, and it became evident that the underlying thrust of economic growth was largely due to a bubble in the technology sector. The chief executive and financial officers of the paragon of privatization, Enron, as well as a litany of other well-regarded and major American corporations and accounting firms – including

WorldCom, Global Crossing and Arthur Andersen – were charged with corporate malfeasance. The events of 9/11 further dampened economic growth in the US. Against this backdrop, President Bush established a 16-member, allegedly bipartisan 'Commission to Strengthen Social Security' to consider how best to implement 'individually controlled, voluntary personal retirement accounts' (President's Commission to Strengthen Social Security, 2001).

Motives for reconstructing social security capital

Aside from the alleged 'common sense' assumption rooted within the neoliberal paradigm that government policy should take a backseat to efficient markets (see Chapter 3), all three attempts to privatize Social Security share a related motive: lack of available financing. This rationale is located in both the public and private sectors. While the government has used numerous arguments to justify privatizing old-age pensions, one strand that has figured prominently in neoliberal attacks on the existing system may be regarded as the 'demographic argument'. This argument posits that, when coupled with a negative savings rate in the US, low birth rates and longer life spans will inevitably lead to less funding available through payroll taxes (Manning, 2000; Blackburn, 2002; Clark, 2003). Analysts at the Cato Institute believe there will be 70 million Americans of retirement age by 2030, twice as many as in 2004 (Cato Institute, 2005). According to White House data, by 2018, the government will begin to pay out more in Social Security benefits than it collects in payroll taxes; and by 2033, the annual shortfall will be more than $300 billion (White House, 2005b). Financing problems also exist outside the federal system. State (e.g. New Jersey, New York, Illinois, Ohio, West Virginia) and local (e.g. San Diego) government pensions, for example, are currently experiencing a massive funding crisis. These public pensions, which are paid for by taxpayers and therefore enjoy an implicit form of insurance, are under-funded by at least $300 billion, perhaps even more (Lowenstein, 2005).

The demographic argument is strengthened by the private sector claim that corporations can no longer keep the 'generous' pension promises (akin to 'gifts') involved in the DB scheme, because workers are living longer and working less. Put another way, by discrediting the common-sense assumption of guaranteed pensions linked to the Social Security system, the US government is seeking to undermine the universal reliance on the public sector for funding upon retirement. Given the higher administrative expenses and pension cost per worker (compared with DC plans) (Ghilarducci and Sun, 2006), DB schemes act as barriers to capital valorization for Corporate America.

Assuming that the demographic argument is valid, some examples of 'credible' options put forth by neoliberal ideologues for dealing with the impending fiscal crisis have included forcing people to save for their old age by either raising revenue through higher payroll taxes or privatizing Social Security – or a combination of both. It is interesting to note an obvious alternative that policymakers have been ignoring consistently: financing Social Security by levying taxes on wealthy individuals, financial institutions and corporations. Instead of pursuing this option, the government has chosen to continue to subsidize 'rational' market forces through negative corporate taxation rates, 'off-shoring' and unwillingness to implement inheritance and wealth taxes (Palan, 2006). Seen from this angle, the official rationale for privatizing Social Security based on demographic arguments helps to explain away the financing problem. It also relieves the government from having to justify its role in *creating* the funding gap through its decision to subsidize capitalists in an effort to assist them in gaining a competitive advantage in the world market. At the same time, this strategy depoliticizes the government's decision to cut levels of social protection for workers by, for example, reducing government funding for welfare, health and education systems and revising the promise that workers have a right to receive a pension at the age of 65.

The erosion of social protection for labour, combined with a surplus of labour that is more dependent on low-wage, temporary or casual work, has led to a situation in which workers repeatedly submit to the exploitative conditions of the labour market (Taylor, 2008). This form of social discipline permits capitalists to overcome the barriers to capital valorization by providing a more disciplined workforce that will yield higher levels of productivity while accepting lower wages. The push articulated in the Ownership Society rhetoric for reliance on the market, as opposed to the government, is closely tied to the growing power of private financial actors in the American political economy (Holloway, 1995; Harvey, 1999, 2005; Krippner, 2005). As noted above, the George W. Bush administration was not the first to cater to the interests of Wall Street. The two previous attempts to privatize Social Security under the Reagan and Clinton administrations catered to the interests of the same financial actors, including insurance companies and mutual funds, which stood to gain from partial privatization of Social Security and further promotion of the DC schemes.

Rapid growth in the number and value of 401(k) plans is telling. The plans grew from zero in 1981 to 10.3 million participants, with a total worth of $105 billion, by 1985; by 1993, the plans represented 18 million participants, with funds worth $475 billion (Blackburn, 2002). This figure has continued to grow as employers have opted to close DB plans to new entrants, encouraging employees to join DC plans. Today, more than 35 per cent of Americans are tied to a 401(k) plan (OECD, 2007). Given their lack of both investment experience and knowledge of highly technical financial terms, most participants opted for well-known brand names in the investment industry – or at least those companies that set out successful marketing campaigns. By 1996 just 20 companies managed 77 per cent of total 401(k) assets, while the top ten firms accounted for 56 per cent of total assets, e.g. Fidelity, UBS Paine Webber, Goldman Sachs, Merrill Lynch & Co., Prudential, Bankers Trust, State Street and so forth. At the end of 2000, 42 million US workers held more than $1.8 trillion in their 401(k) accounts (OECD, 2005: 8). Many of these accounts were reinvested in the stock of the companies for which the policyholders work (Blackburn, 2002: 31). It should not come as a surprise that those in favour of privatizing Social Security are its largest benefactors. Lobbyists retained under the category of 'finance, insurance, and real estate spent over $200 million in 1998 and 1999, ahead of spending on any other category including health and defence' (ibid.: 418).

In the wake of the 2008 sub-prime mortgage fiasco and credit market gridlock, the world's biggest investment banks, insurers, hedge funds and private equity shops have been busy lobbying Washington to let them take over and run corporate pension funds. The prize entailed $2.3 trillion worth of pension plans, including those at IBM, Hewlett Packard and Verizon. According to some analysts, this figure could triple by 2012. The Treasury Department offered a blueprint for lawmakers on Capitol Hill in August 2008, one month before the credit crisis, to allow financially strong entities in well-regulated sectors to acquire pension plans. According to the Director of the Pension Benefit Guarantee Corporation (PBGC), the federal insurer of last resort of corporate pension plans, such a move would create '*greater security*' (*BusinessWeek*, 2008; my emphasis).

It should also not come as a surprise that the financial institutions involved in 401(k) investments pocket a huge slice of investors' returns through fees and costs. According to John C. Bogle, founder of the Vanguard mutual fund firm, over several decades these fees and costs add up to 80 per cent of the return going to money managers, with only 20 per cent received by the investor (PBS Frontline, 2006).[9]

Despite the regulatory changes to the financial sector since the Reagan administration, and the subsequent trend toward DC plans, about three-quarters of the corporations listed in America's S&P 500 index have a DB pension fund. The total liabilities of these funds were around $1.4 trillion at the end of 2004. According to the PBGC, which insures company (DB) pension plans covering about 44 million workers, the obligations of single-company DB plans in the US were under-funded by over $450 billion at the end of 2004. Tellingly, as of October 2005, the PBGC agreed to take on an unprecedented $6.6 billion in unfunded pension liabilities from United Airlines. The agency has accepted an increasing amount of pensions in the wake of the 2008 credit crisis. Moreover, according to a spokesperson for the PBGC, the imminent bankruptcy of the 'Big Three' US car manufacturers (General Motors, Chrysler and Ford) means that the federal agency 'would be responsible for about $13 billion of the under-funded benefits should they terminate' (*Fox Business*, 2009).

It is noteworthy that the PBGC is itself in a financing crisis, as it has registered, at the time of writing, approximately $23 billion in the red. Analysts expect this shortfall to increase significantly, as more companies declare bankruptcy and large US corporations continue to enter into Chapter 11 bankruptcy protection. For example, the pension promises issued to workers by Delta Air Lines and Northwest Airlines exceeded the assets in their pension funds by an estimated $16 billion. In October 2005, Delphi, the world's biggest maker of car parts, entered the largest bankruptcy filing in the history of the auto industry, a result of its inability to meet its pension obligations. The once-powerful symbol of US international competitiveness, General Motors, has been moving quickly down the slippery slope of bankruptcy in the new millennium because of, among other factors, problems tied to the pension crisis, which have been augmented by the sub-prime mortgage crisis that emerged in 2007 (Langley, 2008). Other major corporations, such as IBM, Hewlett Packard and Verizon, have decided to freeze their pension plans. In response to this quagmire, President George W. Bush signed into law the Pension Protection Act, on 17 August 2006. According to Bush, the new law establishes 'sound standards for pension funding' (PBS Frontline, 2006). However, when viewed historically against the backdrop of previous pension laws, many pension experts argue that the Pension Protection Act not only makes 401(k) plans more attractive for both employers and employees, but also provides an easier transition from traditional, more secure DB plans to 401(k) schemes.

The meaning of pension provisions has shifted from a guaranteed contract between employer and employee to DC plans, such as 401(k)s. Unlike DB schemes, the 'rewards' of DC plans are not guaranteed, but instead are dependent on the market, i.e. stock markets and, by extension, the economic performance of corporations. It is important to underline that the root cause of this modification regarding old-age security is not simply the changing demographics. As argued thus far, a more critical reading of this situation suggests that the reasons behind the inability of powerful US corporations to meet the obligations to their current and former (retired) workers, despite generous state subsidization, is due to the problem of surplus capital combined with decreasing outlets for profitable investment, both of which have been brought about by the crisis of overaccumulation. A key feature of the crisis has been that investment in production is no longer as profitable as speculative investments in the stock market and foreign exchange markets, as witnessed by the strategies pursued by Enron, Global Crossing, WorldCom and many others (Harvey, 1999). In contrast to the demographic argument, this perspective helps to explain why the US government, through strategies such as the privatization of Social Security, is constantly seeking to expand the parameters of the market (see Chapter 1).

Owing to their asymmetrical effects on different classes within US capitalism, strategies of privatizing social security capital must be legitimated and internalized by beneficiaries of pension plans if they are to be successful. The next section looks at various dimensions of the socialization processes associated with the creation of a culture of dependency in which workers' pension savings rely on financial markets and, by extension, publicly listed corporations.

Constructing a culture of dependency

The construction and normalization of dependency between the stock market and old-age pension savings (social security capital) is lubricated by the nature of money in capitalism. The class nature of the Ownership Society – and its underlying social construct, 'Main Street' – is, in part, concealed by the fact that pension fund capital is largely treated and understood as an apolitical object. In contrast, from a Marxist point of view, old-age savings are essentially a form of money, which implies that they possess social power. The ability of money to act as a great equalizer is an important consideration in understanding how the culture of dependency can appear as an unproblematic, natural occurrence in the market. As a store of value, money possesses social power that can be held over time and allows individuals to choose between present and future satisfaction. Drawing on Marx, Harvey notes that

> Money represents value par excellence, and thereby stands opposed to all other commodities and their use values. Money assumes an independent and external power in relation to exchange because, as the universal equivalent, it is the very incarnation of social power.

> (ibid.: 139)

Marx suggests that there is something very democratic about money, as it erodes class distinction and replaces it with the crass democracy of money, or 'community of money' (paraphrased in Harvey, 1989). In this community, all marks of class (as well as racial and ethnic) distinction and domination are erased. The result is that capitalists, rentiers, landlords, workers, managers and so forth, lose their social identity and become savers, who have a vested interest in the repro- duction of the status quo. This seemingly level playing field acts to distort capi- talist control over the credit system, in which pension savings play a significant role (Harvey, 1989; see Chapter 5).

A prime example of the community of money is the powerful, yet largely myth- ical, image evoked by the notion of 'Main Street', a conflict-free society (Lefeb- vre, 2005) in which middle-class Americans are portrayed as co-existing harmoniously with the super-wealthy in the hopes that they may someday join the latter group (Cypher, 2007). The financialization of everyday life, which is part and parcel of the rise of social security capital discussed in Chapter 1, has led many 'middle-class' Americans to believe that they too can reach the dizzying heights of opulent wealth by 'playing the markets' and 'owning' a piece of Corpor- ate America (Martin, 2002; Langley, 2008). Through the discourse and policy of the Ownership Society, as well as the ongoing debates about labour shareholder activism (Drucker, 1976; Hawley and Williams, 2002; Fung and Wright, 2003), the community of money is infused with a sense of empowerment. Americans are encouraged to view themselves as 'capitalists' as opposed to unskilled and skilled workers. This issue is discussed in more detail in Chapter 5. For now it is import- ant to stress that the community of money, which underlies both the Ownership Society and its closely related construct of 'Main Street', aims to naturalize, and thus reproduce, not only a classless vision of US society, but also a (blind) faith in the market as the ultimate and fair provider of social welfare.

The (false) democratic appearance of the community of money helps to explain how the general privatization of old-age savings has been largely accepted as normal and natural, despite increasing levels of socio-economic inequality. As we saw above, in the Ownership Society, everyone, despite their income, can and should own corporate stocks, real estate and so forth. By partic- ipating in the stock market, for example, *all* Americans are able to reap the benefits of economic growth in the US. Lower-income Americans, like their middle-class counterparts, will then take greater interest in the operations of the stock market, as attested by the spate of television shows, speciality newspapers and websites aimed at catering to the layperson (Martin, 2002; Langley, 2008). The representation of the market, in which the community of money operates, as a harmonious and level playing field also redirects attention away from the underlying reasons why a large portion of US society does not have enough to save (let alone participate in the stock market); namely, the scaled-back welfare system, lack of secure, well-paying jobs and so forth. According to a study by the Economic Policy Institute in 2001, the year that marked the end of one of the longest economic booms in the post-war period, 'one in three working families with children could not afford all their basic needs, such as housing, health care, and food' (Weller, 2004).

In contrast to the smooth and even surface of the US economy portrayed by the creators and supporters of the Ownership Society, prevailing socio-economic trends in the US reveal not only widening income gaps, but a poor–rich divide that is growing at an alarming pace (Mishel *et al.*, 2007). Even the conservative, pro-business weekly magazine *The Economist* observes that,

> In 1979–2000, the real income of the poorest fifth of American households [most of which are represented by African-Americans and Latino-Americans] rose by 6.4 per cent, while that of the top fifth rose by 70 per cent (and the top 1 per cent by 184 per cent). As of 2001, that top 1 per cent nabbed a fifth of America's personal income and controlled a third of its net worth
> (*The Economist*, 2005; see also Cypher, 2007).

By attempting to encourage people to turn to the market for greater access to commodities, choice of commodities and economic freedom, the Ownership Society acts as a form of social discipline by transforming the individual from a passive recipient of social programmes to an active investor in the economy, someone with a stake in the financial system. Through its emphasis on creating opportunity and access (not to mention the ideologically skewed concept of 'good citizens'), the Ownership Society falsely appears to be concerned with constructing a level playing field for old-age pensions in the US, especially as a means of allegedly addressing the growing gap between the rich and poor.

The growth of market-based DC plans since the 1980s is a representative case of class assimilation vis-à-vis retirement savings (Marcuse, 1964). As we saw above, although DC plans are riskier than their DB counterparts, there exists what some commentators have referred to as an 'irrational' attraction of workers to individual accounts: 'It is ironic that employees seem to prefer the new species of retirement plan, although it might not be good for them' (Ghilarducci and Sun, 2006). Part of this explanation can be located in the discourse of risk, which is almost exclusively discussed in finance as economic risk and, in turn, largely reduced to incomprehensible code in the form of algebraic equations and Wall Street jargon that is intelligible only to a select few. In part, the explanation is also linked to the manner in which risk is presented as a normal and natural feature of the largely technologically driven new economy. The 2001 Annual Report of President Clinton's Council of Economic Advisors, for instance, stated that 'the rewards of the New Economy are associated with risk, since the economy depends more heavily than before on financial markets, which remain volatile' (Martin, 2002: 32). It should be noted that these remarks were penned at a time when stocks yielded a very good return of around 7 per cent in real terms, more than enough to compensate for additional risk. But, as the economic pundit Paul Krugman observes, a 7 per cent rate of return is not a natural constant (Krugman, 2005).

Rarely, if ever, is the social dimension of risk raised to the same level of significance as economic risk when discussing investments. Moreover, in the culture of investment, which is fuelled by the financial and advertising industries, the common-sense assumption is that higher risks are associated with higher rewards. Put another way, in the high-risk society that characterizes the current era of financialization (Chapter 1), 'workers, businesses, and countries must start thinking like investors in the financial markets, where the only way to consistently achieve [economic] success is to achieve risk' (Martin, 2002: 34). Given that discussions of risk use the sanitized language of mathematics, Niklas Luhmann suggests that 'the question of who or what decides whether a risk is to be taken into account *or not*' is avoided (Luhmann, 1993: 45). The US government's refusal to update legislation relating to the managers of DC plans, discussed below, also acts as a legitimizing agent that enforces the idea that investment in a riskier retirement plan is a rational economic decision that will no doubt result in higher rewards. The hundreds of billions of dollars in pension savings that have been lost through speculative activities tied to financial crises – such as those that swept across several so-called emerging markets in the latter half of the 1990s and in the Enron-style debacles of Corporate America in the early 2000s – are interpreted as glitches in the system (or weak corporate governance practices), as opposed to systemic problems in neoliberal-led capitalism (see Chapter 3).

Expanded opportunities or increased insecurities? A closer look at the power of social security capital

To throw critical light on the capitalist nature of the Ownership Society's primary policy prescriptions – namely, personal individual accounts – it is useful to critically explore two basic issues of the wider terrain of the private pension scheme to which the personal accounts belong. First, to ascertain whether or not the market is, indeed, a more rational domain than the government in dealing with old-age pensions, I look at the weaknesses surrounding the federal law regulating pension systems: the Employee Retirement Income Security Act of 1974 (ERISA) (Clark, 1993). This law emerged as a reaction to a litany of banking and investment scandals in the early 1970s and sets minimum standards for most voluntarily established pensions in private industry to provide protection for individuals in these plans. This discussion provides the foundation for my analysis of a second issue, the question of the market's ability to provide greater access and choice vis-à-vis the private pension system (DC plans).

Labour economist Teresa Ghilarducci has suggested that ERISA has not kept pace with the evolving pension and investment world. This policy lag with respect to the private pension system is indicative of neoliberal restructuring over the past several decades, with its emphasis on less government intervention and its preference for market-based solutions. The ideology of the Ownership Society builds on the neoliberal view that private pension funds should be unhampered by government legislation, as individuals are expected to trust market-based pension options. To elaborate on this observation, we will concern ourselves with some of the limitations of ERISA identified by Ghilarducci, as they reflect the inability of the market to provide social protection for workers. First, recall that the alleged key benefit of the Ownership Society is the ability of individuals to control their pension savings, and that this ability empowers individuals by freeing them from dependence on government handouts in the form of Social Security. However, 401(k) plans have a dismal track record in terms of encouraging savings and adequate coverage of full-time workers (temporary, casual and part-time labour are not covered at all). This has much to do with the decision of the US government to disallow tax credits for working families with incomes below $50,000, to encourage them to invest in pension savings; conversely – and the class bias is shown here – the tax cuts in 2001 and 2003 were intended to encourage high-income families to save for retirement. According to William Greider:

> Studies have confirmed that personal accounts have generated 'very little net savings'. While every worker could participate in theory, the practical reality is that only the more affluent families could afford to take full advantage of the 401(k) tax break – sheltering their annual 401(k) contributions from income taxes. But typically they did so simply by moving money from other conventional savings accounts into the tax-exempt kind. The bleak reality is reflected in those 401(k) account balances. Of the 48 million families who hold one or more of the accounts, the median value of their savings is $27,000 (which means half of all families have less than $27,000). Among older workers on the brink of retiring (55 to 64 years old) who have personal accounts, the median value is $55,000. That's only enough to buy an annuity that would pay $398 a month, far short of middle-class living standards.
>
> (Greider, 2005b; see also Cypher, 2007; Mishel *et al.*, 2007)

Furthermore, ERISA does not address the fact that changes to pension coverage are caused by serious structural shifts in the labour market. Research has shown that pension protection is actually shrinking, despite the proliferation of 401(k) accounts and the alleged prosperity of the 1980s and 1990s. In the private sector, fewer employees participate in pension plans of any kind now compared with 20 years ago, down from 51 per cent to 46 per cent (the DB company pensions that once covered 53 per cent now protect only 34 per cent). The value of pension wealth, meanwhile, fell by 17 per cent for workers in the middle and below, mainly because their voluntary savings were weak or non-existent, yet soared for those at the top, leading to 'an upsurge in pension wealth inequality' (Wolff, 2006).

According to Ghilarducci, 401(k) plans may effectively lead to unequal coverage as companies exercise the option for coverage of select individuals. In their attempts to escape non-discrimination tests regarding pension plans, corporations persuaded the government to create a safe harbour for employers providing 401(k) plans. Although employers are not required to match their employees' 401(k) contributions, many employers do so for a wide range of reasons, such as remaining competitive in the labour market, responding to workers' bargaining strength and/or satisfying corporate responsibility aims. By providing a generous match for all who elect coverage, employers can avoid non-discrimination tests. Under the safe harbour rule, however, employers also have the option of including all workers and thus making a smaller match. As Ghilarducci observes, 'the insidious outcome is that most employers pick the first option and only the highest paid elect to be covered. The highest paid employees receive a generous match – and the generous tax-exemption contribution' (Ghilarducci, 2004: 4).

The above result leads to another limitation of the ERISA: it does not influence the manner in which corporate management formulates pension plans. The ERISA data from the employer cost index show that employers are not increasing their emphasis on pensions. During good economic times, the compensation growth that did occur was paid in wages and not in pensions. This, in turn, reflects the impulse to reward employees immediately after a bout of high sales and/or high profits, to boost productivity and company loyalty (Ghilarducci, 2000). According to the theoretical underpinnings of the Ownership Society, a market-led pension system would allow for more control and choice. The question that arises is: Do policyholders have control over their pensions? Robin Blackburn points out the legal reality that pension fund assets possess features exceeding those needed to administer the pension. Indeed, the lack of rights accorded to policyholders prevents them from wielding power in the way that equities – even non-voting shares – can confer a degree of leverage over management (cf. Ghilarducci, 1992; Clark, 1993; Blackburn, 2002). Put another way, current US law denies any rights to the collective entity of policyholders covering a particular industry or company (Blackburn, 2002: 129). This, in turn, reinforces the above claim that pensions are 'investments without representation' (Rifkin and Barber, 1978: 96). The ERISA, unlike laws in most other industrialized countries, does not require worker representation on investment boards. The lack of labour representatives leads to concerns over agency, perhaps most notably when pension sponsors or fiduciaries follow procedures that maximize their interests and not the interests of those they are meant to represent (Ghilarducci, 2000). The government, by way of the ERISA, has signalled that it is not interested in either creating a legal mechanism to ensure social accountability or in giving a voice to private pension holders – both of which would enable private pension holders to influence corporate policy regarding the nature of their pension schemes (Chapter 5) and, more generally, investment decisions regarding their deferred wages. Another limitation of the ERISA is the absence of an insurance scheme to protect policyholders of private pension plans, such as 401(k)s. Through the ERISA, the PBGC was established to insure DB payments (up to a certain limit) in case the employer becomes bankrupt. The government has to provide this insurance, because no insurance company will take on the risks. The problem is that the PBGC does not protect DC plans, such as those held by employees of, for example, Enron, WorldCom, Global Crossing and so forth. The capitalist nature of the ERISA comes through in full force here, as 'US law requires the [pension] industry to abide by the standards the industry itself defines' (Blackburn, 2002: 129). The proponents of the Ownership Society have neither addressed changes to the ERISA nor the PBGC (cf. Clark, 1993).

Choice and access in Social (in)Security?

We now turn to the question of whether greater dependency on the market has delivered on its promises of increased choice and access for all Americans with regard to the pension system. Citizens for Tax Justice, a research and advocacy group founded in Washington, DC, over a quarter-century ago, estimates that tax cuts, along with massive government borrowing needed to pay for the cuts and increased defence spending, will add $3.8 trillion to the national debt over six years. Over the next ten years, the richest Americans – the top 1 per cent – are slated to receive tax cuts amounting to approximately half of a trillion dollars. The $477 billion in tax breaks that the George W. Bush administration has targeted for this elite group will average $342,000 per person over the decade (Citizens for Tax Justice, 2005a).

According to the non-partisan Centre on Budget and Policy Priorities (CBPP), '[a] conservative estimate suggests that federal policies are costing states and localities about $185 billion over the four-year course of the state fiscal crisis' (Lav, 2003: 3). In the name of the global war on terrorism, the Bush II administration has shifted health costs from the federal government to states, forcing states to pay for the unfunded mandates of the Homeland Security, election reform and No Child Left Behind programmes (Feldstein, 1998). As a result, states and local communities have responded by raising taxes and cutting social services. President Bush also raided Social Security to help pay for these cuts (Center for American Progress, 2004). The US government's move to axe social welfare at both the federal and state levels has sought to bolster 'corporate welfare' through the reduction of corporate income tax. In the early 2000s, the Bush II administration ensured that corporate income tax had reached its lowest level since the early 1980s and the second lowest level in approximately 60 years. Corporate tax loopholes actually cost more than companies paid in income taxes in fiscal years 2002 and 2003 (Citizens for Tax Justice, 2005b).

The ERISA and the Ownership Society are market-based solutions engineered by the US government to maintain and reproduce neoliberal-led forms of restructuring as this relates to the corporate–financial nexus (Chapter 1). The push for DC pension plans and an ownership-based system are strategies to avert taxation on the wealthy, including corporations, at the expense of the middle and working classes. The market-based strategy inherent in the ideology of the Ownership Society also depoliticizes and declasses Social Security by pushing it into the domain of the faceless and unaccountable mechanisms of the marketplace, while helping to further finance Corporate America, which has grown dependent on the constant flow of funds from pension savings (Blackburn, 2002). The upshot of this move has also been the individualization of pension savings. Since the 1980s, many workers have been forced to invest their savings in a highly volatile financial system, which, for many Americans, is technical to the point of incomprehension. As Holly Sklar notes: 'At a time of rising support for socially responsible business, Bush's Ownership Society offers less social responsibility, less opportunity and accelerating disinvestment in the future' (Sklar, 2005).

Conclusion

As I have argued throughout the chapter, the Ownership Society is not a phenomenon distinctive to the George W. Bush administration. Instead, the Ownership Society should be understood as a feature of ongoing attempts to restructure and socially reproduce neoliberal-led capitalism in the US. By studying the capitalist nature of the Ownership Society, two broad components of the changing nature of neoliberal rule in the US are made evident: (1) the expansion of social security capital to help fuel financial markets and, by extension, Corporate America; and (2) the attempts to discipline labour by attempting to socialize millions of working-class Americans to abrogate their right to Social Security through increasing dependence on the market to augment and protect old-age savings. The ideological tenets of the Ownership Society also act to reassert the legitimacy of middle-class Americans putting their trust in the stock market. This translates into the establishment of market-based, DC plans as the preferred investment means to enjoy financial security during retirement.

The contradictory and highly unstable foundation upon which this promise of economic security has been constructed is illuminated by events of the past decade: the corporate accounting scandals of the early 2000s; the sub-prime mortgage crisis of 2007, which resulted in over one million, mostly low-income Americans with poor credit ratings losing their homes to bank foreclosures; and what is regarded as the worst economic crisis in the post-Second World War era – the 2008 failure of the credit system, which had its roots in housing finance. Aside from dispossessing tens of millions of Americans of their pension savings and/or family homes, these crises have also served to increase the already high levels of income inequality in the US, which by certain measures is more pronounced than in developing countries in regions such as Latin America.[9] Furthermore, the spate of financial and corporate crises over the past decade has cast critical light on the pro-market policies of old-age savings. The lack of regulatory control vis-à-vis private pension funds, as well as structural limitations to savings rates set by the government – e.g. tax legislation, minimum wage level, secure jobs, lack of adequate subsidization of other social programmes and so forth – have led to increased insecurity and vulnerability for millions of Americans. The two major beneficiaries of the Ownership Society thus far have been Wall Street and high-income families, who typically had minimum financial assets of $364,000 in 2001 (Weller, 2004) and have been spared the increased taxation needed to assist in paying for Social Security.

The assimilation of lower-income and middle-class Americans into the private pension system and, relatedly, the stock market, has at least two further implications – both of which serve the dominant interests of US society. On the one hand, given that the attainment of workers' future lifestyles depends on the profitability of Corporate America, environmental concerns, human rights abuses and labour standards begin to take a back seat to the 'bottom line'. In this context, it is easier for corporations to provide band-aid solutions to their actions at home and abroad through the feel-good rhetoric of SRI (see Chapter 7). On the other hand, the assumption that speculative activities are necessary to achieve economic gain embeds itself more deeply into the minds of the construct of 'Main Street' America. Economic risks become desirable and logical in order to achieve material wealth in old age, as well as to pay off high levels of consumer debt, such as mortgages and credit cards. This mindset has the effect of further legitimizing the growing role of DC plans over the more secure DB plans. Although the Ownership Society has not resulted in concrete policy changes to date, it has played an important ideological role in bolstering the long-standing assault on Social Security and, more generally, the privatization of old-age pension savings. More to the point, the ideology of the Ownership Society and its false claims of empowerment, security and freedom have served to legitimate the neoliberal assumption that the market, as opposed to the state, should be the preferred and trusted partner in providing old-age security for all Americans – an idea which, in the end, assists in strengthening the corporate–financial nexus. In the wake of the 2008 credit meltdown, for instance, the Bush II administration made clear that any form of regulation that restricted the freedom of the market would only threaten the American way of life and undermine the ability of free markets to help Americans overcome the detrimental effects of the crisis by creating prosperity and hope (*Bloomberg.com*, 2008).

While it may seem anachronistic that the Ownership Society emerged at a time when Corporate America was at its nadir – both in terms of its stock value and confidence levels – the ideological reinforcement and material reproduction (as well as expansion) of the Ownership Society may be viewed as a necessary political intervention to reproduce the disciplinary features of social security capital so as to maintain the corporate–financial nexus, both ideologically and coercively. As discussed in the next chapter, both the cause of and the solution to the crisis of Corporate America were found in the corporate governance doctrine. This move has had the effect of deepening the contradictions inherent in neoliberal-led capitalism and, more specifically, the Ownership Society, while depoliticizing and neutralizing the conflicts associated with these paradoxes.

3 Repoliticizing corporate governance

Scandals, struggles and the Sarbanes–Oxley Act

Between 2001 and 2002, a barrage of corporate scandals affected a quarter of the largest corporations in the American economy. Institutional investors, many of whom had their pension assets tied up in these firms, lost over $300 billion during this period (Greider, 2005a). The downfall of Enron in 2001 represented one of the largest bankruptcies under Chapter 11 in US history, and the term 'Enronitis' came into vogue. The term has been used by the media and the academic community to refer to a widespread 'illness' afflicting extremely powerful and once highly regarded publicly traded firms in Corporate America, such as Adelphia, Halliburton, Kmart, AOL Time Warner, Dynegy, WorldCom and so forth. Observers have described the ailment as involving insider trading and a lack of transparency in corporate and government operations, which has contributed to the meltdown of financial markets around the world (Wei and Milkiewicz, 2003). Interestingly, the disease has been portrayed as an isolated and rare virus caused by the excesses of corporate management, which have largely been driven by greed and a lack of oversight. In other words, the root cause of Enronitis is believed to be weak corporate governance practices, not the underlying contradictions and relations of power linked to the largely deregulated financial market and liberalized corporations.

In response to Enronitis, the Bush II administration launched the Public Company Accounting Reform and Investor Protection Act of 2002, also know as the Sarbanes–Oxley Act (hereafter, Act or SOX). The Bush II administration has portrayed the Act not only as a regulatory mechanism aiming to transform the way in which publicly traded companies control their internal processes, but also as the single most dramatic legislation enacted in the world of commerce since the creation of the New Deal (1933–1938); or, in the words of President George W. Bush, 'the most far-reaching reforms of American business practices since the time of Franklin Delano Roosevelt' (White House, 2002). The question that emerges is why, in an era marked by pro-market reforms and an emphasis on minimum government intervention for the purpose of stabilizing investment, did the Bush II administration choose to describe the Act with reference to the New Deal, especially given the latter's implications of 'big government'? Was this simply a rhetorical exercise to appease disgruntled shareholders and to assuage the fears of potential investors, or is there something more complex at work, involving American capitalism and its prevailing form of neoliberal governance?

In this chapter, I attempt to explore and explain the motivations behind this seeming incongruence between dominant laissez-faire policies on the one hand, and regulatory protection of shareholder interests on the other.

There have been wide-reaching implications of the SOX for the US economy and the livelihoods of millions of Americans, many of whom depend on the stock markets to augment their old-age savings (Blackburn, 2002; Sweeney, 2002; see also Chapter 1). Despite these implications, the Act has not been subjected to critical investigations in the social sciences. This condition of apathy is itself, I suggest later, symptomatic of the pre-eminence of mainstream corporate governance theory and practice. Where debates about the SOX have emerged in academia, they have remained firmly grounded in technical analyses of legal studies and managerial sciences. These discussions shed light on the technical strengths and weaknesses of the Act, but they ignore social and political considerations. Moreover, the debates tend to be confined to questions regarding either the effectiveness of legislation in curbing fraudulent behaviour of corporate executives, including boards of directors (Longnecker, 2004; Peters, 2004; Tracey and Fiorelli, 2004; Weismann, 2004; Westbrook, 2004), or as ways to strengthen transparency and accountability at the firm level in order to protect shareholder value (Van den Berghe and De Ridder, 1999; Cioffi, 2000; Vives, 2000; MacAvoy and Millstein, 2004).

Without conflating the differences between these various perspectives and authors, it is possible to identify a common preoccupation in the debates: What constitutes good corporate governance and how can it be maintained to achieve economic stability and efficiency in the operations of publicly traded firms? According to one of the world's leading management consultancy firms, McKinsey & Company, 'Not since the mid-1980s have we seen such a clear political, investor, and corporate focus on corporate governance. SEC and stock exchange reviews are ongoing, intensified investor pressures are visible, even the president has proposed governance reform' (2002a: 1). The corporate governance doctrine is not a discipline per se, but an emerging field of inquiry about the nature of managing the various interests involved in publicly traded corporations. While corporate governance has its roots in the study of law (Blair, 1995), it has become the pre-eminent analytical framework in understanding the internal and external dynamics of publicly traded firms across a variety of disciplines, including the social sciences, as well as in media and policy circles.[1] Put another way, the corporate governance doctrine guides and rationalizes policies affecting corporate behaviour, such as the SOX. As noted in the previous chapter, the corporate governance doctrine is concerned with understanding how a firm's key participants (i.e. shareholders, management and the board of directors) achieve the ultimate goal of a profit-seeking firm: the highest possible earnings for its shareholders, also known as 'maximization of shareholder value' (Monks and Minow, 2001). Given the prominence of this framework, it should not come as a surprise that the rationale of the SOX was largely portrayed in terms of a need to deal effectively with the root cause of the crisis: weak corporate governance practices (e.g. fraud, lack of transparency and accountability).

My main objective in this chapter is to transcend and, at the same time, question the dominant position of corporate governance theory and practice by situating the SOX within the relations of power, contestations and contradictions that characterize capitalist society. I argue that despite its representation as an attempt to protect shareholder value through the establishment of 'far-reaching reforms' of the corporate sector, the manner in which the cause of the crisis has been analysed and subsequently resolved re-legitimates the same neoliberal policies that have contributed to bringing about the scandals in the first place,[2] namely, self-regulation of corporations and financial deregulation. Moreover, and relatedly, as suggested in the previous chapter, the dominance of the corporate governance framework is not an innocuous occurrence. Like many fields of study, it is highly political, subjective and arbitrary. This is reflected in both the manner in which it has interpreted the causes underpinning the recent wave of crises and, by extension, the solution it puts forward for solving the problem(s) associated with the debacles. Like any body of knowledge, mainstream theorizations of corporate governance speak on behalf of certain interests. It is therefore important to know whose interests are being promoted in the dominant discourse surrounding the Act. Indeed, it must be kept in mind that the corporate governance doctrine, and by extension the SOX, is an integral feature of the prevalent policy and ideological orientation of neoliberalism (see Chapter 1). Given the neoliberal assumptions inherent in mainstream corporate governance theory, it has the power to 'explain away' the recent scandals in myopic, technical and individualized terms, thereby depoliticizing the struggles and underlying contradictions rooted in neoliberal-led restructuring of capital accumulation.

This chapter is organized in four main sections. The first section lays the analytical groundwork by discussing the main concerns of the corporate governance framework and providing an overview of the key response by the US government to the recent wave of corporate scandal: the SOX. The second section begins to draw the links between neoliberalism and corporate governance by identifying three common-sense assumptions embedded in the latter. This section attempts to (re-)draw the inherent connection between the production of corporate governance knowledge and the practice of corporate governance expressed in policy formation. The third section sets out to deconstruct the neoliberal assumptions underpinning corporate governance and, by extension, the SOX, by situating them within the wider framework of neoliberal-led restructuring of capitalist society. This is achieved, first, by identifying a basic contradiction in neoliberal capitalist society, and, second, offering an alternative explanation to each of the common-sense assumptions discussed in the second section. The final section concludes by considering the political and social implications of corporate governance, particularly its ability to legitimate and reproduce two key features of neoliberalism within the US: the self-regulating corporation and financial deregulation.

The official response to 'Enronitis': the corporate responsibility initiative and the SOX

Framing the problem within the parameters of the corporate governance doctrine

This section is concerned with demonstrating how debates surrounding the latest wave of corporate scandals have been framed within the wider corporate governance discourse, particularly regarding the latter's emphasis on continued self-regulation, transparency and accountability of management to shareholders. To facilitate this discussion, it is useful to outline the main tenets of the so-called 'agency problem' that sits at the crux of corporate governance and finds expression in the official response to Enronitis. Within modern forms of corporate organization, managers are seen as the agents of shareholders (also known in agency theory as 'principals'), and are therefore expected to engage in activities that maximize value to shareholders by increasing the market price of the shares. Ensuring that managers remain accountable to shareholders is the cornerstone and defining feature of Anglo-American forms of corporate governance (cf. Lazonick and O'Sullivan, 2000; Jensen, 2000; O'Sullivan, 2000, 2003; Monks and Minow, 2001; Aglietta and Rebérioux, 2005). This objective is not easily achieved, however, given the deep mistrust of corporate managers by shareholders and other suppliers of finance (i.e. banks). In other words, 'principals' are deeply suspicious of whether executives *truly* have their best interests at heart, especially given management's distant proximity from market discipline (Berle and Means, 1932; Scott, 1997). As Adam Smith once argued, corporate managers 'are not as careful with "other people's money" as with their own, causing the interests of the owners of a joint-stock company to diverge from that of its managers' (quoted in Swedberg, 2003: 76). Thus, the study of corporate governance is primarily concerned with understanding and providing solutions to the 'principal–agent problem' by ensuring that the interests between principals (i.e. the shareholders) and agents (i.e. managers and the board of directors) are aligned as fully as possible (Shleifer and Vishny, 1997).

To ensure that the objective of maximizing shareholder value remains at the top of management's list of priorities, institutional investors use various incentives, such as tying managers' pay to the company's economic performance through stock options and stock grants, tying executive compensation to dividend payouts and so forth. According to neoclassical economic theory, the very structure of the free market will also ensure that the interests of agents and principals remained aligned. The constant threat, for instance, of hostile takeovers of underperforming companies will discipline managers to pursue the goal of creating shareholder value (Goldstein, 2000; Bivens and Weller, 2005). As I elaborate below, the economic reasoning behind this position is that the market serves as the best incentive and corrective to what is considered irrational behaviour on the part of corporate executives. In short, irrational behaviour, as it is understood here, essentially involves unnecessary risk taking or negligent or irresponsible management practices that adversely affect the firm's ability to meet the objective of shareholder maximization.

The legal solution to the 'agency problem': the SOX of 2002

> This law says to every dishonest corporate leader: you will be exposed and punished; the era of low standards and false profits is over; no boardroom in America is above or beyond the law.
>
> (President George W. Bush at the signing ceremony of the SOX – White House, 2002)

The SOX has been portrayed by the government as the most important and far-sweeping securities legislation affecting public companies since the SEC was formed in 1934 under the New Deal (Ribstein, 2002; Strahota, 2002; Westbrook, 2004; Mitchell, 2007). Among its many responsibilities, the SEC was mandated to carry out two central objectives: (1) 'to provide investors with information about public offerings of securities'; and (2) 'to prohibit misrepresentations, omissions and other fraudulent acts in the offer or sale of securities'[3] (Weismann, 2004: 1003). In keeping with its regulatory role, the government gave the SEC the responsibility of implementing the Act for all issuers, both foreign and domestic. According to its supporters, the SOX makes it easier for the SEC to facilitate the prosecution of securities fraud. Resonating with the concerns of corporate governance theory, one of the main ways the SEC is to accomplish this task is by placing

> greater responsibility on senior management and directors, particularly independent directors and audit committee members, by requiring these actors to take a substantially more proactive role in overseeing and monitoring the financial reporting process, including disclosure and reporting systems and internal controls.
>
> (Strahota, 2002: 6; see also Tracey and Fiorelli, 2004)

Given the density and length of the Act (Lander, 2004), the present analysis will be limited to some of its more pertinent features. One of the Act's key innovations was the creation of an independent Public Company Accounting Oversight Board (PCAOB).[4] Among its various roles, this private sector, non-profit organization is mandated to address 'off-balance-sheet' transactions, i.e. the financing or raising of money by a company that does not appear on the company's balance sheet, such as the notorious Jedi I and II products created by Enron executives.[5] In this capacity, the PCAOB assumes the duty of setting standards for accounting reports.[6] Moreover, several provisions in the Act attempt to improve existing SEC rules by: barring auditors from doing non-audit work for audit clients (§201); insisting on the rotation of audit partners after five years (§203); requiring corporate audit committees to select auditors (§202); and restricting the auditing of a member of a firm whose senior management has been previously employed by the auditor (§206) (Ribstein, 2002). While decisions regarding the hiring, firing and retention of auditors are left to an independent audit committee of the client's board of directors, and not to senior management, the audit committee and oversight mechanisms are still subject to the control of the Chief Executive Officer (CEO). This, in turn, results in a questionable situation in which the monitored chooses the monitor (Skyes, 2000; Elliot and Schroth, 2002).

Although the PCAOB has some disciplinary clout, it does not possess subpoena power. According to former SEC Commissioner, Harvey Pitt, 'We do not want it to have subpoena power. While subpoena power sounds like it might be very useful, only the government possesses subpoena power' (PBS Frontline, 2002; Weismann, 2004). Instead of devising mechanisms for establishing oversight of the internal operations of publicly traded firms, the SEC sees its role as creating an environment that will empower corporations. Companies are therefore expected to create, implement and self-police 'improved disclosure' without SEC scrutiny to ensure that disclosure accurately reflects risk (ibid.). Given that the interpretation and administration of the SOX by the SEC favours self-regulation as a key response, some legal theorists have concluded that the Act and the PCAOB will add very little to pre-existing regulatory guidelines and statutory framework (Peters, 2004; Weismann, 2004).

In summary, the SOX was formulated within the parameters of corporate governance and, therefore, was designed to strengthen corporate governance practices in publicly traded firms. It did so by introducing mechanisms (self-regulatory checks and balances) that could encourage a realignment between the interests of agents and principals. The corresponding solution was not only highly technical and localized within certain 'expert' circles, such as the PCAOB, it was also based on the principle of self-regulation – allowing corporate management to police themselves. However, this raises a deeply political question: Why, despite the fact that history has proven the failures of self-regulation, does the US government, and by extension the SEC, continue to tow the laissez-faire line? The ineffectiveness of the SOX is revealed in the ongoing litany of high-profile corporate abuse, ranging from fraud to misrepresentation of financial data, such as options backdating,[7] and involving companies such as Hollinger International in 2003, Vivendi Universal in 2003, Tenet Healthcare in 2003, Freddie Mac in 2003, DPL Inc. in 2004, and more recently, American International Group, Inc. in 2005, to name a few. Who gains from this continued policy stance, and why? To address these questions, we need to delve more critically into the corporate governance framework in order to grasp the inner, capitalist nature of the SOX.

Common-sense assumptions underpinning corporate governance

The significance of 'common sense' and neoliberalism: repoliticizing corporate governance doctrine

No one can deny that corporate greed, weak transparency practices and account-ability standards played a role in the recent wave of corporate scandals. I suggest, however, that this crisis had deeper causes than simply a failing of man-agement to adhere to good corporate governance practices. To transcend and repoliticize this dominant framework, we need to re-link corporate governance to neoliberal-led capitalism. The main goal in this section, therefore, is to move beyond mainstream representations of the corporation and its connotations of neutral and objective relations between the so-called 'agents and principals' in order to expose how the corporation is connected to the reproduction of neoliberal-led capital accumulation.

It bears repeating that corporate governance did not emerge in a vacuum, but rather was forged within the context of neoliberalism. The spirit of laissez-faire, or market-led growth, which forms the cornerstone of neoliberalism, is not new to the US. Indeed, the belief that unfettered market forces lead to economic stability and growth was firmly entrenched in the US prior to the New Deal (Fligstein, 1990; Mitchell, 2007; cf. Cerny, 2008). Laissez-faire economics *re-emerged* as a dominant premise of US-style neoliberalism when President Reagan came to power in 1981. As noted in Chapter 1, neoliberalism is often associated with minimum state intervention in the economy and rests on two basic premises: (1) the market, as opposed to the state, should take the lead in terms of decisions surrounding economic and social policy-making, since com-petition among rational, self-interested individuals will allocate resources more efficiently than the government; and (2) there is a harmony between private profit maximization and the general interest of society, which is to say that eco-nomic growth, brought about via policies of deregulation, liberalization and pri-vatization, will lead to more prosperity for all citizens (Hymer, 1970). These principal ideological tenets can help us understand the roots of the neoliberal assumption undergirding the importance of the self-regulation of corporations, as well as financial deregulation – both of which are discussed later in this chapter.

In order to critically elaborate on the common-sense assumptions of main-stream corporate governance theory embedded in the SOX, it is important to understand the significance of the term 'common-sense assumption'. How does knowledge allow for control through consent rather than through coercion? According to Antonio Gramsci, certain types of knowledge, such as the assump-tions underpinning free market reforms of neoliberalism, appear at particular periods of time, in specific material circumstances, and reflect specific configura-tions of social power. Gramsci referred to this prevailing form of knowledge as hegemony (Gramsci, 1992). A constituent element of hegemony is common sense, which is a site for political contestation and struggle (Augelli and Murphy, 1988: 17). Common sense emerges from historically and spatially specific ideologies, social mythologies and scientific doctrines, such as the free-market tenets entailed in neoliberalism. The dynamism of common sense lies, in part, in the underlying contradictions of capital accumulation and, in part, in the struggles inherent in its direct ties to relations of power within capitalist society, represented in the present study by powerful capitalist interests, corporate executives, boards of directors and state officials.

Building on Gramsci, Mark Rupert suggests that common sense is a dynamic concept that is neither univocal nor coherent, 'but is continually transforming itself, enriching itself with scientific ideas and with philosophical opinions which have entered ordinary life' (Rupert, 1997: 16). It is 'fragmentary, incoherent and inconsequential, in conformity with the social and cultural position of those [regular] people whose philosophy it is' (ibid). 'Regular people' may be understood here as referring to those individuals (skilled and unskilled or waged and salaried workers, the unemployed, under-employed and so forth), who pay the highest price when debacles occur, and whose livelihoods and savings are dependent on the ability of corporate executives to deliver promises of maximizing shareholder value – a term which is itself fraught with ambiguity and thus open to subjective interpretation (Froud *et al.*, 2000).

The common sense of corporate governance doctrine

Recognizing that corporate governance is not a homogenous area of study, I present below three key assumptions that push research in this area beyond the purely technical prescriptions found in existing mainstream 'critiques' of corporate governance discourse in order to uncover the underlying power relations at stake. While by no means exhaustive, these assumptions shed light on the neoliberal nature of corporate governance and assist in transcending the dominant view of the SOX and its alleged aim of strengthening shareholder value.

The first assumption underpinning the corporate governance doctrine, touched upon earlier in discussing the agency problem, pertains to the belief that competition between rational, self-interested economic actors will lead to efficient market behaviour. This optimal environment, the theory goes, will ensure the alignment between principals and agents, resulting in the maximization of shareholder value. As William Lazonick and Mary O'Sullivan observe, the majority of US financial economists and policymakers believe that the market is always superior to organizations in the efficient allocation of resources. Based on this assumption, agency theorists argue that because corporate managers are undisciplined by the market mechanism, they would opportunistically use their control over the allocation of corporate resources and returns to line their own pockets, or at least to pursue objectives that were contrary to the interests of shareholders (market participants) (Lazonick and O'Sullivan, 2000: 16; see also Fama, 1980).

Central to the above position is what neo-classical economists refer to as the efficient market hypothesis (EMH). According to the EMH, rational financial markets, possessing perfect knowledge, will act as a check on the system, punishing profligate corporate managers through investment strike and capital flight by, for example, engaging in the 'Wall Street Walk' (shareholders selling shares when they are unsatisfied with management). Eugene Fama, known for his work on asset pricing and portfolio theory, devised the EMH in the 1970s. For Fama,

> an 'efficient' market is defined as a market where there are large numbers of rational profit-maximizers actively competing, with each trying to predict future market values of individual securities, and where important current information is almost freely available to all participants.... In other words, in an efficient market at any point in time the actual price of a security will be a good estimate of its intrinsic value.
> (quoted in Soederberg, 2004: 104; see also Fama, 1970)

The assumption of the efficient market has been thrown into disrepute by high-profile historical events such as the hedge fund blowups – most notably, but not exclusively, associated with the Long Term Credit Management debacle – and the mortgage mess and credit market crisis linked to the sub-prime mortgage scandals, which began in 2007. Questioning this key premise of the corporate governance doctrine is, therefore, critical – a task taken up later in this chapter.

The second and related assumption inherent in the neoliberal understanding of corporate governance is that the relationship between agents and principals is believed to occur on a smooth and even playing field. As we saw in Chapter 1, the corporate governance doctrine is founded upon the pluralist principles imbued in liberal democracy. This pluralist understanding of corporate relations (Dahl, 1956) rests on the assumption that no entity exercises a monopoly of representative activity. For instance, with the establishment of the New Deal, and the passing of the 1933 Securities Act and the 1934 Securities Exchange Act, lawmakers attempted to establish a process of corporate accountability based on the model of America's own liberal traditions of political accountability. Recall the observation of Monks and Minow from Chapter 1, that 'Just as political democracy acted to guarantee the legitimacy of governmental or public power, the theory went, so corporate democracy would control – and therefore legitimate – the otherwise uncontrollable growth of power in the hands of private individuals' (2001: 107). This legitimation occurred by ensuring that corporate democracy was enshrined in the principle of one share, one vote. The contradictions and limitations underpinning the assumption of corporate democracy are discussed in detail in the next chapter.

The third and final assumption of the corporate governance doctrine, and one that is deeply embedded in discussions surrounding the SOX, is that the state is a neutral terrain that is a separate entity from the economy. Following John Locke, one of the main intellectual influences upon the American constitution, the state is a classless entity reflecting the common good of society.

> Political power is that power which every man having in the state of nature, has given up into the hands of the society, and therein to the governors whom the society hath set over itself, with this express or tacit trust that it shall be employed for the good and the preservation of their property.
>
> (Locke, 1690: Chapter 15: 321)

This position resonates with the position of mistrust articulated in mainstream corporate governance discourse regarding government intervention in the efficient operations of the market. The state, as the embodiment of the common good, is able, through its legal apparatus such as the SOX, to ensure the natural morality of the market. It follows, therefore, that laws, as an extension of the state, are viewed as a natural (classless) institution resting above both the market and civil society (Luhmann, 1993; Renner, 1949).

Taken together, the common-sense assumptions identified here share an objective understanding of the market that is devoid of any considerations of contestation, contradictions and relations of power. They also masquerade as truths that are, in reality, highly subjective political arguments for legitimating the self-regulation of corporations and deregulated financial markets – both of which represent an integral feature of Enronitis.

Deconstructing the common sense of the corporate governance doctrine

> The myth that holds that the great corporation is a puppet of the market, the powerless servant of the consumer, is, in fact, one of the services by which its power is perpetuated.
>
> (John Kenneth Galbraith quoted in Monks and Minow, 2001: 4)

An underlying contradiction of the doctrine

It is useful to begin this section by identifying one of the basic contradictions upon which neoliberal corporate governance and the SOX turn. Despite the efforts of policymakers and pundits of neoliberalism, the US economy has largely failed to reach goals promised by free-market ideologues and policymakers (Bourdieu, 1998; Pollin, 2003; Saad-Filho and Johnston, 2005; cf. Cerny, 2008). Since its emergence in the early 1980s, there has been very little sign of sustained growth in terms of productivity rates, standards of living, job security and overall economic stability – all of which is made evident by the alarming levels of corporate, consumer and public debt,[8] as well as the increasing frequency and depth of the manifestations of crisis. Indeed, in addition to the recent corporate scandals, the economic landscape of the US has been marked by a savings and loans debacle in the 1980s, a stock market crash in 1987, corporate scandals in the early 1990s and the collapse of the Long Term Credit Management fund in 1998, to name just a few examples. Emerging in 2007, the sub-prime lending crisis had its roots in the housing bubble; it now threatens the stability of world financial markets. While these scandals are not homogenous in nature, they do share at least three general features. First, they pose legitimacy problems for the neoliberal paradigm. Second, they are connected to the underlying crisis of overaccumulation (to be discussed presently). Third, they detrimentally affect an increasing number of so-called 'Main Street' investors and their pension savings, as well as other innocent bystanders, such as workers employed either directly or indirectly by corporate behemoths (see Chapter 2).

Instead of electing to implement state-led regulations aimed at protecting society from the irrational behaviour of market forces, the state has responded to each crisis with more market-based solutions, such as the SOX, therein deepening, as opposed to resolving, the above contradiction. As will be demonstrated below, solutions to the problems associated with neoliberal-led capital restructuring are said to be in the interests of shareholder value. In reality, state intervention is geared towards the reproduction of the conditions for capital accumulation. The body of knowledge of mainstream corporate governance assists the state in overcoming attacks on the legitimacy of neoliberal polices, most notably deregulated financial markets and self-regulating firms, largely due to its technical, apolitical and, therefore, sanitized discourse. The state finds fault almost exclusively with the misalignment in principal–agent relations, and therefore concentrates attention on issues of fraud, accountability of boards and CEOs and lack of transparency, as opposed to neoliberal-led forms of capitalist restructuring that have benefited a relatively small number of powerful and wealthy people. Indeed, for many Americans, living standards have stagnated or declined over the past several decades, while the burden of work and insecurity has grown (Piven, 2004; see also Chapters 2 and 5).

In what follows, various expressions of this contradiction are examined in light of the three neoliberal assumptions underpinning corporate governance: the efficient market hypothesis; the neutral state and its embodiment of the common good; and the pluralist and democratic nature of principal–agent relations. Since the goal is to view these three moments as integral features of capitalist society, there will be some overlap in the discussion. The assumptions should not be understood as rigid structures, but rather as fluid social relations of power.

Efficient market hypothesis or short-term speculation?

The first assumption of corporate governance holds that the market will effectively resolve the principal–agent problem, therein ensuring that the actual price of a security (company share) is a good estimate of the company's intrinsic value (Toporowski, 2000). However, the wave of scandals over the past quarter of a century have suggested otherwise. To critique and transcend these tenets of the 'scientific doctrine' of neoliberalism, it is useful to situate the scandals within a wider framework than that offered by mainstream corporate governance theory. In doing so, the debacles are no longer viewed as isolated occurrences, but rather as a manifestation of the general tendency of capital accumulation towards overaccumulation. As Marx observed, economic growth under capitalism is a process of internal contradictions, which frequently erupt as crises (Marx, 1991; Harvey, 2005). The dominance of fictitious capital (i.e. the flow of money capital not backed by any commodity transaction) in relation to the possibility of future labour as a counter-value is a defining characteristic of the crisis of overaccumulation that has plagued the US – as well as countries all over the world – since the 1970s.

By no means has the crisis in the US been an even and homogenous occurrence, particularly in terms of its spatial and temporal dimensions (Harvey, 1999). Nonetheless, it is possible to make some general observations vis-à-vis corporate activity. Instead of investing in plant modernization and therefore preparing for long-term international competitiveness, for example, corporate management has largely sought to increase shareholder value through short-term returns on corporate investment through stock repurchases, mergers with competitors, acquisitions of highly profitable firms and larger leveraged buyouts of unrelated businesses. As Manning observes, 'By the mid-1980s, corporate expansion was driven largely by business acquisitions rather than investment in more modern plant and capital equipment' (Manning, 2000: 51; see also Mitchell, 2007). Despite attempts by the neoliberal state to deal with this crisis through corporate welfare strategies – reducing the negotiating power of labour unions and slashing social welfare services and jobs, as witnessed by the massive layoffs that took place during the 1980s and 1990s, and again in 2006[9] – management has opted to overcome what it perceives to be the barriers to capital valorization (e.g. falling rates of profitability, inability to meet health and pension benefit packages of their workforce and so forth) by pursuing the more lucrative outlet of monetary investments. According to Keynes, the organic intellectual whose ideas guided much of economic policymaking in the pre-neoliberal era, the attraction to liquid investments is that they often pay better, at least in the short term, than real long-term investments in production (Patomäki, 2001).

This strategy is, of course, not new. Both capitalists and the state sought, as their predecessors in the late nineteenth and early twentieth centuries had done, to overcome the barriers to capital valorization by relying on financial markets (the credit system) to both prop up and stimulate the economy. Since the 1980s, greater dependence on financial markets than on the productive sphere – coupled with increased demand for credit by the public sector, corporations and consumers – has placed more pressure on the state to deregulate financial markets. In turn, this has had the effect of creating more opportunities for corporate executives to engage in short-term speculative activities to meet the goal of maximizing shareholder value. An important consequence of financial deregulation has been what Richard Minns, drawing on Elmar Altvater's (1988) work, describes as 'arbitrage capitalism'. This term refers to a situation in which an investor

> exploits differentials in market returns within similar asset categories (certain shares in energy companies, for example, may be paying less than others, while their underlying value appears similar). It uses short-term assessments of market movements and advantage, on the assumption that

prices may indeed get out of line with the underlying values, but only for a short time, during which profits can be made.

(Minns, 2001: 157)

This investment practice is at the root of many of the recent scandals of the early 2000s, such as Enron, WorldCom, Global Crossing, Dynegy and so forth.[10] In these cases, the underlying problem was not simply greed or lack of transparency, as stressed by the mainstream corporate governance discourse, but the reliance on arbitrage capitalism as a restructuring tool to reconcile the firm's lack of profitability, and on stock prices as a reaction to barriers imposed by the crisis of capitalism.

The widening gap between fictitious values in the credit system, which manifest in inflated stock prices (or bubbles), and money tied to real value (Harvey, 1999: 265–266) was greatly facilitated by the dramatic expansion and growth of the stock markets that occurred during the Clinton administration (1993–2001). During this period, markets registered an unprecedented annual growth rate of 15.3 per cent (Pollin, 2003). This growth had little to do with real economic developments however (Altvater, 2002). The reliance on monetary capital over productive capital has also incurred high levels of debt over the years. According to the renowned corporate consultants, McKinsey & Company, 'Much of the growth in global financial assets over the past 25 years has come from a rapid expansion of corporate debt' (2006: 2).

One of the largest suppliers of finance to publicly listed corporations in the neoliberal era has been pension funds (Monks and Minow, 2001; Blackburn, 2002). Pension funds, both public and private, are not only the largest institutional investor in the US (Minns, 2001; OECD, 2005), but also the largest institutional investor globally. This has been facilitated by state-led attempts to privatize large pools of workers' deferred wages. In the US, the value of some employees' pension funds now surpasses the value of the company for which the employees work (Blackburn, 2002). As discussed below, the greater involvement of 'Main Street' in financing corporations is characterized by an underlying contradiction. On the one hand, this situation has led to a growing vigilance of shareholders over their future pension savings, and thus a greater emphasis on the maximization of shareholder value (Brancato, 1997; Clowes, 2000). On the other hand, because the custodians of workers' deferred wages, namely money managers of pension and mutual funds, operate within the wider context of arbitrage capitalism, they also seek to increase shareholder value for their clients by the same methods. As Adam Harmes notes, money managers

are evaluated and paid based on their ability to retain old clients and attract new ones, and this means that they must produce strong performance numbers on a quarterly basis. So while the retirement savings that make up mutual funds and pension funds may have long-term horizons, the men and women who manage these funds often do not.

(Harmes, 2001: 36)

Lured by high profit/earnings ratios[11] – indeed the highest since the Great Crash of 1929 – institutional investors are prone to gambling, especially during times of economic downturn (Minns, 2001; Blackburn, 2002). Key public pension funds – such as CalPERS and the Arkansas Teachers' pension scheme – invested in Enron's infamous off-balance-sheet partnerships. CalPERS earned a 23 per cent return on its $250 million investment. Three years later, however, CalPERS encountered problems when its management wanted to reclaim its capital stake. The resolution of this issue was a conversion of CalPERS' claim into a $500 million stake in a new, Raptor-style investment vehicle (ibid.: 32). The real victims, of course, are workers, who depend on the health of a corporation to earn a living wage and/or future pension payouts.

Arbitrage capitalism did not progress naturally as a by-product of efficient and competitive market forces, but instead was the result of key policy decisions, which acted to deepen the above contradiction. In 1999, for example, the Glass–Steagall Act of 1933 was effectively repealed by the Clinton administration through the introduction of the Gramm–Leach–Bliley Financial Services Modernization Act. The 2001 *Economic Report of the President* clearly stated the virtues of financial deregulation, which would 'allow consolidation in the financial sector that will result in efficiency gains and provide new services for consumers' (Pollin, 2003: 32). It was not efficiency gains that dominated the financial scene, however. Arbitrage capitalism dominated, greatly facilitated by the political decision to remove the Glass–Steagall Act, which was long-regarded as one of the cornerstones of the New Deal. Designed in the hopes of preventing a repeat of the events associated with the Great Crash of 1929 by ensuring that commercial banks could receive no more than 10 per cent of their income from the securities markets, the Glass–Steagall Act created a firewall between bankers and brokers. Put another way, the Glass–Steagall Act ensured that a

> firm could not be both an investment bank (organizing the funding of firms' investment activities) and a commercial bank (handling chequing and savings accounts of individuals and firms and making loans); nor could it be one of these two types of banks and an insurance firm.
>
> (MacEwan, 2008)

The Glass–Steagall Act, therefore, had important ramifications for corporations, institutional investors, investment banks and other financial actors engaging in speculative activity, as it placed limitations on securitization measures (i.e. the extension of credit through stocks and bonds).

The replacement of the Glass–Steagall Act by the Gramm–Leach–Bliley Act effectively dissolved the barriers to securitization by opening up more space for financial actors (money managers, corporate managers and so forth) to convert long-term assets into short-term commitments for investors (speculation) (Pollin, 2003). For example, as corporate, consumer and public debt loads continued to grow in the US, so too did financial instruments, especially speculative credit derivatives, more formally known as 'asset-backed securities'[12] (ABS). While

the supporters of ABS claim that these instruments act as a useful form of protection (also known as 'hedging') for investors, it should also be kept in mind
that ABS are designed to profit from debt via speculative activities. As Robin
Blackburn observes, during the 1990s credit derivatives not only became very
popular among institutional investors (e.g. pension funds), but also, and more
specifically, among large banks tied to corporations, such as Enron's creditors:
J.P. Morgan Chase & Co. and Citibank. 'The Bond Market Association estimates the asset-backed securities market in the US alone grew from $315 billion
in 1995 to over $1 trillion 2001' (Blackburn, 2002: 30).

The validity of the EMH is called into question by such speculative activity.
It is difficult to justify the assumption that corporate management acts in the
interests of shareholders when the money managers of institutional investment
funds, such as pension funds, enter into the realm of short-term, speculative
activities to maximize shareholder value for their clients. This should not come
as a surprise, given that mutual and pension funds are under intense pressures to
perform strongly in the very short term (Harmes, 2001). The self-regulatory
nature of corporate governance, which places the brunt of responsibility on the
shoulders of shareholders under the maxim of *caveat emptor* ('let the buyer
beware'), becomes problematic in a situation in which monetary capital, as
opposed to productive investment, is viewed as the primary means of achieving
shareholder maximization.

Neutral embodiment of the common good? Or a capitalist state?

The objective of this section is to interrogate the assumption that the state represents a neutral terrain, existing as an entity separate from the economy, with its
own particular interests, yet also representing the embodiment of the common
good. In contrast to these liberal conceptualizations, Marxists view the state as
encompassing more than government and its traditional legislative, executive
and judicial functions. Instead, they see the state as a historical form of capitalist
social relations, implying that the state's existence depends on the reproduction
of those relations. Seen from this angle, we are not just dealing with a state in
capitalist society, but a *capitalist* state, since its own continued existence is tied
to the promotion of the reproduction of capitalist social relations as a whole
(Holloway, 1995: 121, my emphasis).

One of the key requirements for recreating the conditions of capitalist production is that the state must maintain a veneer of class neutrality by assuming an
autonomous relationship from the sphere of production and exchange (Hirsch,
1986). Thus, while liberal conceptualizations of the state are correct to capture
this façade of impartiality (i.e. through the term 'the common good'), this nonetheless remains a fetishized appearance (i.e. a democratic and neutral, *classless*
structure). As Holloway explains, the fact that the state

> exists as a particular or rigidified form of social relations means, that the
> relation between the state and the reproduction of capital is a complex one:

it cannot be assumed, in a functionalist fashion, either that everything the state does will necessarily be in the best interests of capital, nor that the state can achieve what is necessary to secure the reproduction of capitalist society.

(1995: 121)

As will become evident below, while the policies undertaken over the past several decades to deregulate financial markets tend to favour corporate executives over shareholders, the motivating factor is not an appeasement of certain capitalist interests – although this may be a by-product of certain forms of intervention. Instead, the policies must be viewed as an attempt by the American state to secure the successful reproduction of neoliberal-led capital accumulation.

One way the state achieves the guise of impartiality is through the creation of bourgeois laws. As the legal scholar Karl Renner argues, the law is not an objective, neutral force, but reflects the power relations within capitalist society (1949: 53). Laws are therefore 'created with the intention of producing economic results, and as a rule they achieve this effect' in the interest of recreating capitalism (ibid: 56). The fact that the SEC, a central regulatory agency, is staffed and administered by 'technical experts' and 'impartial' actors and thus is seemingly 'objective' (based on the 'science' of the theories of finance, accounting and economics) also serves to conceal the subjective and highly political forms of state intervention involved in reproducing the corporate–financial nexus. The SEC, for example, is a quasi-regulatory body largely comprised of non-elected officials,[13] which has as its mandate the primary mission of protecting investors and maintaining the integrity of the securities markets.[14] Beyond its fetishized appearance, however, the SEC is a satellite apparatus of the capitalist state, and therefore assumes similar roles and contradictory forms of intervention. As such, the SEC is not only a seemingly neutral regulatory agency, but also provides a legitimizing function for the status quo, particularly the laissez-faire approach to the behaviour of corporations and their relations to financial markets. The legitimating function of the SEC lies in its ability to serve as an impartial mediator between management and shareholder groups. Because, in theory, the agency is empowered by the state to intervene legally in corporate affairs, it wields a level of authority vis-à-vis 'principals' and 'agents'. As in the case of the SOX, US Congress grants the SEC power to implement relatively tough regulatory measures in the interests of promoting good corporate governance practices. For example, the SEC is empowered to regulate indirectly the behaviour of corporations through disclosure laws and listing requirements. However, the SEC has never exercised these powers and has opted for non-intervention (Ribstein, 2002: 13). Seen from this angle, the SEC fulfils its legitimation functions through depoliticization techniques by: (1) sanitizing highly subjective and political decisions through technical, and therefore exclusionary, language; (2) shifting the focus of the struggle away from the state to an unelected satellite apparatus; and (3) mediating the conflicts between 'agents' and 'principals' by devising non-binding measures to achieve greater accountability and transparency among 'agents', while ensuring the re-creation of the status quo.

Protecting shareholder value in a pluralist environment?

The power relationships that run through each of the common-sense assumptions underpinning the corporate governance doctrine are neither rigid nor static, but are continually transformed. The impetus for change does not derive from some functional external force, but from social struggle and contradictions that emerge within the very nature of capitalist accumulation, including periodic crises of overaccumulation. When these crises manifest themselves in Corporate America, the response by many institutional investors, especially public pension funds, has been to effect change in corporate behaviour and policy through shareholder activism, e.g. voting and dialogue (Brancato, 1997; Monks and Minow, 2001; Greider, 2005a). The ultimate threat of shareholder activism is to resort to legal action, or, as will be seen in Chapter 7, engagement in divestment campaigns. While the state cannot effectively mediate shareholder activism, it can intervene to mitigate the latter, more potent, form of activism by leveraging its powers over the legal apparatus.

The US government sought to delimit the power of shareholders through the implementation of the Tort Reform in 1995, more formally referred to as the Private Securities Litigation Reform Act (PSLRA). The primary objective of the PSLRA was to minimize the number of what the state considered 'frivolous' class action 10(b) suits in federal courts (Friedman and Freeman-Bosworth, 2001). One of the main provisions of the reform was to establish a 'safe harbour' for forward-looking statements[15] made by publicly traded companies. The reasoning behind this was to promote the dissemination of financial information to analysts and investors, and improve market efficiency (cf. Sale, 1998; PBS Frontline, 2002). There is another, more ominous, use for forward-looking statements, however. They have often been employed to encourage a particular view of the health and competitiveness of a company, despite the fact that the numbers used to compile this profile are based on future events and/or future financial results (Sale, 1998; cf. Friedman and Freeman-Bosworth, 2001). As discussed earlier, within the wider context of arbitrage capitalism, the central preoccupation for investors is not whether corporations will perform well in the long term, but how short-term financial markets perceive the company's ability to drive up the stock price. Drawing on Keynes' oft-cited example of the beauty contest, Robert Pollin observes that

> What becomes central for investors is not whether a company's products will produce profits over a long term, but rather whether the short-term financial market investors *think* a company's fortunes will be strong enough in the present and immediate future to drive the stock price up. Or, to be more precise, what really matters for a speculative investor is not what they think about a given company's prospects per se, but rather what they think

other investors are thinking, since that will be what determines where the stock price goes in the short term.

(Pollin, 2003: 15; see also Patomäki, 2001)

An important consequence of the PSLRA was the weakening of shareholders' bid to hold managers accountable by effectively removing a major mechanism for punishment and compensation for wrongdoing. Ironically, however, more lit-igation has been filed and more settlements have been made for larger dollar amounts since the passage of the PSLRA. According to Lynn Turner, SEC Chief Accountant from 1998 to 2001, these increases do not reflect loopholes in the PSLRA; rather, the increase in financial fraud lawsuits is due to the fact that there has been more financial fraud (PBS Frontline, 2002; see also Sale, 1998; cf. Peters, 2004). In response to this growing wave of lawsuits, President George W. Bush signed legislation in February 2005 to discourage multi-million-dollar class action lawsuits: 'Class action suits seeking $5 million or more would be heard in state court only if the primary defendant and more than one-third of the plaintiffs are from the same state' (*Guardian*, 2005). In 2007 the SEC attempted, once again, to diminish shareholder voice, through a controversial process aimed at curtailing or even eliminating 'the right to file shareholder resolutions' (Social Investment Forum, 2007b). This move sent shockwaves throughout the share-holder community. The SEC backed down from its proposal in reaction to a major backlash from shareholder advocates and other powerful institutional investors. Nonetheless, the regulatory agency is still committed to defending its attempt to limit the rights of shareholders to participate in the nomination of boards of directors, an issue discussed in more detail in the next chapter (ibid.).

The above scenario differs starkly from the picture painted by mainstream corporate governance theorizations. While the fetishized portrait may be that no specific actor of corporate governance exercises a monopoly of representative activity, the relations of power imbued in capitalist society and further strength-ened by the capitalist state tell another tale. To ensure return on their investment and to meet the needs of old age, workers are required to expose themselves further to exploitative conditions in the workplace, including job insecurity due to downsizing and takeovers, and looming threats of bankruptcy. The unequal and exploitative relationships between workers and management are discussed more fully in Chapter 5. For now, it is useful to highlight two points that reflect these relations but are glossed over by the fiction of corporate democracy (see Chapter 4) and ignored by the SOX.

First, free-market enthusiasts understand CEO compensation (largely in the form of stock options)[16] to ensure an alignment of interests between 'principals and agents'. However, over the neoliberal period, the executive–worker pay ratio has risen astronomically and, in many cases, unjustifiably – especially in light of productivity growth (Brennan, 2005). According to the US Bureau of Labour Statistics, 'CEO compensation swelled from 85 times what workers earned in 1990, to 209 times in 1996, and 326 times the following year. In 1999, CEO pay surged to a record 419 times the average worker's wage' (*OneWorld.net*, 2005;

cf. AFL-CIO Executive Pay Watch;[17] see also Chapter 5). The state has consistently refused to close an accounting loophole by adopting legislation, such as that put forward by the Financial Accounting Standards Board in 1993, which would effectively allow companies to record stock options on their balance sheets and, therefore, encourage management to reveal the true value of their corporation (Hu and Noe, 1997). After almost a decade of battles with regulators, US companies are, as of the 2006 fiscal year, required to expense their stock options. It has been reported, however, that hundreds of companies are using a tactic known as 'accelerated vesting' to overcome the new legislation. To illustrate,

> options traditionally become effective over a period of years after they are granted and are cancelled if the recipient leaves the company. By making options vest in 2005 rather than in future years, companies can bury the cost in the footnotes of their 2005 paperwork. That boosts earning in 2006 and beyond.
>
> (*BusinessWeek*, 2005)

Backdating scandals involving firms such as Apple Inc. and Hewlett Packard, to name but two, exemplify attempts by executives to exploit loopholes in the new legislation.

Second, through neoliberal measures (e.g. the privatization of pension plans) over the past two and a half decades, workers' old-age savings have become less secure and more dependent on the performance of the company for which the employee works. Unlike the more secure DB plans in which employers bear the investment risk, DC plans are subject to more volatility as the 'participant's benefits depend solely on the amount of the contribution and the return earned on investing it, the employee bears all the investment risk' (Federal Reserve Bank of San Francisco, 2003). According to the Federal Reserve Bank of San Francisco, the slowdown in the stock market has led to a nearly $1 trillion shrinkage in the value of private pension fund assets. At the market's height in 1999, 'these assets were worth $4.63 trillion; in 2002, they were worth $3.69 trillion. In the case of defined contribution plans, the burden of these losses fell on the beneficiaries rather than on the sponsoring firms' (ibid). This trend will continue as the 2007 sub-prime mortgage crisis deepens and spreads throughout 'Main Street' America (see Chapter 2). The material and ideological features of the social reproduction of mass investment culture are examined in the next chapter.

Recently, there has been discussion around reforms that would mandate limits on the concentration of stock to no more than 5 per cent in any single security (VanDerhei, 2002). Nonetheless, DC plans for employees of many large, publicly traded firms are substantially composed of company stock. For some large corporations, a full 43 per cent is invested in company stock; other companies require employees to have more than 75 per cent in company assets. In addition, most plans impose some restrictions on the sale of company stock, such as a prohibition on trades until the age of 50, or requiring employees to hold company stock for a prescribed period. Both examples point to the social consequences of dispossessing and impoverishing the great mass of producers to guarantee the unlimited expansion of capital (Marx, 1991; see also Chapter 1).

Conclusion

At the outset of this chapter we asked why the Bush II administration would opt to compare the SOX to the New Deal, especially given the apparent incongruity between, on the one hand, the free-market emphasis of the dominant neoliberal paradigm and, on the other hand, the 'big government' implicated in the New Deal of the 1930s. As the above discussion makes clear, the answer is that the characterization was more than a rhetorical exercise; indeed, it represented some of the key contradictions of neoliberal-led forms of capitalist restructuring, as well as its reproduction, in the US. On one level, the capitalist state sought to restore investor confidence by signalling to shareholders and potential investors that it would step in and ensure that corporate management pay heed to maximizing shareholder value. Despite the fact that this intervention took a legal form (the SOX), the agency responsible for its implementation, the SEC, chose to interpret the law in a manner that favours self-regulatory measures. The rationale for such a decision was based on the dominant framework in describing and prescribing corporate behaviour in the US, namely, corporate governance. According to the assumptions imbued in corporate governance, the most effective way to ensure the stabilization of investment is to expose management to competitive and rational market forces, as opposed to state regulation.

On a deeper level, the SOX served to recreate the very conditions that brought about the scandals in the first place: the growing dependence of self-regulated corporations on deregulated financial markets to falsely augment shareholder value. In contrast to the veneer promoted by neoliberal ideologues and policymakers, the primary characteristics of neoliberal accumulation strategies have been the debt-led growth of corporations, and increasing tendencies towards speculative activities. Aside from encouraging unstable forms of economic growth, the existing accumulation strategy depends on the steady influx of financing, most of which is derived from workers' (waged and salaried) pension savings. By situating the SOX against wider legal reforms, such as the PSLRA, as well as the inherently unequal relationships between shareholders and management, it becomes clear that the Act does not lead to further social protection of workers' savings via the strengthening of shareholder value; it instead leads to further exposure to the exigencies of a short-term, highly speculative market.

While the power of shareholders has been delimited by the capitalist state in an effort to overcome the barriers of capital valorization, the problem remains that the ongoing failure of 'agents' in corporations to deliver shareholder value to 'principals' also destroys the conditions of existence of neoliberalism. The persistent inability of the state and publicly listed corporations to deliver sustained economic growth and rising living standards instead of speculative bubbles in the new millennium (first the stock market in the early 2000s and, from 2007 onward, the sub-prime mortgage crisis), 'exhausts the tolerance of the majority and lays bare the web of spin in which neoliberalism clouds the debate and legitimates its destructive outcomes' (Saad-Filho and Johnston, 2005: 5). The ability of mainstream corporate governance discourse to depoliticize struggle by explaining away the underlying relations of domination and exploitation can be challenged only by exposing its subjective, political and class-based bias. Scholars should begin to strive to understand the contradictions, relations of power and contestation within and outside corporations by examining critically the political and ideological content of the corporate governance doctrine as an integral feature of neoliberal restructuring of capitalism.

The next chapter seeks to develop a broader understanding of the limitations and paradoxes underpinning the corporate governance doctrine and its connection to the corporate–financial nexus by focusing on one of the most controversial issues in corporate governance in the post-Enron era, namely, the 'equal access proposal' and its implications for corporate democracy. The importance of the equal access proposal lies in the fact that it represents an attempt by 'owners' to contest the SEC's decision to limit the rights of shareholders to participate in the nomination of directors of publicly listed corporations. A closer and more critical look at the relations of power underpinning the equal access proposal will help to throw light on the continued disempowerment of shareholders vis-à-vis corporations and the state, illuminating more fully the capitalist nature of the corporate–financial nexus in contemporary USA.

4   Deconstructing the myth of corporate democracy

The case of the equal access proposal

Equal access is quickly becoming one of the fiercest corporate governance issues being debated ahead of US companies.

(*Financial Times*, 2003)

One of the key roles of a board of directors is to monitor management. An independent board of directors is, therefore, viewed as one of the cornerstones of good corporate governance practices, and crucial to the protection of shareholder value. The absence of board independence has been widely cited as one of the chief reasons for the Enron-style debacles of the early 2000s (MacAvoy and Millstein, 2004). The architects of the SOX sought to correct lacking or weak board independence by creating and uniformly imposing high levels of external monitoring of directors in all publicly traded companies in the US (Babajide, 2007). Many observers and practitioners have been critical of the effectiveness of this solution, arguing that the mere requirement that the majority of a company's board members be independent from management does not guarantee that this will translate into rigorous accountability efforts in practice. Various, high-profile institutional investors and shareholder groups have suggested that a possible solution to the lack of board independence would be to revise the SEC rules to allow for an easier process for shareholders to nominate candidates for a company's board of directors. This mechanism is formally known as the Proposed Election Contest Rules (hereafter: equal access proposal or equal access).

Not everyone is supportive of the equal access proposal. Corporate executives, who collectively represent a highly influential lobby group in the US, have been vehemently opposed to equal access (Business Roundtable, 2004). The SEC has also continued to make it difficult for shareholders to nominate and remove directors (*Pensions & Investments*, 2007a). In July 2007, for example, the SEC offered two primary proposals to resolve the disputes around equal access, both of which had the effect of reducing shareholder voice. First, the SEC proposed that a minimum of 5 per cent ownership in a corporation would be required if a shareholder wished to sponsor proxy resolutions. To put this number in perspective, according to ownership data of the top 25 publicly listed corporations, only a handful of major financial corporations, such as Berkshire

Hathaway Inc., Barclays Global Investors, Fidelity Management & Research and so forth, hold over 5 per cent of shareholdings (The Conference Board, 2007a). Second, the SEC proposed that shareholders either be limited or prohibited 'to nominate members of corporate boards' (Social Investment Forum, 2006). The Social Investment Forum (SIF), a formidable alliance of 500 shareholders and shareholder groups in the US,[1] vehemently opposed these proposals, suggesting that they represented a further violation of shareholders' rights and interests in public corporations. The SEC was originally expected to reach a resolution regarding equal access during the 2008 proxy season. Aside from clarifying its position regarding rules permitting management's exclusion of certain share-holder proposals related to the election of directors (SEC, 2007), the SEC has not, at the time of writing, undertaken any major ruling on the equal access pro-posal. For all intents and purposes, the ruling of this highly controversial pro-posal seems to have been indefinitely deferred. Whatever decision is to be reached, if any, the struggles for equal access will continue to represent a fertile battleground, given the Hobson's Choice inherent in the two proposals put forward by the SEC.

Given its significance to shareholder activism and its ability to shed critical light on the constitution of corporate power in neoliberal-led capitalism, the equal access proposal demands close and critical analysis. That said, there are two specific and overlapping objectives in this chapter. First and foremost, I analyse the political and social meaning of the equal access proposal by re-opening questions about a cornerstone assumption upon which the corporate governance doctrine stands – the pluralist and democratic nature of relations within publicly listed corporations, an issue introduced in Chapter 3. Second, I examine more deeply the basic premise upon which corporate democracy rests by critically exploring the separation of ownership from control. Taking both objectives together, this discussion will serve to further underscore the limita-tions to shareholder power in the Ownership Society (see Chapter 2), as well as critically enhancing our awareness of the corporate governance doctrine. My main argument is that the equal access proposal, and its underlying premises linked to the separation between ownership and control, not only distorts and masks the capitalist nature of the corporation, but also depoliticizes the power relations therein by recasting them in democratic and classless terms. The pro-posal represents an overly optimistic framework that is antithetical to meaning-ful change within the corporation. In fact, it serves as a vehicle for the capitalist state (via the SEC) to continue its strategy of curbing shareholder activism (see Chapter 3), especially 'anti-value' activism such as public and labour pension funds. We discuss this in more detail later in the chapter.

I develop my argument through four main sections. The first section lays out the case for equal access to the corporate ballot and the importance of an inde-pendent board as a function of good corporate governance. The discussion high-lights key issues raised by proponents and detractors of equal access. The second section concentrates on the main premises of managerial theory by exploring a chief assumption underpinning the equal access debates and, more generally, the cornerstone of corporate governance theory and practice: a belief in the separation of ownership from control. This section draws on The Conference Board's database of the landscape of ownership of the largest (financial and non-financial) publicly listed corporations in the US, in conjunction with analytical insight from the long-ignored 'class-fractionalist'[2] perspective to critically examine the managerial model. The third section highlights the relevance of understanding public corporations, and the uneven relations of power therein, as integral features of capitalist society by revisiting two common-sense assumptions discussed in Chapter 3: (1) the pluralist and democratic nature of social relations within corporations; and (2) the neutral state. The fourth and final section concludes by restating the argument and main points of the chapter.

Reforming corporate governance: debating equal access

A brief history of equal access

Equal access is not a new issue among shareholder activists. According to the Investor Responsibility Research Centre, individual investor Kurt Wulff sponsored a number of resolutions in the 1980s calling on companies to give shareholders a low-cost way to run alternative candidates by allowing them equal access to management's proxy statement.[3] The flurry of corporate scandals in the early 2000s, coupled with dissatisfaction toward the SOX, helped to reinvigorate the debates around equal access. In 2002, for instance, two noted corporate governance activists, James McRitchie and Les Greenberg, put forward a proposal to the SEC requesting that Rule 14a-8(i) be amended to allow shareholder proposals to elect corporate directors (SEC, 2002). The AFSCME is a major, union-sponsored pension plan representing the largest union for workers in the public service, and wielding pension funds that collectively hold more than $850 million in assets (*Pensions & Investments*, 2007a). On 1 December 2004, the AFSCME proposed a by-law amendment that would permit an investor (subject to certain qualifications) to include in AIG's (American International Group Inc.) proxy materials for the 2005 Annual General Meeting the name of a candidate for election to the board of directors. AIG attempted to exclude this proposal under SEC Commission Rule 14a-8(i)(8) and requested no-action relief from the SEC's Division of Corporate Finance (also known as 'the Division'). Briefly, Rule 14a-8 gives eligible shareholders of US public companies the right to submit proposals for inclusion in the company's proxy materials. This rule is, however, subject to 13 conditions under which the company's management may exclude a submitted shareholder proposal. The Division granted AIG no-action relief. The AFSCME contested this ruling and eventually won the inclusion of the proposal in AIG's proxy materials in 2006,[4] after appealing to the US District Court, Southern District of New York.

Since this decision, the AFSCME has requested that the SEC revise its rules to allow for more direct and easier access by shareholders to the ballot nominating the board of directors. In the current system, there is one ballot for nominations sponsored by the board, and another ballot for nominations sponsored by shareholders and shareholder groups. The mechanics of the separate ballot system are discussed below. For now, it is important to stress that the equal access proposal has been supported by an increasing number of influential institutional investors and investor groups, including: CalPERS, one of the world's largest public pension funds with an investment portfolio of more than $250 billion (market value) at the end of 2007; the Interfaith Centre for Corporate Responsibility (ICCR); and the CII, which represents $3 trillion in shareholder assets. According to Senior Vice President and Special Counsel for Institutional Shareholder Services[5] Patrick McGurn, 'Equal access to board nominations is the holy grail of corporate governance reform. It is a significant reform for institutional investors, as it would provide them with representation on the Board of Directors' (*SocialFunds*, 2003). Unsurprisingly, corporate management and their affiliated, and powerful, lobby groups, such as the Business Roundtable (BR) and the US Chamber of Commerce, have passionately contested the notion of equal access (Business Roundtable, 2004). As will be discussed later in this chapter, the SEC has sided with these powerful economic players from the outset by stifling shareholders on actions related to the equal access issue.

Before turning to this issue, it is useful to examine some of the key assumptions of the equal access proposal. It will become obvious that these premises also reflect the common-sense assumptions identified in Chapter 3.

The case for equal access

Following the losses of millions of dollars of pension savings resulting from the rash of corporate malfeasance at the turn of the century, shareholders, shareholder groups and policymakers were all in the mood for tweaking, albeit to different degrees, what was believed to be the key cause of scandals, namely, board independence. The motivation behind the equal access proposal was to ensure independence of boards of directors by contesting what was not adequately addressed in the SOX (see Chapter 3). Some legal scholars, for instance, have argued that the SOX did not go far enough in directing listing agencies (e.g. NASDAQ, the New York Stock Exchange (NYSE)) and states – the jurisdiction within which the definition of 'board independence' traditionally resides in the US – to modify their board independence standards in order to take into account all associations that might compromise corporate officers, particularly given the strong social networks and personal ties between management and board members (Mizruchi, 1996; Carroll, 2004, Fairfax, 2005; Fogel and Geier, 2007). Seen from this angle, the proposal sought to challenge the 'clubbish atmosphere and somewhat unanimous view that people continue on boards without any challenge' (TheCorporateCounsel.net, 2003).

The significance of board independence in the corporate governance literature may be traced to one of the main preoccupations of agency theory: ensuring that management's interests are aligned with those of shareholders. Board independence is a primary mechanism to establish direct monitoring (Mizruchi, 2004; Zingales, 1998; Blair and Stout, 1999). As we will see later in the discussion, the assumptions of democratization in managerial theory also reflect the deeper theoretical roots of this view of shareholder primacy. Within the parameters of corporate governance theory, the law imposes a stringent and absolute fiduciary duty on the board of directors to ensure that a firm operates with the long-term interests of its owners in mind, namely the shareholders (Hansmann and Kraakman, 2001). From a legal perspective, the board is the corporation's ultimate authority, and therefore wields considerable power and responsibility in ensuring management work towards the creation of shareholder value, which, as noted in previous chapters, is believed to be the chief goal of good corporate governance practice (Aglietta and Rebérioux, 2005).

The selection of company directors, both within the corporate governance framework and corporate law, is viewed largely in democratic terms. Company directors are seen as representing shareholder interests by virtue of the fact that they are elected by the latter group. Current US legislation and most company by-laws permit shareholders to nominate a director for election at any annual meeting. Shareholders also have the legal ability to solicit proxies for the candidate they nominate. Yet, the democratic sheen of a board election quickly becomes tarnished when the process is viewed in practice, wherein it becomes evident that shareholders play an insignificant role in the nomination of directors. In 95 per cent of key US corporations, for example, a nominating committee recommends eligible candidates to the board without active and consultative engagement with shareholders. In the majority of cases, the CEO provides the nominating committee with a 'desirable' list of names. Corporate governance gurus Robert A.G. Monks and Nell Minow describe the rest of the process in the following manner:

> Director candidates are usually interviewed by the full board (including the CEO), and then 'elected' (actually ratified, since they – in 99 per cent of the votes – almost always run unopposed by shareholder vote). In theory, this structure permits the board to evaluate director nominees independently, and to protect against management packing the board with its own allies. But Korn and Ferry found in 1991 that 82 per cent of board vacancies were filled via recommendations from the chairman.
>
> (Monks and Minow, 2001: 178)

One of the main obstacles in ensuring independent boards, as identified by the AFSCME and its supporters,[6] is the existence of separate proxy statements[7] and proxy cards[8] for candidates nominated by the board and candidates nominated by shareholders and others (TheCorporateCounsel.net, 2003). This process allows corporate managers to manipulate the electoral system, as the separate ballot system is an expensive and arduous process. If shareholders wish to place their own board candidate on the proxy, for example, they must engage in a costly proxy contest.[9] The minimum expense of such a contest is $250,000. Management has the upper hand, as they are able to draw on the corporate coffers to oppose the candidacy. 'The height of irony is that a candidate nominated by management needs only one vote to secure a place on the board of directors, even if an overwhelming majority of shareowners oppose the nominee' (*SocialFunds*, 2003; see also Monks and Minow, 2001: 194ff). The supporters of equal access view the separate ballot system as a key impediment to board independence and thus accountability. The proposal to amend Rule 14a-8(i), which the AFSCME submitted to the SEC, seeks to challenge the separate ballot system.[10] The question that emerges is: Who benefits from this *un*equal access to the ballot?

Contesting equal access

It should come as no surprise that several conservative interest groups, think tanks and business organizations, including the BR, a highly influential lobby group of CEOs of leading companies in the US, have strongly advised the SEC to reject the equal access proposal.[11] In its 80-page comment letter, the BR argues that the proposed shareholder access rule would not provide any benefits because the flaw it seeks to address (i.e. the absence of independent boards) does not exist. Given the power wielded by the BR in Corporate America, it is useful to draw on its comment letter to identify the position of management and directors in relation to the Proposed Election Contest Rules.

The BR letter opens by stressing that the proposal for equal access exceeds the statutory authority of the SEC in that the latter is authorized to regulate disclosures in the proxy process only. The regulation of corporate governance, according to the BR, is a matter reserved for state governments. The BR argues that the equal access proposal would not increase shareholder value. Moreover, it maintains that sufficient mechanisms are in place to allow for electoral challenges. However, according to Harvard Law Professor Lucian Arye Bebchuk's empirical findings, these electoral challenges are practically non-existent, largely because of the constraints detailed above, including the heavy costs involved in challenging the existing ballot (Bebchuk, 2005; see also Monks and Minow, 2001).

Notwithstanding these objections, the BR stresses that the market protects shareholder franchise in two important ways. First, there is already a 'dominant presence of independent directors on the board' because of recent changes in stock exchange requirements and corporate practices brought about by the SOX (Bebchuk, 2005: 5). While this may be the case, Bebchuk raises the point that

> it does not obviate the need for the safety valve of a viable mechanism for shareholder replacement of directors. The mere independence of directors from insiders ensures neither that directors are well selected nor that they have the right incentives to advance shareholder interests.

(ibid.: 5)[12]

Second, 'shareholders dissatisfied with incumbent directors can "vote with their feet" by selling the company's stock' (ibid.: 5). Put another way, '[t]he purest form of corporate suffrage takes place in the capital markets, not through regulatory action' (ibid.).

The BR also argues that the equal access proposal will not serve shareholder interests because of the presence of 'collateral objectives' linked to special interest groups. From the point of view of the BR, some institutional investors, particularly the more active union and state pension plans – the same groups that have spearheaded the equal access proposal – might bring and support shareholder access resolutions to advance special interests, such as wages, unionization and benefits, as well as what they deem to be 'other *social* issues', such as environmental protection. The BR believes that these funds 'can be expected to put forward and vote for shareholder election proposals to advance "special interests of their own that are unrelated to the openness of the proxy process"' (ibid.: 7).

The threat of an increased voice from special interest groups, such as labour-led shareholders, in the election of boards of directors appears to be a major preoccupation with key business groups. In a recent speech, Thomas J. Donohue, the CEO and President of the US Chamber of Commerce, remarked that while vocal investors were good for US enterprise, some forms of shareholder activism are more welcome than others. In particular, Donohue drew a distinction between pro-value and anti-value activism. While pro-value activism inspires public involvement in markets and raises returns, anti-value activism is believed to reduce democracy and shareholder value. The key examples given by Donohue of anti-value activism include pro-union policies. The latter are primarily spearheaded by the political and social interests of the top officials from so-called 'activist' funds, such as CalPERS (U.S. Chamber of Commerce, 2006).[13]

The following passage of a letter penned by the Competitive Enterprise Institute[14] and addressed to the SEC in resistance to the shareholder access proposal is worth quoting at length, as it captures the general logic behind corporate management's resistance to increased participation of shareholders, especially so-called 'activist' investors.

> Through pension funds, labour unions and other *anti-market interest groups* have significant stakes in major corporations as well as entrepreneurial new firms. *A shareholder access rule would allow them and other activists to achieve through the board nomination process what they have been unable to accomplish through the political process.* Unions would use this leverage to win card check and neutrality agreements, allowing them to unionize companies without secret ballot elections. They could also put pressure not only on the companies they have stakes in but also their partners and suppliers. The implications go far beyond unions. Everything on the anti-market political wish list from Kyoto-like carbon restrictions, to auto emissions standards, to prescription drug price controls, to animal rights activism, to interfering with defense contractors to advance foreign policy objectives

would be possible. *These initiatives, whatever their merits, belong in the political arena, not in corporate boardrooms where the focus should be on maximizing shareholder value.*

(Competitive Enterprise Institute, 2007, my emphasis)

Yet, as Bebchuk argues, and as is evident in the above discussion, union and state pension fund holdings in the majority of the top 25 publicly listed corporations are far too small to guarantee the passage of shareholder access proposals or even to have a major influence on the outcome of a vote. It has been observed that,

> Indeed, past voting patterns clearly indicate that shareholder resolutions that are brought forward because of their appeal to shareholders with special interests generally do not pass. Shareholder resolutions that focus on social or labour issues generally fail, while those that have attracted majority support are the ones that are viewed by professional money managers as clearly serving shareholder value.

(Bebchuk, 2005: 7)

We discuss the limits to, and contradictions of, labour-led shareholder activism more fully in Chapter 5. For now, it is important to raise the question of why management and directors feel threatened by union and state pension funds, despite the restrictions that they face in the existing system of corporate governance, and despite the fact that these 'anti-value' activists hold insignificant levels of shares when compared to large financial corporations such as Berkshire Hathaway Inc. and the Barclays Group (including Barclays Global Investors and Barclays Bank, among others) (cf. The Conference Board, 2007a). The answer is provided, in part, in the above quotations furnished by the Competitive Enterprise Institute and the US Chamber of Commerce. In their capacity as 'activists', union and state pension funds have drawn considerable attention to excesses of management power and laxity of board oversight. This not only highlights the erosion of shareholder value, but also politicizes corporate governance in such a way so as to reveal elements of social power and its economic foundations. A case in point is the central role unions and state pension plans have played in drawing attention to the ever-widening gulf between workers' wages, executive salaries and stock options (Brennan, 2008; see also Chapter 5).

Underlying assumptions of the debates

What are executives and directors afraid of? Democracy?

(Rapoport, 2003)

As is evident from the above discussion, a key assumption recurring throughout the debates on board independence, and by extension the corporate governance doctrine (see Chapter 1), is the democratic and pluralist nature of social organization. As noted in Chapter 3, pluralism is defined as a system of interest representation in which management, the board of directors and shareholders are organized into voluntary, competitive, non-hierarchical categories that do not exercise a monopoly of representative activity within their respective categories (Dahl, 1956). Moreover, the role of the state, or, in this case, the SEC, is a reflection of the outcome of the competition among these various social categories. As such, for the proponents and opponents of equal access, the key to either improving or damaging the status quo is found in changing the rules of the SEC.

In keeping with a more narrow definition of democracy based on competitive elections (e.g. the one share, one vote principle), shareholders are believed to have the power to 'elect' directors by 'voting' for their choice of 'nominees' (SEC, 2002). On the one hand, through the proposed mechanisms of separate ballots, advocates of the equal access proposal strive to ensure that representative democratic relations are respected in the running of corporations. By allowing shareholders' power to change board members at the general will, democracy, in this sense, is understood as a necessary condition to limit the excesses of management (Bebchuk, 2007). If shareholders, for instance, disapprove of their representatives, they will be able to 'throw the bums out' (SEC, 2002). On the other hand, opponents of the equal access proposal believe any changes to the meaning of an independent board will dilute democratic relations within the corporation and, by extension, threaten the creation of shareholder value. In other words, by invoking the state to change the laws governing independent boards, it is believed that there is a danger that the rational forces of the unfettered market (shareholder value) and democracy could be distorted by special interests, such as unions and state pensions, that seek to impose social concerns over and above the goal of creating shareholder value.

I argue that framing these debates within a pluralist and democratic perspective fails to adequately examine the underlying power relations rooted in capitalism, which condition the processes and outcomes of Corporate America. In effect, this neoliberal view of the world obscures the limitations of equal access and its role in reproducing the status quo, especially with regard to the ongoing depoliticization of resistance inherent in the corporate governance doctrine (see Chapter 1). Before elaborating on this argument, it is important to examine more fully the premise of the pluralist and democratic assumption in corporate governance, namely, the separation of ownership from control.

The analytical roots of corporate democracy: the splitting of ownership from control

In their path-breaking study, *The Modern Corporation and Private Property*, Berle and Means (1932) argued that publicly listed corporations in the US were characterized by the separation of ownership, usually by families, from control. As we discussed in Chapter 1, this split was believed to have occurred through the evolution of industrial society, whereby companies needed to draw on constantly increasing pools of disposable wealth, thereby transferring the ownership form to a wider and more diverse base. In this context, direct owner-control became progressively more attenuated to the point where 'owners' were effectively removed from any control over the actual operations of the business (Scott, 1997: 2). For Berle and Means, the implications of the ownership–control split were profound, especially in the way we think about capitalism. As Scott explains,

> The power of control becomes divorced from legal ownership, and it is no longer appropriate to regard the enterprise as a capitalist one at all. It is, instead, a managerial enterprise, subject to management control, and it is effectively free from the constraints of capitalist property ownership. The managers are able to run the enterprise with a more general public interest in mind. The 'democratization' of shareholdings means that if the business system is still to be described as capitalist, then it must be described as 'People's Capitalism'.
>
> (Scott, 1997: 31; see also Drucker, 1976)

In contrast to later managerialist theorists, Berle and Means were not optimistic that the split between ownership and control would result in further democratization of US society. On the contrary, they surmised that management control would lead to the rise of a powerful class of professional managers who would be insulated from the pressures and demands of shareholders, as well as wider society. Management control occurs when the individuals able to dominate the composition of the board of directors are almost totally divorced from the legal ownership of the corporation (Berle and Means, 1932). The authors warn that managers and even 'elected officials' (the board of directors) represent a self-reproducing oligarchy, who are not accountable to the owners they are believed to represent (Mizruchi, 2004). Furthermore, the rise of management control and unchecked corporate power had potentially serious implications for the democratic character of the US (Mizruchi, 2004).

Social scientists writing during the 1950s and 1960s, and later corporate governance theorists working primarily in the fields of finance and law, have continued to accept the Berle–Means thesis regarding the split between ownership and control – with one notable difference: these scholars have presented a more benign reading of managerial power, especially with regard to its implications for democracy, than Berle and Means. For these theorists, 'the separation of ownership from control actually led to an increased level of democratization in the society as a whole' (ibid.: 579). One reason for this new reading on the consequences of the separation of ownership from control, which includes a rejection of the argument that managerial control represents a dangerous form of concentrated economic power, is due to the fact that after 1920, most sociologists held the view that there was an effective break-up of the ruling class. As Ralf Dahrendorf noted, business leaders in advanced industrialized countries had become a plurality of competing, differentiated groups (Zeitlin, 1974; Mizruchi, 2004: 583). Thus, the absence of a ruling class, coupled with the fact that managers of large firms were employees of corporations, as opposed to its owners, shifted the issue of control from class orientation to a pluralist structure (Dahl, 1956; see also Chapter 3).

With regard to the equal access debates, there are at least two relevant and overlapping consequences of the continued acceptance of the separation of ownership from control. First, as highlighted above, the alleged ownership–control split has been associated with increased forms of democracy in society, including the corporation (Mizruchi, 2004). Second, because capitalist classes are viewed as having transferred their power to management, class theory is no longer applicable to understanding capitalist society. Maurice Zeitlin notes that 'a class theory of contemporary industrial society, based on the relationship between the owners of capital and formally free wage workers, loses its analytical value as soon as legal ownership and factual control are separated' (Zeitlin, 1974: 1075). Closely tied to a rejection of class analysis is the dismissal of a Marxist-informed analysis, which strives to understand the relationships within and outside corporations, most notably the relations of domination, class conflict and social reproduction that are believed to characterize capitalist society (cf. Carroll, 2004; Aglietta and Rebérioux, 2005; van Apeldoorn and Horn, 2007; Overbeek *et al.*, 2007; Brennan, 2008).

The 'fractionalist' challenge: the ownership–control split as a pseudo-fact?

> It might at first seem needless to say that before social facts can be 'explained', it is advisable to ensure that they actually are facts ... pseudo-facts may ... serve to deflect attention from critical aspects of social structure, determinant social relations, and basic social processes. They may inspire not merely 'explanations', but 'inferences' and 'theories' as well, which further confuse and obscure social reality.
>
> (Zeitlin, 1974: 1074)

Aside from critical investigations into the questions of the ownership–control split by economic sociologists in the 1960s and 1970s (Kolko, 1964; Zeitlin, 1974; Kotz, 1978), this position has remained devoid of either radical commentary or empirical investigation (Scott, 1997; Mizruchi, 2004). Zeitlin's seminal work, which appeared in the mid-1970s, revealed major empirical flaws in Berle and Means' 1932 study. Zeitlin notes that 'numerous scholars over the years have cited the work by Berle and Means (when giving citations at all) as the main or only source of their assertions that ownership and control were split apart in the large corporations' (Zeitlin, 1974: 1082). The former debates about the viability of the separation of ownership from control are detailed and complex. It is, however, important to discuss two important facets of these debates: (1) the methodological limitations in establishing the ownership–control split; and (2) some of the main conclusions drawn from competing studies of the alleged separation of ownership from control.

Before addressing these points, two caveats are in order. First, the objective of this section is not to prove or disprove conclusively the existence of a separation of family or individual ownership from control (which, I suggest, is quite limited given the methodological problems involved), but rather to demonstrate that the ownership–control split is more complex and inconclusive than allowed for by mainstream corporate governance literature. This, in turn, has significant ramifications for debates over equal access and pluralist forms of corporate democracy. Second, there is a distinction between the Marxist-informed framework upon which I draw to deconstruct the managerialist view of democracy and the fractionalist approach, which is also a strand of Marxism, represented here primarily by the seminal work of Zeitlin and his critique of the Berle–Means thesis. The need for this distinction relates to the first point. Zeitlin's variant of Marxism and its analytical and empirical emphasis on class fractions (e.g. finance capitalists) were integral to his deconstruction of the Berle–Means argument and general debates about the nature and role of the capitalist class in the United States (Zeitlin, 1989). For the purposes of this chapter and the overall argument of the book, a broader theoretical understanding of the corporation as a feature of contemporary capitalist society, i.e. less focus on particular capitals, is more appropriate (see Chapter 1).

According to the fractionalist perspective, at least two methodological problems exist in proving the separation of ownership from control in publicly listed corporations. First, it is difficult to determine

> who are the actual 'beneficial owners' of the shareholdings held by the 'shareholders of record'. Shareholders may appear in the name of voting trusts, foundations, holding companies, and other related operating corporations in which the given family has a dominant interest.
>
> (Zeitlin, 1974: 1086)

Much of the research has drawn on guesswork based on inside information and newspaper sources (e.g. Fortune 500 listings), which have quasi-scientific standing in the business community. But, as John Scott observes, a lot of

> difficulty arises from the use of 'nominee' accounts by shareholders. While the ownership of each share must be registered in the company's share register, shares are often listed under anonymous accounts or 'street names' that conceal the identity of the beneficial owner. Even where access to the register is achieved, it may not be possible to identify the leading sharehold ers because of the prevalence of such nominee holdings.
>
> (Scott, 1997: 63)

A second methodological problem involved in establishing the separation of ownership from control is the treatment of intercorporate holdings. Scott explains that Berle and Means drew on a category of control based on a legal device, which allowed them to distinguish between immediate and ultimate control.

While the immediate control of such an enterprise may be exercised through a legal device, its ultimate control, Berle and Means held, was the same as that of its parent company. An enterprise subject to 'immediate' minority control – which for Berle and Means required 20 per cent of shareholdings – by an enterprise that was itself controlled by management, was to be regarded as subject to 'ultimate' management control. This distinction between immediate and ultimate control tends to overstate the significance of 'management control' and can lead to unwarranted conclusions about the autonomy of the internal management of enterprises controlled through legal devices (Scott, 1997: 62). In his critique of the managerialist model of boards, for instance, Mizruchi argues that while board members 'may appear to be passive, disinterested, and fully co-opted', none of this necessarily indicates that they lack power vis-à-vis management, especially when the firm experiences financial difficulties (Mizruchi, 2004: 597).

Another weakness in the ownership–control split is the reluctance to engage with competing perspectives. In his extensive review of the literature, Zeitlin observes that studies which appeared at the same time as that of Berle and Means but which contradicted the notion of the separation between ownership and control – e.g. Anna Rochester (1936) and Ferdinand Lundberg (1937) – were ignored by mainstream social science. Drawing on the same corporations used in Berle and Means' study,

> Lundberg found that 'in most cases [the largest stockholding] families had themselves installed the management control or were among the directors', while several others were 'authoritatively regarded in Wall Street as actually under the rule of J.P. Morgan and Company'. 'Exclusion of stockholders from control, within the context as revealed by Berle–Means', Lundberg concluded (pp. 506–508), 'does not mean that large stockholders are excluded from a decisive voice in the management. It means, only, that small stockholders have been [excluded].'
>
> (Zeitlin, 1974: 1083)

Despite the tendency across the disciplinary boundaries of economics, sociology, law, management sciences, and so forth, to accept the Berle–Means thesis, there has been little attempt, aside from Larner (1970), to update Bearl and Means' study of the rise of management control of the 500 largest non-financial corporations in the US (Mizruchi, 2004). Indeed, since the 1970s, there has been no attempt either to problematize the methodology of the study of the separation of ownership from control, or to engage with the conclusions of those studies that challenged the Berle–Means thesis. Yet, some of the findings from these studies seriously challenge the position that class is no longer relevant in understanding the corporation. For instance, the conclusion of the studies conducted by Kotz (1978), Kolko (1964), and the US Congress House Banking and Currency Committee, Subcommittee on Domestic Finance, more popularly referred to as 'The Patman Report' (1968), suggest that family control of non-financial corporations was evident through their ownership interests and control of major banks. The

Patman Report concluded that 'the major banking institutions in this country are emerging as the single most important force in the economy. The Subcommittee warned that growing bank control may result in restraints of competition and poses serious conflict of interest problems' (Kotz, 1978: 10).

Institutional shareholding reflects a move towards much greater concentration in corporate capital. This fact led The Patman Report to observe as early as 1968 that

> the trend of the last 30 or 40 years toward a separation of ownership from control because of the fragmentation of stock ownership has been radically changed towards a concentration of voting power in the hands of a relatively few financial institutions.
>
> (Scott, 1997: 68)

This situation has continued since the 1970s and accelerated in the 1980s with the rise of neoliberalism and the latter's emphasis on financial deregulation and privatization (see Chapters 1, 2 and 3). Based on recent statistics furnished by The Conference Board, a global and pre-eminent business membership and research organization, institutional investors held 67.9 per cent ownership in the top 1,000 corporations in the US in 2005, up from 46.6 per cent in 1987. As Table 4.1 shows, the principal owners of company shares are financial intermediaries, such as investment banks, insurance companies and mutual funds.

Drawing on the above data and our brief survey of the methodological limitations regarding the ownership–control split, two related observations can be made. First, while there has been a decline in family ownership, there is not sufficient evidence to suggest that family ownership and control have altogether disappeared in Corporate America. While all cut-off thresholds regarding minority control are arbitrary – Berle and Means, for example, employed a 20 per cent cut-off while Larner imposed a 10 per cent limit – Scott has suggested that thresholds 'can be justified if there is supporting evidence on the overall distribution of shareholdings' (ibid.: 61). Drawing on Herman's (1981) findings, Scott suggests that in the post-war period, holdings of 5 per cent or less are unrealistic bases for control in even the largest firms, and that owners of 5–10 per cent may exercise, at best, a very limited form of minority control (Scott, 1997: 61).

Seen from the above perspective, Table 4.1 and data collected from The Conference Board (2007) reveal interesting points regarding the landscape of ownership of the top 25 publicly listed corporations in the US. Although US institutional investors own a significant portion of shares in the largest corporations, the last column on the right-hand side of Table 4.1 ('Total held by all institutional investors') shows that in each of the 25 corporations a considerable proportion of shares – ranging anywhere from 23 per cent to 81 per cent – are held by non-institutional investors, e.g. non-US institutional investors and/or individuals, US individuals or family members, key officers, or members of the board. Because of the unavailability of complete and comprehensive information on corporate ownership and 'nominee accounts', it is difficult to

Table 4.1 Percentage of holdings of US institutional investors of the 25 largest US financial and non-financial corporations

Company	All (%)	Top 5 (%)	Top 10 (%)	Top 20 (%)	Top 25 (%)	Total held by all institutional investors (%)
Exxon Mobil Corporation	50	13	20	26	28	50.0
General Electric Company	57	15	22	31	33	56.6
Microsoft Corporation	71	19	28	38	41	71.2
Citigroup Inc.	62	20	27	35	38	62.0
Bank of America Corporation	58	16	24	32	34	57.8
Wal-Mart Stores, Inc.	35	10	14	19	21	35.0
Proctor & Gamble	57	14	20	28	30	57.0
Pfizer Inc.	62	13	20	30	33	62.0
Johnson & Johnson	61	18	24	32	34	61.0
American International Group, Inc.	63	19	27	35	38	63.0
Altria Group, Inc.	72	21	30	44	47	72.0
J.P. Morgan Chase & Co.	64	17	24	34	37	64.0
Berkshire Hathaway Inc.	19	9	12	14	15	19.0
Cisco Systems, Inc.	64	17	24	33	36	64.0
International Business Machines Corp.	46	14	19	26	27	46.0
Chevron Corporation	60	17	24	32	35	59.8
Intel Corporation	52	13	18	27	29	52.0
Wells Fargo & Company	65	18	26	35	39	65.0
AT&T Inc.	61	22	30	39	42	61.0
The Coca-Cola Company	60	22	28	38	41	60.0
Google	77	30	40	52	55	77.0
Verizon Communications Inc.	57	16	22	32	34	57.0
PepsiCo, Inc.	66	14	21	30	34	66.0
Hewlett Packard Company	72	19	28	38	41	72.0
The Home Depot, Inc.	64	18	25	34	37	64.0
Wachovia Corporation	54	18	25	31	33	53.7

Source: The Conference Board (2007b).

Note
* Calculations based on available data for 2005 and 2006.

ascertain who actually owns these shares. In other words, there is not enough evidence to suggest definitively that individuals and families have not retained the power to intervene in corporate affairs and to ensure that their views are influential by mobilizing votes in sufficient numbers, either through ownership of large blocks of shares or the acquisition of voting control over the shares owned by others, or by influencing state officials to create or recreate legal laws to protect their interests, as discussed in Chapter 3 (Scott, 1997: 15–16). It does imply that both the corporate and financial realms of social interaction are more intertwined, uneven and muddied than the corporate governance literature assumes.

Second, although there has been significant growth in terms of financial shareholdings in the form of institutional investment (ibid.), the landscape of ownership regarding financial shareholdings is highly uneven. With regard to the 25 companies listed in Table 4.1, the largest blocks of shares held by single US institutional investors are represented by major financial institutions: Barclays Bank held 5 per cent or more shareholdings in seven corporations; Fidelity Management and Research held more than 5 per cent (but less than 10 per cent) in two corporations; Capital Research and Management Corporation held more than 5 per cent (but less than 10 per cent) in one corporation; and Berkshire Hathaway Inc. held 5 per cent (but less than 10 per cent) in two corporations (The Conference Board, 2007a). As pointed out earlier, while the number of these shares does not have a significant impact vis-à-vis the control of the corporation, they have the potential of exercising a limited form of control. There appears to be a major gap between the ownership levels of these large banks and investment funds compared with the amount of shares held by activist funds, such as public pension funds. According to the data collected from The Conference Board, only three public pension funds (CalPERS, New York Teachers' Retirement System, and New York State Common Retirement System) registered within the top largest institutional investors among the 25 biggest corporations. Aside from one case where CalPERS ranked as the eighth largest shareholder in Berkshire Hathaway Inc. (controlling only 0.5 per cent of the overall holdings, largely due to the small percentage of company holdings held by US institutional investors, see Table 4.1), these pension funds ranked below the top 15 institutional investors, registering shareholdings from 0.4 per cent to 0.6 per cent.

Two points are worth emphasising here. First, the relatively small amount of shareholdings of public pension funds in the top publicly listed corporations in the US does not include their ownership in publicly listed financial corporations, such as Barclays and Citicorp, which wield relatively more clout in the 25 listed corporations. Second, the overall (direct) holdings of public pension funds are relatively small, which puts into perspective the influence wielded by this category of institutional investor, labelled as a dangerous 'special interest' with the potential, according to the US Chamber of Commerce and the BR, to engage in anti-market behaviour.

Repoliticizing equal access

When viewed in conjunction with the analysis laid out in the first three chapters of the book, the above perspective allows us to identify and move beyond at least two common-sense assumptions imbued in the equal access proposal, and the corporate governance doctrine more generally. First, the relations between shareholders, boards of directors and management do not occur on a level and pluralist playing field, but are instead embedded in the relations of power, contradictions and struggles of capitalist accumulation. Related to this point is the fact that the corporation itself is a social relation of capitalism, as opposed to a rigid object devoid of politics and class interests. Recall, for instance, that any form of contestation that challenges the status quo should, as stated above by the Competitive Enterprise Institute, take place in the political arena of the government as opposed to what has been regarded as the purely economic space (market realm) of the boardroom. Second, the state is not a neutral actor but instead a central force in guaranteeing the reproduction of capitalist society, including the unequal relations of exploitation and domination therein. This is evidenced, for example, by the state's role in depoliticizing class-based resistance, which emerges from the contradictions of capital accumulation and, more specifically, the corporate–financial nexus (see Chapter 1). We look at each point in turn.

The corporation as a social relation of capitalism

With regard to the first point, and in contrast to the managerialist model, the corporation is more than an economic institution and legal structure over which either managers or financial capitalists possess effective control. There is more to the corporation than its superficial image of an economic actor and/or artificial (legal) person. Beneath this veneer lies a complex and dynamic social relation that reflects, and is rooted in, the power, struggles and contradictions of capitalist society. In contrast to the managerialist model, the separation of ownership from control does not imply a dismissal of class relations within capitalism. While the granting of primacy to one power bloc (e.g. financial capitalists) over another (e.g. industrial capitalists), is not a useful way of understanding the complexities of relations of power and domination within corporations, this does not imply that class is no longer useful. A different reading of Marx does not concentrate on class fractions per se, but rather the role of social classes within the wider capitalist mode of production. In other words, the analytical usefulness of class relations lies in its ability to help us conceptualize the interconnections between the relations of exploitation (as the economic form of class relations) and the relations of domination (as the political expression of class relations) (Clarke, 1978). While it is true that the legal separation of ownership from control changed the manner in which corporations were managed, this split did not erase the essential capitalist character of the corporation (Carroll, 2004; Brennan, 2005, 2008). This is seen in at least two ways. First, corporations, despite the control–ownership configuration, are still required to extract surplus value from labour power through exploitative practices. This social relation in turn wields hierarchical forms of domination over workers (both skilled and unskilled) to ensure that surplus value, and later profits and dividends, are realized. Second, corporations do not exist in an artificial context of a marketplace driven by rational and efficient actors. Instead, as discussed in Chapters 1 and 3, corporations operate and define the wider terrain of capital accumulation (including the credit system), which is contradictory, led by conflict and prone to crisis (Aglietta and Rebérioux, 2005).

As I noted in Chapter 1, for Marx, the rise of publicly held corporations was part and parcel of an attempt by capitalists to expand the scale of production and thereby temporarily overcome barriers to capital valorization by creating new forms of credit relations in the form of joint-stock companies. However, despite the changing form of corporations – from state-run, such as the East India Trading Company (Braithwaite and Drahos, 2000), to family or individually owned, to 'social' forms of production (in the sense of not held by an individual) – Marx held that corporations were still capitalist in nature. The 'social' form of the corporation, like its previous incarnation, still presupposes a social concentration of means of production and labour power, and the relations of domination and exploitation that accompany these basic characteristics (Marx, 1991: 567). Put another way, while the *form* of corporate ownership underwent a transformation, its *content* as a capitalist institution based on the extraction of surplus value through exploitative activities – and all the contradictions inherent to it – has remained intact.

The capitalist nature implies that the corporation, encompassing social relations that transcend the limited realm of corporate governance to include workers, the wider community and the environment, retains all of the contradictions inherent in its former form, i.e. as individual property. Recall from Chapter 1, the legal construction of the modern corporation was part and parcel of the need to accumulate under the capitalist system by expanding through the credit system, i.e. raising new funds by creating shares (Harvey, 1999). The fact that corporations 'remain trapped within the capital barriers' implies not only that the social relations within firms (management, workers, shareholders, board members) are affected by the wider contradictions, conflicts and crises within the capital accumulation process, such as the crisis of overaccumulation and the resulting financialization of capitalist society, but also that these very relations can affect the nature of the crisis through various control strategies, such as increasing shareholder value via fictitious capital (capital not backed by assets) (ibid.).

The role of the capitalist state

We now turn to our second point. In contrast to the managerialist perspective, the state is neither a neutral nor an autonomous sphere of influence and power vis-à-vis corporations. The state is a dynamic and historically contingent site of struggle that mediates conflicts and manifestations of crisis in capital accumulation in an *ex post facto* manner. As such, forms of state intervention are never neutral or objective, but speak to particular interests within the class relation, depending on the issue and temporal context. Although not an instrument of class (or class fractions, such as the financial class or industrial class), the state is a *capitalist* state, which means that it intervenes in the economy in ways that will reproduce the social relations of capitalist production, thereby assisting in depoliticizing struggle and smoothing out manifestations of underlying crises and perceived barriers to capital valorization. All of this is another way of saying that the state, including its satellite agencies, such as the SEC, influences the nature of power relations within corporations, and outside corporations in the wider capitalist society. A case in point is the SOX, which, as discussed in Chapter 3, was an attempt to re-legitimate the norm of self-regulation regarding corporations. When examined in the broader context of past rulings, the SOX is shown to be instrumental in hindering, as opposed to facilitating, greater share-holder power vis-à-vis corporate executives.

The SEC appears to have continued this trend with regard to its equal access ruling. Although the SEC announced that it would undertake a full review of proxy rules, in particular Rule 14a-8, it was less than accommodating regarding the growing calls by shareholders and shareholder groups for equal access to the corporate ballot. In the same year that it submitted its proposal to the SEC, the AFSCME submitted proposals to six major US corporations[15] for by-laws estab-lishing that shareholders representing 3 per cent of the company's outstanding shares would have the right to have their nominee included in the company's proxy statement and proxy card. All six companies rejected the proposals, on several counts, under SEC Rule 14a-8. Management and directors of these firms suggested that the equal access proposal would result in proxy contests, that equal access was inconsistent with the proxy rules and that the by-laws violated state law. The SEC ultimately found that the by-laws were excludable under 14a-8(i)(8). The latter section allows for the exclusion of matters related to elec-tion contests, drawing on the precedent of its prior no-action positions in similar cases (TheCorporateCounsel.net, 2003).

In response to these debates, the SEC put forward two proposals in 2007 that many critics view as tantamount to decreasing shareholder voice in the election of boards of directors. The proposals have since been bitterly disputed by many shareholders and shareholder groups (*Pensions & Investments*, 2008b). The first proposed rule attempts to bar shareholder proposals seeking shareholder access to the boards of directors' ballot, while the second rule makes access dependent on a 5 per cent ownership threshold and considerable disclosure by the nominat-ing shareholders (SEC, 2007). To put this 5 per cent benchmark into perspective, few shareholders of America's largest public companies own over 5 per cent (The Conference Board, 2007a). Thereby, this rule sets the bar so impossibly high that it could be exercised only by mega-investors (Save Shareholder Rights, 2007). Those owning such shares are large investment funds and banks, such as Barclays Bank and Berkshire Hathaway Inc. Many of the so-called 'activist' funds (or what the BR deems 'anti-market' activists, most of whom are in favour of equal access) own only 0.5 per cent of shares in these public companies (The

Conference Board, 2007a). In contrast to a pluralist perspective, highly influential lobby groups like the BR and the US Chamber of Commerce wield considerably more political, ideological and economic clout than those shareholder groups pushing for equal access. Moreover, these powerful lobby groups represent the interest of capitalists, as opposed to labour unions and other 'special interest' groups such as public pension funds. This uneven playing field is smoothed over, however, by recreating the myth of democratic relations inside and outside corporations, and by reducing political tensions and class issues to the sanitized and rationalized discourse of economics. Take, for example, the arguments against equal access, which are set within the parameters of shareholder value and *anti*-value, as opposed to *pro*-value, activism.

Conclusion

The equal access proposal aims at ensuring that the checks and balances within corporate governance are realigned to create shareholder value. On the surface, the equal access proposal is a useful intervention to democratize boardrooms and mitigate management's excesses and close alignment with directors. When viewed at a deeper level, however, the corporate governance framework, and its underlying premise of the ownership–control split, provides an incomplete understanding of the reproduction of the status quo with respect to the disempowerment of shareholders vis-à-vis management. While the separation between ownership and control has taken place, this neither implies the absence of the power of social classes in either listed corporations or the American state, nor does it not mean that the relations of social power rooted in capitalist society are insignificant to understanding the reproduction of diminished shareholder voice in the nomination of directors. Yet, the continued existence of the ownership–control split embedded in the corporate governance doctrine ensures that struggles within and outside corporations are viewed in classless and democratic terms.

An important development associated with the rise of corporate governance as a hegemonic neoliberal project in the US has been the emergence of labour-led shareholder activism, which, as will become clear in the next chapter, has continued to depoliticize resistance to corporate power and its capitalist underpinnings.

Part III
The changing forms of, and limits to, shareholder activism

5   The limits to labour's capital and the new activism

Trade unions are believed to have experienced a renewal since the 1990s. Viewed against the backdrop of mass investment culture, this revitalization does not refer to union members' role as workers, but to their role as active shareholders. Union organizations, such as trade union organizations, union-based pension funds, individual union members and labour-oriented investment funds, have become increasingly cognizant of their powers as 'owners' of vast amounts of social security capital (see Chapters 1 and 2), or what some commentators have referred to as 'labour's capital' (Fung *et al.*, 2001). Unlike traditional forms of union activism, which have relied primarily on strikes and picketing to gain concessions from management to improve workers' welfare, the new activism focuses on ensuring that good corporate governance practices are met by way of proxy voting, dialogue and negotiation with management and other shareholders. By flexing their financial clout through shareholder oversight and influence on corporate decision making, proponents of this new activism believe that unions will make more inroads in securing workers' interests than by engaging older strategies to change corporate behaviour (Schwab and Thomas, 1998). In other words, there is an implicit assumption that the maximization of shareholder value, which lies at the heart of corporate governance theory and practice (see Chapter 3), will lead to improved welfare benefits for all, including workers.

Despite the enthusiasm for this so-called 'new activism' and its ability to effect positive social change, observers have conceded that workers still do not exercise meaningful control over their capital (Baker and Fung, 2001; Hebb, 2001). This lack of control is particularly evident in the growing insecurity of retirement income and the ever-widening gap between executive pay and compensation packages on the one hand, and workers' wages on the other (Weller and White, 2001; Brennan, 2005, 2008; Mishel *et al.*, 2007). Two major and overlapping perspectives dominate the explanations regarding the limits to union-led shareholder activism: (1) the weak corporate governance perspective; and (2) the myopic market model. The first explanation locates the majority of blame with the ongoing passivity of shareholders to ensure that management adheres to good corporate governance practices, thereby working toward maintaining shareholder value. The second explanation, the myopic market view, finds fault with the short-term and speculative nature of money managers and financial markets. The shortsightedness by the financial community has, in turn, placed pressure on corporate management to focus on improving the price of company shares as opposed to keeping an eye on the long-term benefits of reinvesting in production processes, worker training and so forth – all of which aid in improving the welfare of workers (Baker and Fung, 2001; Brennan, 2005). My main thesis in this chapter is that while the two explanations mentioned above are helpful in understanding why organized labour continues to wield little control over its pension fund capital, the accounts fail to capture some of the deeper causes of the limits plaguing the new activism, specifically those rooted in the contradictions and power relations of capitalist society. As such, these accounts explain away the underlying causes of the limits to union-led shareholder activism, as well as the depoliticizing tendencies inherent in the corporate governance doctrine. I develop this argument in four main sections. The first section maps the rise and significance of the debates about labour-shareholder activism, and establishes their relevance to changes in both financial markets and corporate governance. The second section identifies the chief limitations to union-led shareholder activism since its rise in the early 1990s and explores the two major perspectives that have been used in the debates to explain the weakness surrounding this novel form of activism. The third section critically evaluates these two explanations, aiming to transcend mainstream analyses by identifying the underlying causes that have led to the weakness in union-led shareholder activism. The fourth section concludes by drawing out the analytical and political limits to the new activism.

The changing landscape of investment in Corporate America

In his controversial book, *The Unseen Revolution: How Pension Fund Socialism Came to America*, Peter Drucker argues that through their pension funds, workers have come to represent a controlling share of equity capital. The growth in pension fund assets, according to Drucker, translates into the 'ownership of the means of production by workers', and therefore a state of socialism. Labour, seen as the source of all value, now receives the 'full fruits of the productive process' through pension savings (Drucker, 1976: 4). While Drucker's analysis of the socialist features of pension funds has proven overly optimistic, at least in terms of the power workers wield over their pension fund capital, his insight into workers' ability to influence corporate behaviour through their pension funds has undergone a recent revival. There are at least two interrelated reasons for this renewal: (1) the astronomical rise in levels of corporate ownership by institutional investors, especially in the form of pension plans; and (2) the growing interest in good corporate governance and its key objective, the maintenance of shareholder value, which has been spurred on by the general increase in shareholder activism since the early 1990s.

With regard to the first point, there has been a staggering increase in ownership levels among US institutional investors (e.g. pension funds, investment companies, insurance companies, banks and foundations) over the past several decades. As discussed in Chapter 1, US institutional investors as a whole have increased their share of US equity markets substantially (The Conference Board, 2007a). Pension funds represent the largest type of institutional investor, with 38.9 per cent of total assets in 2005. Of this category, private pension funds, especially open-ended mutual funds,[1] have experienced the most rapid levels of growth since the 1980s, largely, although not exclusively, due to state-led privatization campaigns within the Ownership Society (see Chapter 2). Private pension funds, for instance, have amassed institutional investor assets totalling 23.8 per cent in 2005 (ibid).

Despite their size, private pension funds, such as DC schemes like 401(k), have not been major sources of shareholder activism. There are at least two reasons for this. First, unlike guaranteed DB plans, employer-sponsored, market-based DC schemes are subject to specific controls under the Department of Labour's ERISA, which limits the ability of money managers to engage in corporate governance activities (Blair, 1995; see also Chapter 2). Second, DC plans (mutual funds) are largely indexed. The significance of indexing for shareholder activism is that 'Index fund managers may have no interest in shareholder activism since they merely adjust their holdings when the mix of the index changes and only want to follow the index, not influence it' (Federal Reserve Board, 2002). For these and other reasons, DC retirement plans have not been at the forefront of holding corporate executives accountable to shareholder concerns, such as the bid for equal access discussed in Chapter 4.

In contrast to DC plans, union-sponsored pension plans, most of which are more secure, DB plans, have played an important role in contesting strategies and decisions made by corporate management (Schwab and Thomas, 1998; Hawley and Williams, 2000). The total institutional investment assets of activist state and local funds are considerably less than their private counterparts; however, public and local pension funds have not only grown relative to the private sector corporate pension funds, but have also devoted a greater percentage of their assets to equities. With a membership base consisting largely of unionized workers, these funds exercise their clout through proxy voting, proxy fights and other interventionist strategies aimed at ensuring good corporate governance practices, making them the most active category among pension plans (The Conference Board, 2007a).

The growing voice of the activist funds relates to the second point concerning the revival of workers' ability to effect corporate change through their pension savings. Most contemporary scholars seem to agree with Drucker's claim that there has been a fundamental shift in power with regard to pension funds since the Second World War, and, by extension, that pensions funds have come to represent new power centres that offer new opportunities to those who dominate them (Drucker, 1976; Rifkin and Barber, 1978; Blasi, 1988; O'Barr and Conely, 1992; Clark, 2000; Fung *et al.*, 2001; Blackburn, 2002). In their extensive and path-breaking study of labour-shareholder activism, Stewart J. Schwab and Randall S. Thomas go so far as to suggest that labour unions are active again, but this time in the form of capitalists (Schwab and Thomas, 1998). The umbrella term 'labour-shareholder activism' captures these new union tactics aimed at protecting their members' interests in a manner distinct from traditional strategies such as strikes and picketing (O'Connor, 2001). For trade unions, this new activism has translated into a powerful presence in the private sector, despite shrinking membership and density in key sectors of the US economy (Moody, 1997; Mishel *et al.*, 2003).

As discussed in Chapter 1, corporate governance, with its emphasis on maximizing shareholder value, became the new management mantra in response to the mergers, acquisitions and bankruptcies that plagued Corporate America during the 1980s. To recap briefly, corporate governance refers to 'the system by which business corporations are directed and controlled, so as to enhance shareholder value'. The maximization of shareholder value describes a strategy in which managers are required 'to pay more attention to increasing the returns on the assets of the firm in order to increase the value of these assets to shareholders and pay less attention to other constituencies, such as employees and communities' (Brennan, 2008: 27; see also Fligstein and Shin, 2005). While labour-shareholder activism has assumed different forms, such as economically targeted investments (ETIs), social screening, and shareholder advocacy initiatives (Hebb, 2001; see also Chapter 7), the main strategy to effect change in publicly held corporations has been shareholder advocacy through proxy proposals, or, put another way, filing resolutions that appear on corporate proxies on which all shareholders are to vote during proxy season.[2] Indeed, as Maureen O'Connor (2001) notes, union-led activism largely involves submitting precatory (advisory) shareholder proposals.

Before continuing this discussion, it is instructive to provide a brief excursion into the basics of shareholder proposals. The procedure of submitting a shareholder proposal is regulated by the SEC Rule 14a-8. Any shareholder, who has continuously held shares of at least $2,000, or 1 per cent of the company value, may submit at most one proposal of 500 words or less per annual meeting (Tkac, 2006). The content of the proposal may be contested, as was the case with the equal access proposal discussed in Chapter 4, by the firm's management, which can petition the SEC to exclude a proposal on one of the four following grounds: (1) the proposal reflects a personal grievance; (2) the proposal requires the firm to violate state, federal or international law; (3) the proposal relates to operations accounting for less than 5 per cent of the firm's assets, sales and revenue; or (4) the proposal relates to the company's ordinary business operations (ibid.: 4). The last point is the one that most corporations cite when attempting to exclude proposals that management deems as 'anti-value' activism, such as special interests linked to union demands (see Chapter 4). It is important to make clear that even if challenges by management fail and a proposal goes to – and *wins* – a shareholder vote, there is no guarantee corporate behaviour will be affected. This is because management is not required to implement successful proposals. Over the years, unions have gained management attention by submitting changes to company by-laws to make their resolutions binding (O'Connor, 2001; Tkac, 2006).

In their bid to use their shareholder rights to influence managers, unions have sought to align themselves with other shareholders. This alignment has largely been accomplished by appealing to the broader (and common) concern of protecting shareholder value, that is, the economic best interests of beneficiaries, as opposed to specific claims that could further the interests of workers, such as wage increases and other forms of social protection (Weller and White, 2001; Brennan, 2005). In other words, since 2002, unions have shifted their focus on social advocacy and moved their attention entirely to corporate governance proposals (Tkac, 2006). Given the hegemonic position of corporate governance and its guiding principle of shareholder value (see Chapters 1 and 2), union-sponsored pension funds have tried to target issues that will garner a fair amount of support from other non-unionized shareholders, such as executive compensation reform, declassified boards (i.e. boards in which all directors are elected annually), golden parachutes, disclosure of political contributions, an end to 'poison pill' provisions[3] and so on. Some commentators have gone so far as to suggest that the success of union-led shareholder campaigns is dependent on the quality of partnerships and networks that unions forge with other key institutional investors (Schwab and Thomas, 1998; Chakrabarti, 2004). As we saw in the previous chapter, the most powerful institutional investors represent influential financial interests, which, more often than not, reflect the same interests as corporate management. Through these new partnerships, the proponents of this new activism believe that there has been a major realignment of the traditional ideologies and/or relationships between shareholders, workers and managers (Blasi, 1988; Schwab and Thomas, 1998; cf. Useem, 1993).[4]

During the 2006 proxy season, corporations faced more than 200 shareholder proposals from major union-sponsored pension funds, which were responsible for filing the largest number of shareholder proposals of any group. As is evident from Table 5.1, these proposals dealt with corporate governance, largely focusing on executive pay and board accountability, as opposed to social issues (cf. Tkac, 2006). This point is illustrated by the following figures:

> In 2006, 295 of 699 shareholder proposals were introduced by union pension funds. By contrast, for 2006, public pension funds sponsored 31 proposals; mutual funds and other types of equity funds, 23; social or religious funds, 39; and individuals, 280.
>
> (*Pensions & Investments*, 2007b)

Explaining the limits to labour's capital

Despite the rising levels of ownership and novel forms of activism by labour-sponsored pension funds in public corporations, these funds have made little progress in safeguarding the general welfare of unionized workers, especially with regard to protecting pension savings and curbing what many perceive to be excessive levels of executive pay and compensation, especially vis-à-vis workers' wages. This section focuses attention on these set-backs for labour and

Table 5.1 Key proposals of US union pension funds in the 2006 proxy season

Union pension fund	Size of fund ($)	Proposal
United Brotherhood of Carpenters and Joiners of America Pension Fund	558 million	A call for a majority vote to elect directors (i.e. 'equal access proposal', discussed in Chapter 4) and greater linkage of pay and corporate performance
American Federation of Labour-Congress of Industrial Organizations Retirement Fund	180 million	The fund introduced proposals at 28 companies, including resolutions for independence of compensation consultants used by boards
American Federation of State, County and Municipal Employees Staff Pension Plan	850 million	The fund introduced proposals at 27 companies, including one resolution calling for corporations to reimburse shareholders' expenses in proxy contests that meet certain conditions
The International Brotherhood of Teamsters General Fund	100 billion*	The Teamsters introduced proposals at 19 companies, focusing on issues that include backdating of executive stock options and board independence, including separation of the chairman and CEO positions

Sources: *Pensions & Investments* (2007).

Note

* Approximate figure for 2006 representing Teamster-affiliated pension and benefit funds. Letter issued from The International Brotherhood of Teamsters to the SEC on 7 April 2006, accessed on 3 August 2008, available at: www.sec.gov/rules/proposed/s70306/s70306-371.pdf.

elaborates on the two dominant explanations in mainstream debates as to why labour continues to lack control over pension fund capital, especially as this pertains to two key areas: financial markets and corporate management.

Although US capital markets are currently financed by $9.4 trillion of workers' pension fund savings, of which $2.69 trillion are held by public pension funds (The Conference Board, 2007a), there has been a general decline of the average real pension benefit by one-third since the 1980s (Brennan, 2005). Mishel *et al.* (2007) draw on the category of 'retirement income adequacy' in order to measure the ability of individuals to replace at least half their current income based on their expected pension, Social Security benefits and returns on personal savings. According to their study, 27.2 per cent of households headed by someone aged 47–64 expected their retirement income to be *inadequate*. In contrast to the level playing field depicted by the rhetoric of the Ownership Society (see Chapter 2), Table 5.2 reveals how the numbers regarding retirement income adequacy vary along class and racial lines. While there was an improvement in the overall levels of expected retirement adequacy from 1998 to 2001, most gains were wiped out between 2001 and 2004, largely due to the surge of corporate scandals (ibid.). It is expected that these levels will be adversely affected by the 2008 credit crisis.

Table 5.2 Retirement income adequacy,* 1989–2004

Group	1989	1998	2001	2004	1989–2001 Percentage-point change	2001–2004 Percentage-point change
By Race/Ethnicity						
Non-Hispanic White	27.3	40.3	25.4	24.1	–2.0	–1.3
African-American or Hispanic	42.1	52.7	40.0	39.0	–2.1	–1.0
By Education						
Less than high school	39.2	48.6	29.2	46.6	–10.0	17.4
High school degree	24.7	40.9	29.0	28.8	4.3	–0.2
College degree or more	20.8	40.7	25.4	21.2	4.6	–4.2

Source: Adapted from Mishel *et al.* (2007: 270).

Note
* Percentage of households headed by someone aged 47–64 with expected retirement income less than one half of current income.

The myopic market model represents a key perspective in explaining the ina-bility of the new activism to effect change by assuming greater control over old-age savings in order to create long-term wealth, especially as it pertains to protecting the security of workers' pensions. Generally speaking, this view, as employed in the labour-shareholder activism debates, is comprised of two strands. On the one hand, it posits that the dominance of financial concerns driven by the principle of maximizing shareholder value has permeated the man-agement of old-age savings to such a degree that corporate ownership has not been accompanied by commensurate levels of influence and control by US workers, because pensions are not managed directly by their beneficiaries (Rifkin and Barber, 1978; Hebb, 2001). Instead, they are held in trust and invested by money managers in the capital market on behalf of those beneficiar-ies. This has resulted in a situation in which relatively few corporations, state governments or unions manage their employee pension funds in-house. Most give over investment responsibility to bank trust departments, insurance com-panies and independent asset managers (Rifkin and Barber, 1978: 91; cf. Clark, 2000). Jeremy Rifkin and Randy Barber suggest that the transfer, or outsourcing, of daily investment decisions has led to a situation in which trade unions and states have relinquished control over pension fund capital to the financial estab-lishment (Rifkin and Barber, 1978: 11). William Graebner argues that the tension between ownership and control still exists. Despite the fact that workers are owners of a vast amount of money, they have gained none of the power that historically accrues to such wealth (Graebner, 1980; Ingham, 2000).

On the other hand, the myopic market perspective holds that the pressure to rapidly boost returns on capital has not only led to increased risk for pension savers and retirees, but has also compromised other social issues affecting labour as a result of the influence and power of financial markets (cf. Blair, 1995; Baker and Fung, 2001; Hebb, 2001). Put another way, the primacy given to the maximization of shareholder value underpins the perspective that 'short-term increases in stock valuation justify such forms of distress as closing otherwise productive facilities, shifting work to lower-wage or less regulated regions, and selling off pieces of coherent business complexes' (Hebb, 2001: 2–3; Baker and Fung, 2001). This position has been supported by numerous scholars, from a variety of disciplines, who are critical of the meaning and social impact of what they refer to as the ideology of shareholder value (Lazonick and O'Sullivan, 2000; Erturk *et al.*, 2004; Aglietta and Rebérioux, 2005; Fligstein and Shin, 2005; see also Chapters 1 and 2). A case in point is the dramatic increase in share repurchases in the neoliberal era. As discussed in previous chapters, corporations have traditionally raised capital by selling shares on the stock market. Firms have, in turn, traditionally used this capital for productive purposes in order to generate profits for shareholders (dividends). However, since the 1980s the level of share repurchases, that is, firms repurchasing their own shares as opposed to offering shares for sale in new equity issues, has skyrocketed. As David M. Brennan observes,

> During the 1950s, 1960s, and 1970s, firms were, in aggregate, net sellers of equities. In the 1950s, firms raised $1.96 billion per year on average on net new equity issues. For the 1960s, this annual average was $1.16 billion, and the 1970s experienced an average of $5.52 billion per year in net new equity issues ... During the 1980s and the 1990s, however, net new equity issues based on annual averages were –$55.89 and –$69.4 billion, respectively. In the year 2000, net new equity issues were –$150.6 billion. This means that, in aggregate, U.S. firms were repurchasing their own shares in excess of what they offered for sale in new equity issues.
>
> (Brennan, 2008: 89–90)

Institutional investors and corporate management, as opposed to labour, have been the biggest winners of these share repurchases. L. Josh Bivens and Christian E. Weller (2005) argue that the link between the simultaneous rise in share repurchases and poor wage and employment growth is due to the growing influence of institutional investors and their demand for higher levels of return on their shares. Brennan suggests that another aspect of the growth of share repurchases is to be found in the sharp rise in the use of stock options to pay CEOs in order to ensure that they remain focused on increasing shareholder value (Brennan, 2008). As discussed in Chapter 3, the 'carrot' feature of stock options is rooted in the assumption of the corporate governance doctrine, i.e. that agents (management) will act rationally (in terms of 'profit-seeking' behaviour) and align their interests with the principals (shareholders).

A second, related manifestation of the lack of influence of workers over their pension fund capital is the unprecedented increase in the ratio between the compensation of executives and workers in the US over the past two decades. In real terms, average executive compensation has risen to almost 300 per cent of average wages since 1990 (ibid.). According to a preliminary analysis by The

Corporate Library, the average CEO of a Standard & Poor's 500 company in 2006 received $14.78 million in total compensation. This amounts to a 9.4 per cent increase in CEO pay over 2005 (AFL-CIO, 2007). In contrast, the average worker has received less than 5 per cent in pay raises over the period from 1990 to 2006. In fact, wages, compensation and income growth for the typical worker and family have lagged significantly behind the country's rapid increase in productivity, which grew to 81 per cent between 1973 and 2005 (Mishel *et al.*, 2007).[5]

A basic premise of the corporate governance doctrine posits that management should be aptly rewarded with stock options and adequate compensation that will not only attract and retain the best talent, but also ensure that the interests of the so-called agents (executives) are aligned with the principals or owners (shareholders) (see Chapter 3; cf. Fama, 1980). In contrast to this view, there has been a vast and rigorous research that has demonstrated 'a weak or non-existent relation between pay and performance' (Erturk *et al.*, 2008; see also Tosi *et al.*, 2000). Indeed, over the years, executive pay has risen at a much faster rate than the stock market or corporate profits (Institute for Policy Studies and United for a Fair Economy, 2007). Executive pay excesses come at the expense of shareholders and stakeholders, the company, and its employees. According to the AFL-CIO,[6]

> Excessive CEO pay takes dollars out of the pockets of shareholders – including the retirement savings of America's working families. Moreover, a poorly designed executive compensation package can reward decisions that are not in the long-term interests of a company, its shareholders and employees.
>
> (AFL-CIO, 2007)

The recent flurry of stock option scandals in the US is a case in point regarding the abuses linked to excessive executive compensation packages. While the SEC has been investigating as many as 160 companies for possible backdating violations, some observers estimate that there are approximately 700 US public companies that have received or provided manipulated stock option grants (Bebchuk *et al.*, 2006; Brennan, 2008). Stock options, which grant CEOs the right to purchase shares at a set price, usually after the stock's closing price on the grant date, are believed by some to provide CEOs with an incentive to work harder to increase their company's stock price. Recent findings have revealed that CEOs not only have received and cashed-in generous stock options at a time when a company's share price was sinking, but they have also engaged in the practice of 'backdating' their stock options. 'Backdating' refers to a strategy in which executives select a date when the stock was trading at a relative lower price than the date of their options grant, which, in turn, results in an instant profit (see Chapter 3). The *Wall Street Journal* succinctly captured the gist of backdating by comparing it to being allowed to bet on a horse race after it is over (*Wall Street Journal*, 2006).

While the proponents of union-led shareholder activism acknowledge these limits, they have largely been understood and explained as weaknesses related to poor corporate governance practices. According to this perspective, the above problems affecting the welfare of workers can and should be resolved by encouraging workers to undertake a more aggressive role as shareholders and thereby hold the executive accountable. Old-style union tactics are not considered as effective or suitable to achieve these ends. Union-sponsored pension funds can only effectively influence management by drawing on their position as company shareholders rather than workers. As noted earlier, union-sponsored pension funds are most effective when they align themselves with other institutional investors so as to have the greatest impact on corporate management during proxy voting. According to the proponents of this view, this alignment has usually resulted in increased transparency, stronger corporate governance and greater accountability on the part of management (Hebb, 2001: 6; O'Connor, 2001). Various authors credit this new activism with bringing about a major realignment of the traditional ideologies and/or relationships between shareholders, workers and managers in what is framed as a predominantly positive, win–win situation (Blasi, 1988; Useem, 1993; Schwab and Thomas, 1998).

While the weak corporate governance and myopic market explanations point to important and relevant structures and practices that inhibit labour-shareholder activism, they remain incomplete in that they fail to capture the underlying causes of the contradictions and social relations of power linked to this activism. In what follows, I have two interrelated goals: (1) to identify the analytical weaknesses of existing explanations of the limits to the new activism; and (2) to shift analysis to the wider capitalist society. The latter objective entails the following two steps. First, I will explore the role of labour and the neoliberal state *within* the context of capitalist society and the relations of domination therein, establishing an analytical framework that allows us to move beyond the depoliticizing boundaries of the corporate governance doctrine. Second, I will transcend the focus on the short-term nature of financial markets by examining the underlying relations of power and contradictions inherent in the social power of money and the wider credit system.

Transcending the weak corporate governance perspective

I have stressed throughout the book that corporate governance is not a neutral field of study, but rather one that is firmly rooted in the larger and hegemonic neoliberal paradigm. It is useful to recap some of the key criticisms of the corporate governance doctrine introduced in earlier chapters (especially Chapters 1, 3 and 4), as these criticisms inform the following attempt to transcend explanations provided in the labour-shareholder activism debates.

In what follows, I demonstrate that the labour-shareholder activism debates repeat the same common-sense assumptions of mainstream corporate governance theorists in explaining the continued inability of organized labour to exercise meaningful control over their pension funds, particularly with regard to excessive levels of executive compensation packages. This is particularly evident in arguments suggesting that the limits to labour-shareholder activism lie in ineffective strategies pursued by organized labour groups to improve corporate governance, as opposed to the existing legal system. The new activism will fail to garner support from other, non-unionized, shareholders and corporate management if the proposals for reform by union-led shareholder activism are seen as contrary to the fundamental goal of increasing shareholder value. Management groups have claimed, for instance, that most union-sponsored shareholder reform is 'part of a "corporate campaign" designed to win other concessions for workers. Corporate management representatives have even asked the SEC to restrict unions' ability to submit shareholder proposals' (Schwab and Thomas, 1998: 1022). As noted in the previous chapter, the CEO and President of the U.S. Chamber of Commerce, Thomas J. Donohue, drew a distinction between pro-value and anti-value activism. While pro-value activism inspires public involvement in markets and raises returns, anti-value activism is believed to reduce democracy and shareholder value. Some examples given by Donohue of anti-value activism include pro-union policies, which are usually spearheaded by the political interests of top officials of public pension funds (U.S. Chamber of Commerce, 2006). It should be noted that union leaders hold powerful positions on the board of directors in large and influential public pension funds in the US, such as the CalPERS (see Chapter 6). As seen in the previous chapter on the myth of corporate democracy, anti-value activism is portrayed as an attempt by unions to use their role as shareholders primarily to regain strength in collective bargaining and increasing membership institutions (Ghilarducci, 1992: 121; Schwab and Thomas, 1998).

According to many commentators, the legal system does not need to be altered to deal with the new activism or its specific demands, including the issue of equal access discussed in the previous chapter (O'Connor, 2001). Stewart J. Schwab and Randall S. Thomas, for instance, argue that the existing legal and economic framework in the US will keep labour-shareholder activism from dominating debates about corporate governance due to existing fiduciary checks, such as the primacy money managers must place on financial concerns over social concerns (i.e. job security, wages) (Schwab and Thomas, 1998). For her part, Marleen O'Connor freely acknowledges that the National Labour Relations Act does not adequately protect workers' rights against managers, but she says that unions do not require an amendment to the labour code, as they can use their rights as shareholders to exert power over managers (O'Connor, 2001: 67; see also Schwab and Thomas, 1998). O'Connor goes so far as to suggest that 'corporate governance will trump labour laws in importance, and shareholder rights will constitute a new focal point for labour relations in the US in the twenty-first century' (O'Connor, 2001: 67).

The above view, which represents one of the chief positions by those who advocate the weak corporate governance perspective, is based on the understanding that workers can no longer rely on the state to protect their rights or improve their security in the current era of neoliberal-led capitalism. Instead, workers should move away from old forms of activism, which included struggles in and against the state, as well as corporate management, toward market-based solutions that focus on maximizing shareholder value. This premise reflects all three common-sense assumptions inherent in corporate governance theory (see Chapter 3). Proponents of the weak corporate governance perspective adhere to the belief that the neutral state and the existing labour and corporate laws that frame labour-led shareholder activism are unproblematic because they embody the common good of American society. Moreover, proponents argue that the rationality and competitive forces of the marketplace, in which corporate governance is exercised, will lead to equilibrium, thereby ensuring the maximization of shareholder value, which is assumed to be the best outcome. Implicit in this argument is the notion that the rational and competitive process(es) necessary to achieving maximum shareholder value (i.e. the alignment of the divergent interests of workers/shareholders and management) occur on a smooth and level playing field, devoid of relations of domination and exploitation that characterize capitalist society, a fallacy critiqued in detail in Chapters 3 and 4.

Understanding the strengths and limits of labour-led shareholder activism in terms of its ability to meet the requirements of shareholder value does not provide a meaningful explanation as to why labour-led shareholder initiatives are antithetical to shareholder value, as opposed to excessive compensation packages for corporate executives. Furthermore, and more fundamentally, it does not help to explain why there continue to exist growing inequities between executive and workers' pay, or why workers' wages have not kept up with productivity rises in the US over the past several decades (Mishel *et al.*, 2007; Moody, 2007). As discussed in Chapters 3 and 4, shareholder value, which forms the core of mainstream corporate governance theory and practice, is not an irrefutable premise; but instead, an ideology that is subjective in nature, promoting the particular interests of some over others, especially those of the management and board of directors over workers and other stakeholders (cf. Aglietta and Rebérioux, 2005; Brennan, 2008). As several scholars have demonstrated, the goal of maximizing shareholder value has had little to do with economic prosperity since the rise of neoliberal rule in the early 1980s in the US (Lazonick and O'Sullivan, 2000; Fligstein and Shin, 2005).

By moving outside of the depoliticizing tendencies of the corporate governance doctrine and situating union-based shareholder activism within the wider social relations of power and contradictions that underpin capitalist society, we are able to provide a more complete picture of the causes of the main weakness of this new activism. In order to do so effectively, however, two primary issues need to be confronted and transcended in the debates. The first is the failure to grasp the fact that labour is not an economic category but instead a social relation within the wider capital accumulation process, which is marked by conflict between social classes. By ignoring this perspective, the labour-shareholder debates side-step relations of exploitation and domination, reducing complex social interaction between variegated groups and classes to the simplified (depoliticizing) terms of the corporate governance doctrine, which focuses exclusively on the maximization of shareholder value. In treating labour as an economic category, as opposed to a social category, the debates also fail to grasp that labour's subordinate position in the capital accumulation process is not a natural and thus eternal feature, but instead needs to be reproduced by the dominant social forces of society.

Within a Marxist perspective, the defining feature of capitalist society is the necessary exploitation of labour power in order to extract surplus labour, i.e. labour time over and above that which is required to produce the value embodied in the wage. On this view, the subordinate classes perform work for the reproduction of the ruling class, and therefore end up working to reproduce the very conditions of their own subjugation, exploitation and dependence. Marx refers to the extraction of surplus labour in class societies as the exploitation of labour (Fine, 1989; Marx, 1991). Obviously, the reproduction of capitalist society depends on other forms of social discipline and control. The emergence of the hegemonic position of the corporate governance doctrine in academia and policy-making circles is discussed in previous chapters, with an emphasis on: its naturalization (Chapter 3); its attempt to make capitalist society irrelevant (Chapter 4); and its centrality in the ideological and disciplinary (neoliberal) features of the Ownership Society (Chapter 2).

Within the context of the public corporation, the direct and exploitative relation between labour (skilled and unskilled workers) and capitalists (owners of the means of production) is difficult to discern, largely because ownership of the corporation has been dispersed into shares, and the identity of class has been concealed by the homogenizing and harmonizing term 'shareholders' (Renner, 1949; Scott, 1997). The social power of money plays a central role in obfuscating the class nature of exploitation and creating the illusion of democracy. I discuss the role of money in more detail below. For now, it is important to stress that social classes, as discussed in Chapter 4, have not disappeared in either the context of the corporation or, more generally, capitalist society; but rather have been, and are continually being, transformed through the contradictory and conflict-ridden nature of capital accumulation (Marx, 1976; Holloway and Picciotto, 1991; Jessop, 1991). This position is based on the understanding that class is not a thing, but instead is a social and cultural formation that assumes its dynamicism from struggles rooted in the historical unfolding of capital accumulation processes (Thompson, 1991; cf. Scott, 1997; Carroll, 2004).

The second and related issue that must be confronted in order to overcome the limits within the weak corporate governance approach to labour-led shareholder activism is that the state, including its legal regime, is neither a natural nor a neutral object, but an historical social relation that is an integral feature of capitalist society. As discussed in Chapters 1 and 2, the state is neither neutral nor a separate political entity from the market; neither is it an objective actor, nor a mere instrument of class or class fractions (e.g. financial, industrial capital). Instead, the state is a complex, contradictory and dynamic historical social relation that both influences, and is influenced by, the shifting relations of power within capitalist society (Hirsch, 1991). The state plays an integral role in reproducing the subordinate position of labour in the wider capital accumulation strategy. At the heart of this strategy are financial markets and transactions, which are supported by a wide range of neoliberal policies, including privatization, deregulation and liberalization schemes – all of which have affected the power relations between management and labour.

Instead of problematizing the role of the capitalist state, many of the proponents of labour-shareholder activism tend to blame authorless, external forces of globalization and deregulated financial markets for the weakened position of labour vis-à-vis corporate management (Rifkin and Barber, 1978; Fung *et al.*, 2001). In doing so, the debates fail to grasp that the new activism is part and parcel of several decades of strategic neoliberal domination over labour. Greg Albo appropriately refers to neoliberal strategies as the politics of 'competitive austerity' (Albo, 1994). Such strategies have led to, among other things, the dispossession of millions of workers' pension savings, increased levels of personal debt, job insecurity and systematic attempts to discipline labour by threatening workers with investment strikes or capital flight if they do not accept lower wages and a reduction in social benefits (Mishel *et al.*, 2003, 2007; Moody, 2007). The problem with mainstream literature is that it understands competitiveness as a natural, given and rational phenomenon, rather than a constructed strategy that is directly linked to capitalist interests, the ongoing crisis of overaccumulation and state-led policies (Panitch, 1994; Harvey, 2005).

Neoliberal forms of social discipline, as well as commodification strategies employed by both corporations and states, are largely neglected in the labour-shareholder activism debates. For the proponents of labour-shareholder activism, old forms of protest by unionized workers are a thing of the past, since globalization has shifted the goal posts. Cheaper labour and capital in the global South and the domination of financial markets are two major outcomes of globalization. Proponents of labour-shareholder activism uncritically accept that social change is deterministically imposed on labour (seen as an economic category) by the unstoppable and neutral forces of globalization (Bieler *et al.*, 2008). In doing so, they remain blind to the fact that labour-shareholder activism is not only rooted in new forms of exploitation and neoliberal domination, but also assists, to some degree, in reproducing the status quo. The primacy granted to shareholder value in the corporate governance doctrine neutralizes and depoliticizes the class nature of the neoliberal restructuring of labour markets by encouraging workers to focus on aligning themselves with other shareholders to encourage good corporate governance practices, as opposed to winning more substantial gains of ownership. These gains may be regarded as decreased levels of exploitation through increased social protection that is legally mandated, as well as more control over productive processes. In contrast to the proponents of the new activism, I argue that such gains should be achieved by the legal imperative of the democratic state as opposed to the de facto promises made by powerful interests in the private sector.

The legal system in the US has helped pave the way for the successful implementation of neoliberal restructuring of labour relations. On the one hand, US labour law has long been skewed in the interests of employers, which calls into question the pluralist relationships between management and workers. As Dan Clawson and Mary Ann Clawson note, among industrial democracies, US labour law is unique in that it allows employers to actively oppose their employees' decision to unionize. A series of court and administrative decisions over the years have further narrowed employee union rights, while expanding employer rights. Furthermore, while workers are guaranteed the right to strike and may not be penalized for doing so, employers are guaranteed the right to maintain production during a strike and may hire permanent replacement workers (Clawson and Clawson, 1999: 100). On the other hand, aside from the ERISA of 1974, which dictates how far unions can flex their financial muscles, especially with regard to fiduciary requirements governing various types of pension plans (Ghilarducci, 1992; Clark, 2000), there are other notable limits to the power of pension fund activism. As noted earlier, according to the SEC's rule, management can omit shareholder proposals that 'deal with a matter relating to the conduct of the ordinary business' (Tkac, 2006: 4; see also Weller and White, 2001). Through this law, the state ensures that shareholders, including union pension fund activists, keep their resolutions and voting behaviour in line with the overall goal of shareholder value (see, for example, Table 5.1), as opposed to engaging in 'anti-value' activist strategies, which fall under the term of SRI strategies (see Chapter 7). Another legal restriction imposed by the state vis-à-vis labour-shareholder activism, is contained in corporate charters and corporate by-laws (ibid.). Many votes are not legally binding, and to change corporate by-laws often requires that the super-majority wins, which, as previously noted, is a rare occurrence (Tkac, 2006). As noted above by O'Connor (2001), labour groups have begun to challenge corporate by-laws as part of their wider shareholder activism strategies, but the process has been slow and arduous, largely due to the relations of power both within the corporation and wider capitalist society (see Chapter 4).

Transcending the myopic market explanation

... not violence, but credit may be a rather ultimate seat of control within modern societies.

(C. Wright Mills (1964), quoted in Zeitlin, 1989: 111)

[F]inancial markets are cutting our throats with our own money, and it has to stop.

(Leo W. Gerard, International President, United Steel Workers of America, 2001)

While proponents of the myopic market perspective are cognizant of the fact that the dominant, free-market ideology underpinning the current organization of financial markets is neither neutral nor value-free (Hebb, 2001), this perspective incorrectly assumes that the present status of the highly deregulated financial markets is a natural phenomenon that has evolved progressively through the internal processes of the market, or through the unstoppable, external forces of globalization (Baker and Fung, 2001). This assumption leads to at least two problems with the myopic market perspective. First, while the proponents of the myopic market view correctly identify several key weaknesses of the present financial system, such as preference for short-term rewards to boost the price of company stock and the relative power that money managers wield over the investment decisions of workers' pension savings, these characteristics are not natural occurrences, as the myopic market perspective would have us believe. Instead, I suggest that they should be understood as social constructs that not only serve particular interests, but are also inherently conflictual and contradictory in nature. A second limitation of the myopic market perspective is that while the debates on labour-shareholder activism politicize the role of workers vis-à-vis the financial system, the discussions tend to treat the financial realm in an apolitical manner (Langley, 2008). This oversight, I argue, leads to an incomplete assessment and explanation of the limitations to union-led shareholder activism because it fails to engage with the struggles and contradictions that accompany relations of power, that is, those inherent in the wider capitalist society, including the credit system (see Chapters 1 and 3).

In my attempt to move beyond the above two weaknesses of the myopic market perspective, I look at the social power and contradictions entailed in two categories: money and the credit system. These two highly interrelated features, which are central to the financial system and pension fund capital, have been understood in the myopic market debates as neutral objects, devoid of social power in their own right. I draw on a Marxist-informed perspective of money and the credit system in order to draw out the social features of the financial system and the ways in which the status quo is recreated and represented as a natural and apolitical feature of capitalist society. The objective of this exercise is to provide an alternative perspective on how we can better understand the underlying dynamics of the limitations to the new activism, especially in terms of protecting the pension savings of unionized workers.

Despite its centrality to the discussions, the new activism debates do not provide a precise definition of pension fund capital. Based on the applications of this term in the debates, we can deduce that pension fund capital refers to a passive object in the form of a pool of deferred wages or salaries that, in turn, is 'acted upon' by money managers and trustees of pension funds through investment decisions. The aim of, or fiduciary duty behind, these decisions is to ensure that they generate stable growth over the long term through investment in shares, bonds, property and other income-producing assets in order to generate a stable income from which to pay the pensions of its retired members (Scott, 1997: 67; Minns, 2001). The problem, as understood in labour-shareholder activism debates, is that the ability of unionized workers to adequately protect their pension savings is impeded by the dominance of the financial community over daily decision-making processes, as well as the short-term nature of capital markets. While this is true, there is more to the explanation than is provided for in the myopic market perspective.

As explained in Chapter 2, when money and, by extension, pension fund capital, is treated as a social relation embedded in capitalist society, it permits a deeper understanding of the relations of power that run through the primacy of shareholder value and financial concerns, which, according to the myopic market perspective, are the root cause of workers' lack of control over their capital, including the protection of their pension savings. In Marxist theory, money is significant because it conceals underlying social power within the wider capital relation. This social power is concealed in the very nature of money, due to the latter's ability to act as the embodiment of exchange value, for instance, by standing opposed to all other commodities and their use values. In doing so, money assumes an independent, external and, therefore, objective standing vis-à-vis the power relations of exchange (Harvey, 1999). While the interests of money managers have not been well aligned with the long-term interests of unionized workers, there is more to the limitation than the myopic market perspective allows. Specifically, workers' ability to influence the investment decisions of their pension savings (deferred wages or salaries) are restricted by more fundamental barriers involving a complex array of contradictions and limitations surrounding their identity as workers and savers, as well as the very nature of how money is organized by the credit system in capitalist society (Harvey, 1999, 2005; see also Chapter 3).

Marx's notion of the 'community of money' permits us to transcend the surface level explanation provided by the myopic market viewpoint. Marx characterizes capitalist society as a community of money in which social relations are 'strongly marked by individualism and concepts of liberty, freedom, and equality backed by laws of private property, rights to appropriation, and freedom of contract' (Harvey, 1989: 168). As an expression of liberty, for instance, money signals voluntary exchanges between equals on the market. As a relation of formal equality, money represents, or more precisely conceals, exploitative relations as relations of formal equality: everybody is equal before money (Bonefeld, 1995: 183). Money in the form of pension fund capital acts as the great equalizer, as it establishes a bond between divergent interests – e.g. capitalists, landlords, governments, workers, managers and so forth – who lose their class identity and become shareholders, meeting on a level playing field at the annual general meetings of public corporations. Thus, the confrontation between unions and management has moved from the shop floor and the picket lines to the 'democratic' setting of proxy voting (see Chapter 4). Moreover, within the neutralizing and depoliticizing features of corporate governance, divergent class interests and unequal relations of domination among various institutional investors (e.g. public pension funds, mutual funds, private equity funds and so forth) are not only concealed and smoothed over as each group takes on the blanket, and generic, identity of 'shareholders', but also are united in ensuring that corporate management achieves the highest possible return on their investment (Brennan, 2005, 2008).

The relations of power and domination that are inherent in Marx's community of money are taken for granted by the myopic market perspective. Yet, these relations draw attention to the important connection of workers to corporations, and thus the exercise of control over corporate management that is represented in terms of 'shareholder power'. The notion of 'shareholder power' is understood in highly sanitized, monetary terms, such as the number of shares (minimum amount required to vote) and types of shares (common or preferred stock), all of which are portrayed as legal and, therefore, objective rules created by a capitalist state. In this way, the role of labour in the exploitative relations of production vis-à-vis the corporations are severed, sanitized of class relations and depoliticized by the uncritical treatment of the social power of money vis-à-vis social security capital. This perspective is further reinforced by the hegemonic status of corporate governance as the dominant manner not only in which to analyse corporate behaviour, but also in which to engage corporate management, by ensuring that the latter create shareholder value. Within the neutral and socially constructed bounds of corporate governance, all interactions involving a plurality of economic actors (e.g. labour-shareholders, management, the wider shareholder community and so forth) are believed to eventually lead to a harmonious outcome (see Chapters 3 and 4).

The appearance of equality and concealment of exploitation and domination in the community of money is further reinforced, and complicated, in the current era of financialization. The latter describes 'a pattern of accumulation in which profit-making occurs increasingly through financial channels rather than through trade and commodity production' (Krippner, 2005: 181; see also Arrighi, 1994; Holloway, 1995). The dominance of money, as opposed to productive capital, emerges from the deeper crisis and contradictions of capital accumulation, such as the crisis of overaccumulation, which refers to a condition where surpluses of capital lie idle with no profitable outlets in productive investment (Harvey, 2005; see also Chapter 3). The credit system plays an integral role in attempts to overcome barriers to the expansion of capital in times of crisis. Debt-driven forms of accumulation (i.e. consumer, corporate and state debt), which have dominated US economic expansion over the past several decades, are a case in point. As Geoffrey Ingham notes, in the US

> overall debt – corporate and household – can be taken as a rough guide to the level of expansion of the financial sector, which rose from 130 to 150 per cent of the GDP [gross domestic product] in the 1950s to over 250 per cent in the early 1990s.
>
> (Ingham, 2000: 73)

For Marx, credit was a Janus-faced creature in that it represents both swindler and prophet. One the one hand, it exists as a lever for expanded reproduction as it realizes the internal relation of production and circulation without this relation having been performed, i.e. fictitious capital (Marx, 1991; Harvey, 1999). 'On the other hand', Marx argued, 'it develops the motive of capital production, enrichment by the exploitation of others' labour, into the purest and most colossal system of gambling and swindling, and restricts ever more the already small numbers of exploiters of social wealth' (Marx, 1991: 572–573). Aside from its ability to overcome – albeit temporarily and contradictorily – the barriers to capital valorization, the credit system accomplishes another important role in capital accumulation, namely: masking relations of power and exploitation. It is within the credit system, for instance, that money is able to dissociate itself from the exploitation of labour in the form of credit, thereby continuing to perpetuate the appearance of a harmonious, equal and individualistic community of money (Bonefeld, 1995). This acts to depoliticize further the social power inherent in pension fund capital. In the credit system, for instance, pension fund capital in the form of equity holdings in public corporations, appears as a 'mysterious and self-creating source of interest – the source of its own increase' (M ... M') (ibid.: 190). In other words, money appears to increase its value as if by magic. The following quote furnished by legal scholar Paddy Ireland, succinctly captures the fetishization (i.e. the disconnect from the unequal and exploitative social relations of capitalism) that occurs in financial ownership through the objectification of money:

> Some years ago, newspapers in Britain featured an advertisement depicting a man lying on a sofa. We were told that, contrary to appearances, he was working and, indeed, working highly profitably. His money was, so to speak, working for him, albeit in places and ways of which he almost certainly had no knowledge and little interest. Moreover, it was working incessantly, for money, as another advertisement recently pointed out, 'never sleeps'. In reality, of course, the man lying on the sofa was *not* working. But someone, somewhere, certainly was. Indeed, it was these unknown others, dotted no doubt around the globe, working in unknown industries, for unknown wages and in unknown conditions, who were generating the wealth to which the sofa-bound man was entitled to lay (partial) claim by virtue of his ownership of income rights like the joint stock company share. In its way, therefore, the sofa in the advertisement is curiously revealing of the fetishized nature of financial property and interest-bearing capital (money appears to make more money by itself) and the social relations underlying it (it is only able to do so when certain social relations prevail).
>
> (Ireland, 2007: 53–54)

One of the main reasons the credit system can appear sanitized is because it operates in the form of fictitious capital, which refers to a flow of money capital that is not backed by any commodity transaction (see Chapter 3). Put another way, fictitious capital occurs whenever credit is extended in advance, in anticipation of future labour as a counter-value (Harvey, 1999: 265–266). For Marx, the accumulation of capital through investment was represented as

(M ... C ... M') in which money (M) is employed to buy raw materials, machines and labour to produce commodities (C), which are then sold, with the capitalist receiving M' (Marx, 1976; see also Arrighi, 1994). The value of money is not determined through the value it represents in relation to commodities, or, more pronouncedly, in relation to itself, but through the surplus value which it produces for its owner (Bonefeld, 1995: 190). Since the onset of the era of financialization in the early 1970s, corporations and financial institutions have amassed large profits through the creation of fictitious capital ahead of actual commodity production. Financial institutions of all types now accumulate huge quantities of debt as they attempt to make money with borrowed money, including corporate bonds and collateralized debt obligations (CDOs) (Blackburn, 2006). According to the *Wall Street Journal*,

> Corporations are borrowing money at the fastest clip in several years amid a wave of leveraged buy-outs and acquisitions, rising capital expenditures and pressure from shareholders for larger dividends and share buybacks ....
> Non-financial companies saw their debt rise 6.3 percent in the last 12 months .... That is the fastest yearly growth for debt in five years
>
> (Magdoff, 2006: 3)

As discussed in Chapter 1, the chickens came home to roost in 2007 in the form of the sub-prime mortgage scandal, which involved high levels of CDOs, among other risky and opaque financial products (cf. Blackburn, 2006).

Since the connection between money and exploitation is further severed in the credit system, the class-based relations of power within the credit system are generally ignored in favour of a focus on financial markets and financial actors. The latter, especially within the myopic market framework, are seen as the primary culprits in eroding workers' livelihoods – a view that glosses over the relations of power and domination imbued in the credit system (Harvey, 1999). The new activism debates, for instance, understand an increase in the value of pension fund capital as a result of the behaviour of money managers, such as the choice to engage in high risk, short-term ventures, the decision to draw on reliable information and so on (Baker and Fung, 2001). The dependency of workers' savings on financial markets is viewed as a natural phenomenon that involves rational economic actors (agents and principals) interacting on a level playing field to achieve a harmonization of interests. These debates fail to recognize that the construction of pension fund capital is intimately tied to neoliberal forms of restructuring and the disciplinary features therein, which are, fundamentally, a response to, among other things, the inability of corporations to generate adequate levels of profit through production (Minns, 2001). One of the outcomes of the dwindling profit levels of Corporate America has been the rise of private equity firms. These funds purchased more than half of a trillion dollars in US corporations in 2006, which represented a tenfold increase in only three years (see Chapter 1). These new investors wield huge amounts of shares in Corporate America. Private equity firms, for example, hold about 60 per cent of total shares in the beleaguered General Motors. Moreover, the interests of these new investors are antithetical to the interests of unions. Wages and benefits, especially pension benefits, represent the largest costs to companies, and private equity firms are obviously interested in clawing back these costs (*Washington Post*, 2007a); see also Blackburn, 2006).

Finally, the social power of money and the contradictions and struggles played out in the credit system are reproduced and mediated through the capitalist state. In contrast to the myopic market perspective, which views the state as a pluralist institution operating outside the parameters of the market, a Marxist approach to the capitalist state treats the latter as an historical form of social relations of power that is deeply rooted in capitalist society and its particular mode of production and consumption. Although the role and nature of the capitalist state is discussed at length in previous chapters, it is worth underscoring here that the US state has played, and continues to play, a central role in supporting and legitimating class-led strategies carried out through the credit system in order to restructure capitalist society in such a way so as to allow for the continued expansion of capital. The construction, reproduction and expansion of social security capital through the ongoing privatization of pension savings in the form of the Ownership Society exemplifies the central role played by the state (see Chapter 2). Through its ideological and coercive (e.g. legal system) functions, the US state has also played a central role in depoliticizing and delimiting moments of contestation linked to the Ownership Society, including the equal access proposal discussed in Chapter 4 and labour-led shareholder activism. Finally, the state has played a key role in the deregulation of financial markets – both at home and abroad (Panitch and Gindin, 1995; Gowan, 1999; Soederberg, 2004, 2006; Harvey, 2005). This has allowed the superintendents of social security capital, namely institutional investors such as pension and mutual funds, to continually engage in high-risk, speculative activities known more generally as 'arbitrage capitalism' (Arrighi, 1994; Harvey, 2005; Blackburn 2006; see also Chapter 3). These short-term strategies undertaken by money managers should not be interpreted in the narrow confines of either irrational or rational behaviour, as often depicted in the myopic market perspective; rather, they must be understood as part and parcel of the contradictory and conflict-led attempts to overcome perceived barriers to the incessant need to maximize profit.

Conclusion

I have argued that the two major approaches – weak corporate governance practices and market myopia – are insufficient for understanding why organized labour continues to wield little control over social security capital. Specifically, these two approaches fail to provide full explanations as to the limits to the new activism because they do not grasp the underlying contradictions and power relations of capitalist society. These partial accounts regarding the restrictions plaguing labour-led shareholder activism have translated into policy prescriptions that are equally incomplete, reproducing, in turn, the limited scope of labour vis-à-vis corporate power and the wider financial system. Instead of challenging the existing legal or productive structures in order to provide secure and well-paying jobs, or insisting on the re-regulation of financial markets to mitigate arbitrage capitalism, proponents of the new activism suggest that self-regulatory (and thus market-based) strategies – for example, engaging with corporate executives and money managers to help construct good corporate governance practices to ensure shareholder value – will lead to longer-term investment and thus job creation and economic security. The debates, therefore, remain focused on the financial markets and money managers of pension funds as the primary obstacle to protecting labour's capital. They are less interested in pursuing the deeper roots of disempowerment and exploitation within capitalist production as a structural limitation found within the credit system and pension fund capital itself. Taken together, both mainstream explanations act to depoliticize and marketize resistance, thereby recreating the hegemonic position of the corporate governance doctrine, and, relatedly, the dominance of neoliberal discourse and policy.

In the next chapter, we continue to deepen and widen our analysis of the capitalist nature of shareholder activism with regard to the corporate governance doctrine. Moving beyond the confines of the US context, discussion shifts to the global benchmarking initiative of one of the largest public pension funds in the world, CalPERS. Up to this point, we have concentrated on shareholder activism as a form of resistance. Yet, as we have seen in this chapter, the capitalist nature of financial ownership in corporations presupposes that shareholder activism also entails another feature: a mode of domination. While the latter is present at the domestic level in the US, as is evident in our discussion of labour-led shareholder activism, it assumes a more explicit expression at the global level, especially with regard to North–South relations.

6   Corporate governance and entrepreneurial development

The case of CalPERS' Permissible Country Index

Since the early 1990s, pension funds have played a major role in equity financing in emerging market economies. Equity financing refers to the method by which publicly traded companies in the global South raise long-term capital through the sale of shares (equity) to investors rather than through other financing means such as a bank loans (International Finance Corporation, 2006; World Bank, 2007). Notwithstanding the role of foreign direct investment (FDI),[1] which still constitutes the bulk of private capital flows; equity financing has become a significant source of credit for emerging markets (World Bank, 2005).[2] According to the US investment bank J.P. Morgan Chase & Co., corporate debt in the developing world has risen from $21 billion in 2002 to $111 billion in 2006 (*Financial Times*, 2007; World Bank, 2007).

Given their central position in global financial markets, pension funds are believed to be particularly vulnerable to a wide array of risks (Clark and Hebb, 2005). To monitor and manage these risks, pension funds, like other institutional investors, have created various assessment instruments for 'benchmarking' individual non-US public stock markets to determine their ability to support investment. A chief concern of these assessment exercises has been the compliance of strong corporate governance practices in the developing world.[3] Since the 1990s, various institutional investors have attempted to expand their understanding of corporate governance to include non-financial indicators, such as labour standards, which have also been associated by some with SRI. The benchmarking strategy of the largest US-based public pension fund, CalPERS, is an important case in point and will serve as the primary focus of this chapter.

With assets valued at $176.1 billion (as of 2009), CalPERS represents the leading public pension fund in the US and one of the largest in the world.[4] While the majority of CalPERS' funds are tied up in US corporations, an increasing amount is destined for 27 emerging market economies. CalPERS draws on information gathered by its investment assessment instrument – the Permissible Country Index (hereafter PCI or Index) – to identify suitable investment climates. The Index provides an interesting study, as the 'activism' it is purported to reflect embodies the growing trend in corporate governance discourse to assume a greater concern for social issues (Kawamura, 2002: 14).[5] Through the application of its PCI, CalPERS has sought to promote an understanding of corporate governance based on what it terms 'enduring value' in the developing world. The PCI aids CalPERS' Investment Committee in determining, on a quantitative basis, the levels of enduring value in an emerging market by measuring not only economic indicators (market factors), but also social factors (non-market factors) involving equitable treatment of workers, the environment and other commonly shared public assets.

My argument in this chapter is twofold. On the one hand, I suggest that once we move beyond the surface appearance of the Index, it becomes clear that CalPERS' assessment instrument is not only contradictory and conflict-ridden, but also aimed at ensuring that the conditions for continued expansion of capital accumulation in the Third World are obtained and reproduced through the neo-liberal strategy of the corporate governance doctrine (see Chapters 1 and 2). This is largely accomplished through the promotion of the Anglo-American variant of corporate governance, which affords more attention to shareholder value and market forces more generally. The attempt to facilitate the social power of foreign institutional investors in emerging markets is subsequently legitimated and embedded through the ethical gloss of SRI. This move, I propose, is an attempt to ensure the continual extraction of higher returns on investment than are presently available in the advanced industrialized countries, most notably, in the case of CalPERS, the US. On the other hand, the PCI is neither a natural phenomenon, nor has it emerged in an ahistorical and apolitical vacuum. The basic premises and objectives of the Index, including its appeal to 'enduring-value', are firmly rooted in, and informed by, the most recent revision of neoliberal-led development discourse and policy, which the IFC, a sister institution of the World Bank, refers to as 'entrepreneurial development'. This prevailing and overarching capitalist strategy aims not only to encourage greater involvement of the private sector in development, but also legitimates deepening forms of dependency on, and discipline of, transnational capital in emerging markets.

This argument is developed in four sections. The first section discusses the significance of entrepreneurial development as it pertains to ongoing neoliberal revisionism within official development discourse and policy since the mid-1980s. The second section examines the circumstances and assumptions under-pinning CalPERS' rationale for commissioning Wilshire Associates (hereafter Wilshire), a leading investment consulting firm in the US, to devise a comprehensive index for evaluating public stock markets in emerging market economies. The third section deepens this critical investigation of the Index by seeking to understand its capitalist nature, as well as how it normalizes and legitimates relations of domination and exploitation in emerging markets. I accomplish this task by identifying and elaborating on how three key premises underpinning the PCI act to normalize and thus recreate its capitalist nature. The final section draws some conclusions regarding the argument presented in the chapter.

Neoliberalism and the rise of entrepreneurial development

The shifting landscape in global development financing

As discussed in Chapter 1, neoliberalism is a response to the crisis of overaccumulation that swept over much of the world in the 1970s, and which culminated in the debt crisis for large parts of the global South (Taylor, 2006; Harvey, 2007). The statist and redistributive approaches that marked the post-Second World War development paradigm came under attack by those championing a market-based solution to what were considered insurmountable economic problems, including decreasing levels of productivity and concomitant increases in levels of debt, unemployment and inflation (Leys, 1996). Neoliberal ideologues argued that to overcome the manifestations of this crisis, Third World governments needed to give more leeway to the competitive and rational features of a free market, which, in turn, would assist in bringing about 'progress'.[6] The latter term, as with all official post-war development goals, was understood in terms of achieving material prosperity for society as a whole through economic growth. Neoliberalism was promoted throughout the Third World, driven largely by the Washington Consensus, which, guided by International Monetary Fund (IMF) and World Bank policies, pushed for reforms through highly conditional Structural Adjustment Programmes (SAPs). The SAPs forced open the economies of debtor countries to foreign investment through the liberalization of trade and investment regimes, the privatization of state-owned enterprises and economic policies of restructuring and stabilization, all under the watchful eye of the IMF (Stiglitz, 2002). By 1990, these economic policies would, among other things, produce the desired effect of changing the landscape of development finance (see Figure 6.1 and Table 6.1).

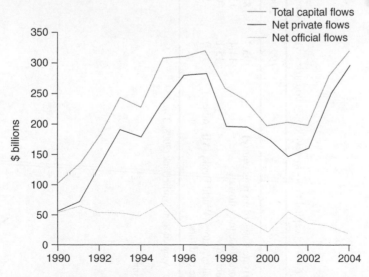

Figure 6.1 Financial flows to developing countries, 1990–2004 (source: World Bank (2005b: 14)).

Table 6.1 Net capital flows to developing countries, various indicators, 1999–2007 (in billion of dollars)

	1999	2000	2001	2002	2003	2004	2005	2006	2007(e)
Net private flows (debt plus equity)	195.7	187.0	164.5	169.1	274.1	412.5	551.4	760.3	1,028.9
Net portfolio equity flows	11.4	13.5	5.6	5.5	24.1	40.4	68.9	104.8	145.1
Net debt flows	15.1	–0.4	4.5	8.9	72.8	128.8	152.4	217.5	409.1
Official creditors (World Bank, IMF, others)	14.0	–5.8	26.8	4.9	–11.7	–26.1	–71.7	–70.5	–3.9
Private creditors	1.5	5.8	–23.0	3.8	84.4	155.2	222.7	288.0	413.0

Source: Adapted from World Bank (2008: 35).

Note
e = estimate.

As these tables demonstrate, private capital flows in the form of FDI and FPI has surpassed public financing in the form of bilateral and multilateral aid and loans. The rise in private capital flows to emerging markets has continued well into the millennium. Net private capital flows to developing countries, for instance, reached a record $1 trillion in 2007 (World Bank, 2008).

As will become clear below, the shift from public-oriented financial flows to private sources is not simply an economic phenomenon, but one that is marked by relations of power and contradictions. For instance, while the majority of CalPERS' assets are invested on a long-term basis in US corporations, the pension fund does hold a substantial amount of assets internationally, e.g. as of February 2005, CalPERS held $3.9 billion in assets in emerging markets. Although this number may seem small compared to its overall holding in the US, it takes on a different meaning when contextualized against the size of stock market capitalization in countries such as the Philippines, Thailand and Malaysia.[7] Seen in relative terms, the amount of equity finance to emerging markets is substantial. Moreover, as will be seen below, the decision to divest from a country has devastating economic, social and political effects. It should be underscored that capital flows to the global South are highly dependent on the nature of neoliberal restructuring strategies in the global North, as well as their fallouts, such as the 2008 credit crisis. The latter have resulted, among other things, in substantially less financial flows to the developing world (ibid.).

Entrepreneurial development and the new conditionality

Mirroring the general tendency to move from public to private sector forms of development financing, the IFC observes that:

> More and more development and aid organizations – multilateral banks, foundations, nonprofits – are looking at an entrepreneurial approach to development. They are asking how they can harness the power of private capital, free enterprise, and social entrepreneurship to bring about needed change.
>
> (International Finance Corporation, 2006)

The objective of this approach, according to the Executive Vice-President of the IFC, Lars Thunell, is 'to bolster the stability of existing capital markets and flows in the developing world by strengthening domestic financial institutions and deepening local currency markets' (ibid.). Thunell goes on to suggest that in order to achieve this goal, 'We need to improve corporate governance, so that more of the up-and-coming companies that are creating jobs can tap into the capital in the global economy' (ibid).

The World Bank's 2005 World Development Report, *A Better Investment Climate for Everyone*, echoes this concern by arguing that economic growth and improved standards of living can be brought about only by facilitating a good investment climate and high level of productivity (World Bank, 2004: 2; see also World Bank, 2007). A good investment climate, for instance, is characterized by low trade barriers, open financial markets and a commitment to ongoing com-modification of all areas of social life through the privatization of health serv-ices, education, old age pensions and basic services. Proponents of the current neoliberal orthodoxy claim that the results of this approach will be universally beneficial, as long as governments practice good governance, such as adopting 'proper' legal and political systems that are universally applicable to both domestic and foreign investors (Soederberg, 2004).

In keeping with the balance between, on the one hand, growth-oriented goals and, on the other, the social and human development objectives of the so-called Second Generation Reforms (SGRs) of the IMF and World Bank (ibid.), the IFC recently made explicit reference to the importance of social accountability for indigenous, publicly listed corporations in the global South to achieve growth, thereby adding a 'social dimension' to entrepreneurial development. In 2006, for example, the IFC introduced new environmental and social standards, or what it calls 'performance standards', to help minimize the negative impact of private-sector projects on the environment and affected communities.[8] According to Thunell, with these new policies, the IFC aims

> to increase the development impact of projects in which we invest. We also seek to give companies operating projects in emerging markets the capacity to manage fully their environmental and social risks and to compete better in a global economy.
>
> (Thunell quoted in Mekay, 2006)

It should be noted, however, that unlike the PCI, the IFC's social standards are not mandatory, but instead rely heavily on self-reporting by companies.

Entrepreneurial development signals subtle changes with regard to global development financing. These modifications warrant explanation as they offer a contextual backdrop for the PCI. In addition to its mainstream definition, entre-preneurial development captures a reconfiguration of power relations in global development finance that involves two interrelated issues. First, entrepreneurial development reflects an expansionary strategy that is directly connected to the continued growth of social security capital, or, seen another way, the widening of the corporate–financial nexus to include US institutional investors in publicly listed companies in the global South. Second, the greater participation of US institutional investors in emerging market economies extends and intensifies the discipline and power of US-based capitalist institutions, such as public pension funds. In this sense, the term 'new conditionality' aptly captures the increasing ability of US capital interests to discipline states and societies in the Third World by defining, quantitatively measuring and ultimately judging which countries are either 'good' or 'bad' investment sites. Good investment sites are rewarded with financing on favourable terms, while bad investment sites are punished by with-holding credit.[9]

The PCI and the shifting geography of development finance

The dual nature of CalPERS' activism

Before turning to a discussion of the content of the PCI and the various revisions it has undergone since its inception in 1987, it is useful to highlight the nature of CalPERS' activism vis-à-vis emerging markets. CalPERS, along with other institutional investors, has long acted as a main driver of shareholder activism in the US, especially with regard to its proactive stance in pushing the good corporate governance agenda. There are important differences, however, in the nature of CalPERS' activism in the US and in the Third World. With a membership base totalling 1.4 million people, largely comprised of unionized, local public agencies of California, CalPERS engages in active ownership with regard to US corporate holdings. According to the CalPERS website, 'Shareowners collectively have the power to direct the course of corporations. The potential impact of this power is staggering. Shareholder activism is defined by a strategy of action that relies primarily on "voice" as opposed to "exit"' (Brancato, 1997). In contrast, when engaging with publicly listed corporations in the Third World, CalPERS prefers exit strategies (i.e. the 'Wall Street Walk') as opposed to exercising its voice (activism) (see Chapter 1). Such exit strategies are seen to be a response to high levels of family and/or state ownership in publicly listed corporations in the developing world, which threaten to limit the ability of CalPERS to exercise 'voice' in the same way it can in the US context.

Another related difference between the nature of CalPERS' activism in the US and the developing world is the level at which good corporate governance practices are observed. Corporate governance can be assessed at a variety of levels: from the national context, involving, for example, rules and regulations making up the regulatory and legal framework of a country, to the company level, which includes appointments of non-executive directors, executive pay, board accountability and so forth (Gul and Tsui, 2004). While CalPERS targets both levels in the context of the US, the public pension fund has decided to centre its attention exclusively on country factors with regard to emerging markets. Although the Index's country-level focus has come under significant criticism by its detractors for neglecting company-level reforms in emerging markets, the rationale behind this move is twofold. First, as a minority shareholder, it can effect very little change in Third World corporations. Second, if change is to take place at the company level, it must be accompanied by 'big picture' reforms at the level of legal and political systems.[10]

CalPERS' shareowner activism in emerging markets is also distinguished by its temporal focus. While CalPERS generally tends to be a long-term investor (holding stock for 7–8 years) in the US, it engages in short-term behaviour when operating in emerging market economies (Blair, 1995). Indeed, given its penchant for exiting emerging markets when broad, national indicators of the PCI point to unfavourable investment conditions, the nature of equity financing falls more into the camp of 'hot money' or short-term investments than more stable, long-term investments such as FDI. This observation stands in contrast to the above definition of equity finance offered by the IFC, which stresses the 'long-term' feature of capital flows. The relatively short temporal nature of these investments also has important consequences with regard to disciplinary features, such as living with the constant surveillance and scrutiny of the PCI, as well as the threat of capital flight and/or investment strike (e.g. when CalPERS blacklists a country from its PCI).

CalPERS' management and board of directors, which include both labour representatives and state officials, strongly believe their proactive stance ensures that companies in which the fund invests adhere to good corporate governance principles.[11] As will be seen below, the PCI was designed to help gauge the degree to which 'best practices' in corporate governance are adhered to by governments in the Third World. Corporate governance refers to the relationships between a company's owners, managers, board of directors and other stakeholders. It is important to underline that although there are many country-specific forms of corporate governance, CalPERS draws on the so-called Anglo-American model, with its emphasis on maximization of shareholder value, as the preferred model for emerging markets. This strategy is based on the conviction that the Anglo-American model is the most desirable for achieving long-term profitability and economic efficiency (Reed, 2004; Soederberg, 2004).

Unlike many of its counterparts in the Third World, the Anglo-American model is widely believed by mainstream observers to be marked by a heavy reliance on financial markets and shareholder input. By contrast, corporate governance models in the developing world are said to reflect relationship-based models of corporate governance that rely on the links between banks, businesses and the government, affording little weight to shareholder input (Clarke, 2000). This arrangement is believed to reduce, among other things, rent-seeking behaviour on the part of economic actors (Hutchinson, 2001). From the perspective of US institutional investors, the immediate problem posed by alternative corporate governance practices in emerging markets is that they deny minority shareholders any significant influence over the management of emerging market economies (cf. Lavelle, 2004). US institutional investors, such as CalPERS, view Anglo-American corporate governance in a more favourable light, as it establishes minority shareholder rights and the protection of private property.

Given the centrality of corporate governance to the Index, as well as to 'entrepreneurial development', it is useful to highlight some of the key features of the Anglo-American model that governments in developing countries are said to be including in their reforms (Clarke, 2000). Darryl Reed explains that the Anglo-American variant of corporate governance possesses some of the following characteristics: (1) a single-tiered board structure which gives almost exclusive primacy to shareholder interests (e.g. the board is elected exclusively by shareholders, who have strong rights grounded in company law); (2) a dominant role for financial markets; and (3) little or no industrial policy involving firms cooperating with government agencies (and labour bodies) (Reed, 2004: 10).

The Anglo-American model reflects the key interests of the PCI, namely, the expansion of capitalist strategies of US institutional investors and the safeguarding of their investments in the Third World through, for example, the creation of minority shareholder rights, protection of private property and financial liberalization. A caveat is needed. The preference for the Anglo-American model is warmly embraced by some capitalists in various parts of the developing world, such as India. Some business interests in the global South favour the American variant, as it, unlike other national models, does not provide a role for the involvement of stakeholders, e.g. employees, suppliers and the wider community (ibid.: 10; Overbeek *et al.*, 2007).

The changing nature of neoliberal investment assessment exercises: the PCI

American businesspeople are going to put capital where they feel they are welcome, where capital is honoured and where they can get good returns.
(John Snow, US Treasury Secretary, *Financial Times*, 14 June 2005)

Against the backdrop of the height of shareholder activism in the US and the modest but growing interest by institutional investors in emerging markets,[12] the CalPERS Investment Committee turned to Wilshire to devise a permissible markets analysis (the PCI) in 1987.[13] As noted above, one of the main objectives of the Index was to gauge good corporate governance practices in emerging markets. With the onslaught of a deep recessionary environment in OECD countries in the early 1990s, coupled with relatively higher growth rates in various areas of the developing world, net equity flows to key areas of the global South began to pick up early in the decade, and then took off in the mid-1990s (World Bank, 2005; see Figure 6.1).

Given its heavy exposure in emerging markets, CalPERS, along with many institutional investors, was directly and adversely affected by the rash of financial crises in the global South during the 1990s, most notably the Mexican Peso Crash in 1994–1995, the East Asian Crisis in 1997 and the subsequent crises in Russia and Brazil in 1998 (Armijo, 1999; Soederberg, 2004). In 1999, the CalPERS Investment Committee sought to redesign the manner in which the PCI assessed the stability and profitability of investment opportunities in developing countries. The amendment was significant as it included non-financial criteria in determining suitable investment sites in the developing world. The methodology of the PCI, for example, was revised to take into account two broad sources from which it was believed risks (defined as 'the standard deviation of returns') emanated in the emerging markets. These were: (1) country factors, which concentrated on a narrowly defined concept of political risk; and (2) market factors, which related to issues such as market liquidity and volatility, market regulation, legal system, investor protection, capital market openness and settlement proficiency and transaction costs.[14]

In response to the Enron-style debacles in the US in the early 2000s and the heavy losses incurred by institutional investors, including CalPERS, the

CalPERS' Investment Committee once again asked Wilshire to revise the instruments of the PCI. The major change to the permissible country criteria was a broader understanding regarding the definition of 'country factors' or political risk, which encompasses the following: (1) transparency; (2) productive labour practices; and (3) an expanded understanding of political stability (see Table 6.2).[15] It should be emphasized that Wilshire is not responsible for determining which factors and sub-factors comprise the PCI; instead, these factors are selected by the CalPERS Board of Directors, although the revised PCI was initiated by both the Treasury Department of California and the former CEO of CalPERS, Sean Harrigan.[16] According to a senior associate at Wilshire, it is the consultancy firm's job 'to find appropriate, credible, independent third-party sources that evaluate the factors and sub-factors'.[17] It is interesting to note that the 'credible, independent' third-party source used to evaluate civil liberties in the global South is Freedom House, which publishes annual rankings of civil liberties by country. For the most part, the Universal Declaration of Human Rights guides the Freedom House findings.[18]

Elaboration on country factors

The first political risk or country factor is political stability. Like the rest of the indicators that comprise the permissible country criteria, political stability is comprised of two parts: a macro-factor and several sub-factors. Political stability (the macro-factor) refers to progress in the creation of basic democratic institutions and principles, such as guaranteed elimination of human rights violations (e.g. torture), and a strong and impartial legal system. Political stability is seen as a vital component in guaranteeing the development of a free market in the Third World, which in turn will attract and retain long-term capital. There are several sub-factors that further define political stability: (1) civil liberties; (2) independent judiciary and legal protection; and (3) political risk.[19] Similar to other PCI factors, each of the three sub-factors comprising political stability is scored out of 3. The highest score is 3 (good) and the lowest is 1 (poor). For a country to remain on the PCI, it must reach a passing score of 2.

Table 6.2 PCI/CalPERS – country and market macro-factors

Country macro-factors (or political risk factors)	Weight (%)	Market macro-factors	Weight (%)
Political stability	16.7	Market liquidity and volatility	12.5
Transparency	16.7	Market regulation/legal system/ investor protection	12.5
Productive labour practices	16.6	Capital market openness	12.5
		Settlement proficiency/ transaction costs	12.5
Total assigned weight	50		50

Source: Adapted from Wilshire Consulting (2005: 4, 11).

The second political risk or country macro-factor is transparency. Wilshire sees this factor as primarily comprising financial transparency, but also including 'elements of a free press necessary for investors to have truthful, accurate and relevant information on the conditions in the countries and companies in which they are investing' (Wilshire, 2005: 6). The transparency factor includes four sub-factors: (1) freedom of the press; (2) monetary and fiscal transparency; (3) stock exchange listing requirements; and (4) accounting standards (ibid.: 6–7).

The third macro-factor is productive labour practices. To assist in the evaluation of this macro-factor, Wilshire identified a credible third party, Verité, a US non-profit research organization that CalPERS has employed since 2000. Verité provides information and analysis of labour protections in 27 emerging markets based on 42 indicators of labour standards compliance – the first such framework of its kind to be used for investment purposes.[20] In 2002, Verité's labour standard analysis contributed to a decision by CalPERS to divest from four Southeast Asian countries. Verité went on record stating,

> We looked at the laws, the institutional capacity to implement the laws and then we looked at what was really going on the ground – child labour, forced labour, freedom of association, and discrimination …. We had in-country researchers in those Southeast Asian countries using questionnaires to interview governments, labour unions, NGOs, and business groups. Then we used more traditional research data to make an overall assessment.
>
> (*BBC World News*, 2002)

The PCI and 'enduring value': the social factor

Despite the fact that neither CalPERS nor Wilshire explicitly uses the term 'SRI' to describe the PCI, and instead insist that the Index assesses good corporate governance practices abroad, CalPERS board member and Treasurer of the State of California Phil Angelides drew on the notion of 'enduring value' in 2002. He did this not only to promote the fact that the revised Index allocates equal weight to both financial and social criteria, but also to justify the decision by the CalPERS' board of directors to exit several Southeast Asian countries. According to Angelides, 'enduring value' should trump short-term economic thinking as a guiding principle for investments.

> These reformers understand that the current *laissez faire*, let 'er rip system damages important social values – equitable treatment of workers, the environment and other commonly shared public assets – and that both workers and retirees (and the state taxpayers who put up the money for public pension funds) have a strong self-interest, personal as well as financial, in husbanding the distant future: a healthy society and strong economy for themselves and their families.
>
> (Angelides quoted in Greider, 2005a)

To demonstrate that its expanded understanding of corporate governance had teeth, CalPERS announced in 2002 that it would pull out of all investments in Thailand, Malaysia, Indonesia and the Philippines. It did so because of financial criteria regarding issues of corporate governance – assessing the openness of a capital market, the sorts of protection offered to investors and how effectively a market is regulated – as well as non-financial issues, such as concerns about social conditions in these countries, particularly with regard to labour conditions in special export zones. As reported by Verité, these zones have been attacked by labour and human rights organizations due to their weak (or non-existent) social protection for workers.

CalPERS' exit strategy had immediate and devastating ramifications for these countries.[21] For example, although the $65 million invested in the Philippines in 2002 represented 0.04 per cent of CalPERS' global fund, it was five times the average daily trading volume on the Philippine stock exchange in 2001. The day the exit of funds was announced, the Philippine Stock Exchange Composite Index tumbled 3.3 per cent, signalling important and immediate economic implications stemming from the pull-out. The decision to divest, for example, triggered a run on foreign investments in the Philippines, causing the economy to suffer and leading to countless job losses. According to the Philippine Ambassador to the US, Albert del Rosario, given the size of CalPERS, it is important to remain on the fund's permissible country listing because it represents the coveted 'seal of good housekeeping', which signals to the global investment community that the Philippines is 'an attractive and viable investment location'.[22]

Although sensitive to the socio-economic consequences of CalPERS' 2002 divestment in Southeast Asia, Robin Blackburn sees the move as 'a striking victory' for the SRI movement, as the countries targeted by CalPERS represent a large portion of the approximately 27 million workers in 800 to 1,000 special export zones worldwide. 'The ban on labour organization in these zones has been an intense concern of the anti-sweatshop movement, and CalPERS' decision is certainly a success for this campaign' (Blackburn, 2002: 517). As will be seen below, Blackburn was not alone in interpreting the revised PCI as an attempt at SRI.[23]

Drawing on the findings of its investment assessment instrument, CalPERS decided to stay away from the Thai, Malaysian, Indian and Sri Lankan equity markets in 2003, despite the fact that 2002 stock market returns averaged (in dollar terms) 136 per cent in Thailand, 82 per cent in India, 30 per cent in Sri Lanka and 23 per cent in Malaysia (ibid.). On the face of it, this decision might suggest that the public pension fund is more interested in establishing what it considers a better investment climate for its money than entering into short-term gains, which are tied to relatively higher risks. This position is supported by CalPERS' claim that its divestures have had a positive effect on the overall governance structures in the global South. According to Wilshire's research, the PCI seems to have an effect on the country and market performance of the selected 27 developing countries (Wilshire, 2005: 15).

At first glance, the PCI appears not only laudable, but also effective in encouraging social and economic change in the governance structures of targeted

Third World countries. The Index ensures that its assessment of individual countries' abilities to support institutional investment strikes a balance between market and non-market factors, such as democratic forms of governance, human rights, fair labour practices and so on. In doing so, the Index has been portrayed by key members of the CalPERS board of directors as able to effect broad, positive change in the Third World.

To begin to look beyond the rhetoric of entrepreneurial development and the expanded meanings of corporate governance, it is useful to highlight some of the key criticisms levied against CalPERS. What becomes clear in this discussion is that much of the attention given to the latest revision of the Index has rested on the tension between social concerns and fiduciary responsibilities.[24] The limits to this perspective are discussed in more detail in the next chapter. For now it is helpful to identify some of the underlying contradictions in the debates with regard to the PCI.

Financial versus social concerns: the PCI and its detractors

Critics of the PCI are quick to point out that when viewed against the backdrop of the losses incurred by CalPERS in the Enron-style debacles, CalPERS board members – ten out of 13 of whom are union members, union officers or current and former politicians, and most of whom depend, or depended, on union support and endorsement – have used the PCI strategically to further their own careers. According to some observers, CalPERS' attempt to grandstand its ethical investment, as opposed to engaging in market activism, was driven by votes, not a social conscience.[25]

> In the boom years of the 1990s, CalPERS outperformed most other public employee pension funds; but in the down years of 2000 and 2001, it performed at an average of one percentage point below its peers – a difference of millions of dollars. The fund's value dropped from a high of $177 billion in October 2000 to about $149 billion in July 2002.
>
> (*Wall Street Journal*, 2002)

In that same year, CalPERS pulled out of Southeast Asia, citing poor labour standards and human rights records as the primary reasons for its exit (ibid).

The concern for social issues expressed in CalPERS' investment Index appealed to the California taxpayer and union members. But some suggest the inclusion of social issues in investment criteria was a tactic aimed at riding 'the SRI wave', which took off after the 1999 anti-globalization protest at the World Trade Organization (WTO) meeting in Seattle, and which has since been harnessed by a highly lucrative ethical investing business. In 2003, the ethical investing industry represented total assets under management of $2.16 trillion. This number rose to $2.29 trillion in 2005.[26] Detractors of the PCI also argue that by choosing to divest from four Southeast Asian countries in 2002, despite the fact that they were registering high returns, CalPERS neglected its fiduciary duties to its shareowners (Edwards, 2002). In 2002, Indonesia and Thailand were among the world's ten best-performing equity markets in US dollar terms. According to one observer,

> the use of (public employee retirement system funds) to subsidize economic development efforts is inappropriate …. The greatest good a (state pension fund) can do for its state is to maximize return on investments and reduce the contributions necessary from taxpayers.
>
> (Monks and Minow, 2001: 128)

Another major criticism levied against CalPERS, and one which sheds light on the politicized nature of 'knowledge' with respect to the Index, centres on the fund's inconsistent usage and incorrect rating process of the PCI. After intense lobbying by the Philippine government and the Filipino community residing in the US, CalPERS reversed its decision to blacklist the country in May 2002. The financial reverberations were immediate: stocks in the Philippines immediately rose 1.3 per cent and the Philippine peso soared to a 12-month high. However, in February 2003, Wilshire once again advised CalPERS to divest from its Philippine holdings. Instead of heeding this advice, CalPERS devised the concept of a 'cure period'.[27] Reinforcing the deep-seated idea that Third World countries suffer from 'lack of progress' and 'backwardness', the 'cure period' was designed to offer one year of grace before CalPERS would liquidate its investments in any emerging market that slips out of the public pension funds' permissible list. In March 2004, Wilshire announced that the Philippines was to receive an overall score of 1.86, well below the passing score of 2.0. This announcement caused the Philippine stock index to plunge to its lowest point in six weeks. Despite the Philippine's failing grade, and after intense lobbying by the Philippine government and wider Filipino community, CalPERS issued a statement in April 2004 that it would remain in the Philippines. On 19 April 2004, Wilshire changed its overall score of the Philippines from 1.86 to 2.12.[28] This position clearly reveals the internal inconsistencies of the PCI initiative, as well as its fickle politicization with regard to social concerns in the Third World.

Profits over people?

The 'progressive sheen' of the PCI cannot be divorced from the wider relations of domination and exploitation involved in delivering the ultimate investment goal: a relatively higher return on CalPERS' original outlay than the fund can earn by investing in a publicly listed corporation in the US. This is evident in the following two examples: (1) the blatant disregard of social factors by CalPERS' private equity funds, which invest on behalf of CalPERS in the Third World; and (2) CalPERS' recently revised position regarding investments in China.

With regard to the first point, the PCI guidelines and their goal of building enduring value do not extend to CalPERS' private equity funds, which invest on behalf of the pension fund. The problem that arises here is twofold. First, these private equity funds hold investments in countries that have been blacklisted by the PCI, e.g. China. Second, private equity funds are not concerned with the social criteria of their investments. In 1998, for instance, CalPERS' union-based members were shocked to learn that its pension fund had played a central role, albeit indirectly through its investment in a private equity firm operated by New York financier Wilbur Ross, not only in the suppression of a strike in South Korea, but also the imprisonment of 20 Korean trade unionists.[29] The unwilling-ness of CalPERS' board of directors to impose accountability and transparency regarding their private equity funds makes patently clear the political (public relations) nature of the PCI, as well as the overriding significance of short-term gain over 'enduring value'.

The second point regarding the limitation of CalPERS' enduring value strat-egy involves the formulation of a new policy regarding investment in one of the most lucrative markets in the world: China. On 1 January 2007, CalPERS' investment board selected three private emerging market equity firms (Alliance-Bernstein, Dimensional Fund Advisors and Genesis) to invest on CalPERS' behalf in China. In addition to this, CalPERS has invested approximately $400 million in China's real estate market – primarily in retail and office development in Shanghai and Beijing. The reason for this decision is that the potential rates of return in China are simply too high to ignore,[30] and outweigh the country's dismal overall PCI score of 1.6 (with individual scores of 1.3 on political stability, 1.0 on labour conditions, 1.7 on legal systems, 1.5 on openness to foreign investment, 1.3 on capital market openness and 1.3 on transparency). It goes without saying that CalPERS' Investment Board is willing to turn a blind eye to the primary aim of the enduring value initiative, namely, to build 'a healthy society and strong economy'.

The new investment strategy is described by CalPERS Board President and active trade unionist Rob Feckner[31] in the following manner: the pension fund

> will allow selective investments in good companies in these countries while maintaining our strict standards for investment and keeping a sharp eye out for risk. By allowing investment in selected public companies that meet our standards, we could encourage others to also qualify by raising their stand-ards to meet our investment criteria.[32]

It should be noted that this company-level investment policy has been expanded beyond China. In 2006, former State of California Controller Steve Westly argued that CalPERS be permitted to invest in US depository receipts or global depository receipts[33] of companies based in countries that failed to meet the requirements of the PCI. Westly and other board members noted that CalPERS was being excluded from the burgeoning Chinese stock market (*Pensions & Investments*, 2007c).

In December 2006, the CalPERS Investment Board announced that it would expand its $4.8 billion emerging market portfolio to include companies in for-merly prohibited countries, such as Pakistan, Russia, Morocco, Colombia, Egypt and Venezuela on a company basis, despite their failure to achieve a passing score on the Index. CalPERS noted that publicly traded companies in these and all countries should adhere to the (self-reporting) Global Sullivan Principles, International Labour Organization (ILO) standards and the UNPRI. In 2007, CalPERS committed a $500 million allocation to corporate governance funds that will invest in emerging markets not restricted by the PCI policy and the steep opportunity costs (about $401 million) that the Index is said to have incurred over the past five years. 'Because any corporate governance funds will have to press portfolio companies to change their cultures, there is no reason to be bound by the emerging market list [PCI]', Chief Information Officer (CIO) Russell Read told the CalPERS board (*Pensions & Investments*, 2007c).[34] This position is indicative not only of the deepening and widening of the corporate governance doctrine, but also the internalization of its discipline by various social forces.

Questions regarding the degree of compliance required by the portfolio company, how adherence will be monitored and by whom remain unanswered. If we take the US as a precedent, CalPERS' company-level investment strategy will inevitably be organized around market-based, self-reporting initiatives, i.e. voluntary as opposed to mandatory programmes. Another question that continues to be unaddressed is how, according to the logic of the CalPERS PCI, can 'good' corporate governance, and 'enduring value' more generally, be achieved when productive labour practices, transparency and so forth are virtually absent? The answer seems to lie in the neoliberal belief that left to their own 'rational' devices (i.e. the continued absence of mandatory legal requirements at the national or global levels) profit-seeking firms possess the political will to effect progressive change for their workers. However, the authoritarian political environment and, by extension, repressive corporate governance practices in many of these once non-permissible countries leave active shareowners without the ability to effect change. The neoliberal doctrine is, at best, wishful thinking; at worst, it is a poor attempt to white-wash the decision of CalPERS Investment Board to value high, short-term returns over the establishment of 'enduring value'.

While the above criticisms are useful in highlighting the political features of the PCI, they fail to unveil critically the capitalist nature of the Index and lay bare how and why this strategy is reproduced. The primary reason for this neglect lies in the fact that the debates assume the Index to be a merely economic and technical instrument. In this, they fail to understand the connection of the PCI to the wider discourse and policy of entrepreneurial development and the underlying paradox from which both capitalist strategies emerged. The commentators involved in the above mainstream debates fail to understand that the 'progressive sheen' of the PCI cannot be divorced from the wider relations of domination and exploitation involved in delivering the ultimate investment goal: a relatively higher return on CalPERS' original outlay than the fund can earn by investing in a publicly listed corporation in the US.

Constructing discipline and dependency in emerging markets

This section moves the analysis to a deeper level in order to explain how and why the reproduction of the discipline and dependency of Third World corporations on western-based institutional investors occurs. As I have argued, the Index does not represent an innocent assessment exercise, but rather assists in the recreation of conditions for the continued spatial expansion of capital accumulation while seeking to deal with the above-mentioned paradox underpinning global development finance: the tension between the continual search for profitable outlets to increase shareholder value of social security capital, on the one hand, and the growing impoverishment of the masses in the Third World, on the other. As demonstrated below, the reproduction of neoliberal forms of discipline and exploitation inherent in the Index is accomplished largely through coercive measures, such as exit strategies, as well as the construction of specific forms of knowledge that act to naturalize the 'new conditionality' imbued in entrepreneurial development.

The capitalist nature of the PCI can be revealed and understood by identifying the following three overlapping assumptions. First, the content of the Index – as well as its larger frame of reference, entrepreneurial development – perpetuates the common-sense assumption that development is a neutral and universal concept, which aims to promote material prosperity through growth. This premise, a central feature of post-war development, assists in naturalizing the new conditionality and its primary goal: the establishment and maintenance of new forms of spatial expansion of capitalism in the global South, especially with regard to equity finance. Second, the PCI relies on an economistic frame for assessing the investment potential of countries. This perspective is assumed to be scientific and, therefore, unproblematic. The portrayal of the Index as based in scientific knowledge further distorts the exploitative and disciplinary features of capitalist society by treating capital as an object, as opposed to a social relation. Moreover, the insistence of the IFC that equity finance is an important and necessary component in achieving 'development' has permitted the PCI and, more specifically, CalPERS, to appear as an equal partner in development, as opposed to an economic actor that seeks to engage in exploitative activities necessary for the creation of profit. Third, the content of the Index assumes that the Third World is culturally homogeneous and its governance structures (legal, economic and corporate) are backward. Through this objectification process, also reinforced in the first and second assumptions, the PCI represents highly complex, national social formations in ahistorical and apolitical terms. Subsequently, this move not only primes a developing country to be objectified, and thus understood in terms of categories that measure its ability to provide a good investment site, but it also renders the disciplinary action to withhold funds or subject the country to a 'cure period' as an unproblematic and indeed necessary strategy to ensure market stabilization.

The neutrality and universality of 'development'

The Index and entrepreneurial development have remained above critical reproach largely because they resonate well with the deep-seated, Western common-sense understanding that economic growth leads to progress. As Gilbert Rist observes, this understanding of 'development', which has dominated official discourse and policy since the end of the Second World War to the current entrepreneurial development model, 'offers the promise of general abundance, conceived in biological imagery as something "natural", positive, necessary, and indisputable' (Rist, 2002: 214). The debates have remained silent on the question of how and why the knowledge contained in the PCI is readily accepted by policymakers, the media, shareowners and scholars as a social fact.

Before continuing with an examination of the universality of 'development', a caveat is in order. While the PCI represents an attempt by US investors to influence political and economic structures and practices in emerging markets to safeguard their investments, the Third World should not be viewed as a homogenous 'victim'. By this I mean that many political elites and local capitalists have been actively campaigning either to remain or to get listed on the Index. By helping to signal to foreign investors that a country is creditworthy, capital also becomes less expensive through lower interest rates and more favourable repayment schedules, as a good investment site is deemed a relatively low risk. In other words, while *all* capitalists favour and benefit from the reproduction of the domination of capital over labour, some capitalists gain more from Western attempts to politically and socially configure this domination through, for instance, the Anglo-American variant of corporate governance.

To transcend the technical and economistic treatment of the Index, it is important to question the assumption of progress, as this highly political concept beats at the heart of the official understanding of development. Progress is defined in terms of material prosperity, which is, in turn, generated by economic growth. According to the PCI and the rationale for entrepreneurial development, the ability of countries to attract equity finance assists in obtaining growth. The IFC, for instance, insists that harnessing the power of private capital and free enterprise – represented as 'positive' power – is necessary to bring about needed change in the developing world (International Financial Corporation, 2006). This change will, in turn, reduce economic risks and protect shareholder value by ensuring that the 'underdeveloped' countries strive toward establishing 'good' (read: Anglo-American) corporate governance practices through, for example, implementing 'well-functioning' (universal) legal and political systems, modernizing stock exchanges, stabilizing capital market flows, decreasing commission rates and other transaction charges and so forth. The questions that emerge here, but are rarely posed in the dominant discourse, are: On whose terms is change in the 'developing' world 'needed'? Who benefits from this change? And, what social, political and cultural dislocations are associated with this change, and why?

To address these questions, it is useful to combine the capitalist nature of the PCI with an interrogation of its cultural dimensions of knowledge and the production of social space. This approach reveals that the key sources of power of the PCI lie not only in the coercive features of the Index (e.g. exit strategies, blacklisting 'bad' investment sites, cure periods), but in its ability to normalize and therefore reproduce the knowledge rooted in official development discourse and policy. What is at stake here is concealed by the neutrality of the term 'development', namely the production of knowledge and exercise of power over the Third World (Escobar, 1995: 9). Following Arturo Escobar:

> Most forms of understanding and representing the Third World are still dictated by the same basic tenets. The forms of power that have appeared act not so much by repression but by normalization; not by ignorance but by controlled knowledge; not by humanitarian concern but by the bureaucratization of social action. As the conditions that gave rise to development became more pressing, it could only increase its hold, refine its methods, and extend its reach even further .... [T]he materiality of these conditions is not conjured up by an 'objective' body of knowledge but is chartered out by the rational discourses of economists, politicians, and development experts of all types.
>
> (ibid.: 9)

To grasp the inner nature of the PCI and its ability to replicate the conditions of capitalism by normalizing and universalizing the meaning of good investment sites, I highlight two ways in which the spatial dimension of knowledge production is rooted in capital relations of exploitation and domination (Lefebvre, 1991). First, entrepreneurial development and the PCI are social constructs forged by particular individuals, groups and institutions within social space (ibid.; Harvey, 2001). As we saw earlier, entrepreneurial development represents an intensified phase of neoliberal-led development policies and practices over the past several decades. Two novel attributes of this neoliberal variant are: (1) more explicit and direct control of financial actors vis-à-vis policy formation, such as the 'new conditionality'; and (2) the increasing presence of foreign investors in the global South accompanied by stressing the 'social' aspects of good governance, or SRI.

Moreover, the space within which the knowledge of 'entrepreneurial development' and the PCI is both produced and reproduced is also crucial in understanding the production of power (Lefebvre, 1991). For instance, both the PCI and the IFC are located in, and in turn reflect the dominant capitalist interests of, the US. In an attempt to deal with the effects of the tendency toward overaccumulation (see Chapter 1), US institutional investors such as CalPERS expand geographically into new regions by exporting capital, extending towards the creation of what Marx referred to as the world market (Marx, 1991). David Harvey describes this as a process of the spatial displacement of capital (Harvey, 2001). The latter refers to a strategy in which capitalists seek outlets for their surplus capital by 'opening up new markets, new production capacities and new resources, social and labour possibilities elsewhere' (Harvey, 2003: 64). As Marx suggested, 'If capital is sent abroad, this is not done because it absolutely could not be applied at home, but because it can be employed at a higher rate of profit in a foreign country' (Marx quoted in Harvey, 1999: 434). Marx's observation resonates well with Wilshire's emphasis on the importance of economic growth as the primary motivation for investing in developing countries. According to Wilshire, growth 'is the reason for investing in the emerging markets, including superior relative expected returns and an expanding opportunity set for investment. Last year [2005] the emerging markets collectively out-performed their developed markets counterparts globally' (Wilshire, 2006: 2). Second, as discussed above, equity finance is not an object, but has its base in money, viewed here as an integral moment of the social relations of capital. Seen from this perspective, money and, by extension, equity finance, wields social power. Those who wield this social power also seek to cultivate command over spatial organization. Authority over the use of space becomes a crucial means for the reorganization and reproduction of social power relations (Harvey, 1989).

This command over space, and the subsequent power struggles to resist it, are hidden within the discourse and policy of the PCI and entrepreneurial development. One such expression of this power is the ability of US capitalists and their state to construct forms of knowledge that assist in protecting US surplus capital abroad, for example, in the form of social security capital (see Chapter 2). The manner in which a specific variant of corporate governance is championed over others is a case in point. Despite the fact that the Anglo-American variant of corporate governance bred the largest and most socially devastating forms of business fraud in US history during the early 2000s, the general consensus among mainstream scholars, policymakers and the media is that corporate governance models in the global South are 'weak' and 'underdeveloped' compared with their American counterparts. This clearly reflects the lack of objective forms of 'scientific' knowledge that inform these mainstream perspectives. Key aspects of the Index's 'country factors' involve changing national legal and political systems to protect private property, liberalize financial markets and make labour markets more flexible. However, the political and legal systems of a country are not undifferentiated, ahistorical features of 'investment sites'; rather, they are complex historical products of class-led struggles rooted in nationally specific colonial and post-colonial power relations. Thus, a basic prerequisite for the implementation of Anglo-American reforms contained in the PCI is a fundamental reorganization of *the total social relations of production and exchange* in a given social formation. For instance, given the high concentration of family-owned, publicly run corporations in East and Southeast Asia, minority shareholder rights cannot be guaranteed by mere technical changes without ensuring major social and political struggle and dislocation through the implementation of neoliberal forms of social engineering (Zhuang *et al.*, 2000). The naturalized understanding of 'development' allows the PCI (or, more specifically, the money managers of CalPERS) to conceal its role in promoting imperial practices that are required to guarantee the expanded reproduction of capital in the context of Third World countries.

Economics as 'scientific' knowledge: naturalizing the hegemony of the market

Despite its emphasis on country factors (or political factors), the PCI grants primacy to the economy. Both the means and end of the Index are to promote a well-functioning market by granting it as much freedom from government intervention as possible. This position is firmly rooted in the hegemonic understanding of economic growth and the material prosperity it generates. The hegemony of the theory of market episteme reduces all aspects of life to the needs and proper functioning of the market. This serves to remove, and therefore sanitize, the political, material and cultural aspects of societies while recasting them ahistorically in terms of the neutral realm of science. In doing so, economics is represented as somehow embodying a scientific and, therefore, accurate representation and truth about the world (Teivainen, 2002). As Escobar notes, there is a close, albeit distorted, connection drawn between the scientific knowledge of economics, and its implicit claims to neutrality, and what he refers to as the 'cultural code', or cultural discourse of economics. Economists do not see their science as a cultural discourse; instead their knowledge is assumed to be a neutral and objective representation of the world and truth about it (Escobar, 1995: 59).

One of the main reasons why economics is treated, and largely understood, as a science is because it places rationality as a dominant value in its paradigm. This is evident in the country and market factors that comprise the PCI. Within the parameters of the Index, the market or economy is viewed in harmonious terms, removed from the messiness of politics, social power and history, an utterly rational world, made even more abstract through mathematical calculations used to gauge the quality of investment potential of a country (ibid.: 65). The basic premise driving this view is that the economy is comprised of rational actors whose behaviour can be readily explained and understood through observation, measurement and prediction. It follows from this that rational behaviour is innate and, therefore, only alterable if and when forces external to the market, such as the state, distort the competitive environment through, for example, rent-seeking activities or weak legal systems that fail to protect private property. The assumption that markets are inherently rational, so long as they are left to their own devices, is an important feature of the cultural code of economics. This assumption serves as the cornerstone of the Index's ability to recreate the status quo by neutralizing and thus normalizing disciplinary relations of exploitation and domination. It does so in the following two ways.

First, the understanding that markets are inherently rational depoliticizes, and therefore naturalizes, the knowledge upon which the PCI attempts to exercise its disciplinary power. It removes any problematic issues, such as social conflicts, contestation over material power and so forth, from the political and cultural realms and recasts them in terms of the sanitized and neutral realm of science. While CalPERS claims that its revised Index gives equal weight to market and country factors, for instance, it should be underlined that the country factors have been selected to encourage governments of emerging markets to pursue the neoliberal utopia of unregulated freedom of the market. Country factors are scored on the basis of how well national governments provide the proper conditions (e.g. legal entitlements, sound economic policy based on fiscal austerity, financial deregulation, trade liberalization and so on) for market actors to flourish under the conditions of competition to promote economic growth.

Second, the assumption of the rationality of the market allows CalPERS to continue to place the blame for economic crises or slowdowns at the door of the developing world, thereby justifying ever-more intrusive forms of surveillance and control through neoliberal knowledge. Given the assumption of rational and efficient behaviour on the part of financial actors such as CalPERS, the occurrence of crises is easily blamed on internal factors of state failure, or in neoliberal parlance, the poor governance structures and lack of sound macroeconomic fundamentals in developing countries. As we saw above, the PCI was subject to revision each time a major crisis occurred, whether it originated in the global South (e.g. the Mexican Peso Crash) or in the US (e.g. the sub-prime mortgage scandal). The underlying assumption in each revision of the Index was not an acknowledgement of market failure, but rather of state failure to provide a free-market environment. Crony capitalism, rent-seeking behaviour and weak legal systems are blamed for having led to the distortion of the competitive tendencies of rational economic actors. By locating blame with Third World countries, CalPERS' revised Index mirrors, and therefore legitimizes, the knowledge produced by the IMF, World Bank and G-7 countries in reaction to the major financial crises that occurred during the 1990s, which culminated in the creation of various codes and standards, including corporate governance, imbued in the 'New International Financial Architecture' (Soederberg, 2004).

An important consequence of neoliberal knowledge rooted in the 'economics as science' assumption, is that it has served to naturalize, normalize and, therefore, reproduce not only the corporate governance doctrine writ large, but also, and specifically, the Anglo-American variant, which, as we saw above, relies more heavily on market forces. The assumption here is that, in the presence of good governance structures, such as the democratic and legal systems found in the US, there will be less chance of market failure; that is, financial actors like CalPERS will act rationally. Ironically, the recent Enron-style debacles in the US reveals that the same short-term, speculative and irrational 'herd behaviour' is at play in the highly deregulated financial markets of the First World as in the Third World (Patomäki, 2001; see also Chapter 3).

Critiques of the cultural discourse of economics have tended to overlook the fact that while the assumption of rationality appears to legitimize the reductionism that occurs in the portrayal of economics as a science, it also helps to cloak the social power inherent in capital by treating the latter as some sort of neutral object or thing. This can be seen in the treatment of these terms by international financial institutions (IFIs) and economists. The IFC, for example, understands equity financing as a 'method' in which capital is raised by publicly traded companies; while for economists like Hernando de Soto (2000), capital is a 'force', devoid of power, that helps to raise the productivity of labour and thus contributes to wealth creation. The ability of CalPERS' investment in publicly listed corporations in the developing world to increase in value is believed by the IFC and de Soto to occur through harmonious and equal relations (both of which take place on a level playing field) between rational market actors (buyers and sellers). These conditions are predicated on the ability of the state to provide the right atmosphere (good governance), so as to encourage free market competition. The state does so by ensuring, for example, that universal laws apply to both foreign and local capitalists regarding the protection of private property, the expression of 'voice' in the management of corporations, the existence of a sound macroeconomic policy framework (liberalized financial system), the avoidance of formulating policy that encourages rent-seeking behaviour and so forth. For de Soto, the creation of capital rests on the institutional structures and processes found in Western societies, or, as he puts it: 'an implicit process buried in the intricacies of its formal property systems' (ibid.: 46).

There are at least two immediate and interrelated outcomes in treating capital as a 'thing', as opposed to a social relation. First, the dominant treatment of capital as an object devoid of social power fails to acknowledge the exploitative relationship that occurs between capitalists and labour in the creation of surplus value. Investors, like CalPERS, hold titles of ownership and receive interest (dividends). The latter are not generated in thin air but, to share in future surplus value production, must at some point confront labour (Harvey, 1999: 276). Second, by treating capital as a thing, the cultural code of economics conceals the role and class nature of the bourgeois state, and thereby depoliticizes and declasses the gloss of 'good governance' in which the country factors of the Index are encased. While good governance practices acknowledge the role of the state in creating the ideal conditions for the untrammelled freedom of the market, they do so by representing the state as a set of neutral institutions and policies, thereby concealing its repressive and ideological functions. Thus, the content of the Index masks the capitalist nature of the state and its role in recreating the conditions for expanded reproduction of capital accumulation, through, for example, the establishment of good governance principles. The technical and economic aspects of the Index also downplay the historical configuration of relations of power within a particular national formation. These aspects can delimit the degree to which Anglo-American forms of good governance can be effectively and swiftly implemented (e.g. the one-year 'cure period') without deeper social conflicts and/or possible threats of economic and political destabilization.

Following Marx, capital (or, in the case of equity finance, money circulating as capital) is not a thing, but a social relation that takes on historically specific meaning in a class-based society in which the means of production rest with one class (capitalists) (see Chapters 2 and 5). Within this societal context, capital cannot increase in value, or turn a profit, without confronting labour through exploitative and unequal relations. Unlike the picture painted by de Soto and the IFC, profit is not generated in a conflictless relationship between labour and capitalists, but instead is fraught with social antagonisms. Seen from this perspective, the bourgeois state is required to intervene in order to mediate struggles and thereby recreate the conditions of accumulation. As David Harvey argues:

> The free market, if it is to work, requires a bundle of institutional arrangements and rules that can be guaranteed only by something akin to state power. The freedom of the market has to be guaranteed by law, authority, force, and, *in extremis*, by violence .... Free markets, in short, do not just happen. Nor are they antagonistic to state power in general, though they can, of course, be antagonistic to certain ways in which state power might be used to regulate them [for example, the interventionist style of the developmental state model, or forms of corporate governance that give emphasis to stakeholders as opposed to shareholders].
>
> (Harvey, 2000: 178)

As Harvey rightfully argues, capitalist states help mediate conflicts largely through the depoliticization of struggle through ideological forms of intervention (media, education, religion and so forth) and/or repressive processes (military, police, legal system). Bourgeois states are also called upon to deal with periodic barriers to capital accumulation, which occur in the form of economic and political crises. In these cases, bourgeois states – in both developing and developed countries – are required to intervene to establish political, including legal, structures to ensure the social reproduction of capitalist society (see Chapter 1).

Cultural homogenization and objectification

The act of denying a country its individual history, culture and political characteristics objectifies national social formations, allowing 'scientific' assessments of its investment potential to be undertaken. This process of 'othering' also permits capitalists to control social space within these countries by naturalizing the importance of reducing all economic, political and social activities to the goal of convincing investors that the country is a good investment site. The country categorization of the Index is rooted in cultural imperialism, which feeds off, and is reinforced by, what Edward Said refers to as 'orientalism', a process that manifests through the spatial (re-)organization of capital (Said, 1979; Escobar, 1995: 9). An example of this process may be found in the manner in which the PCI establishes two main investment categories involving 24 'developed' countries and 27 'emerging markets'. This representation demarcates and recreates a geopolitical space, using imaginative geographies to showcase the evolutionary phases of 'progress' across the globe. For instance, a large majority of the world's population (approximately 140 countries) that fall outside the two categories of the PCI are viewed not only as high risk, and therefore unworthy investment sites, but also as failures of development, because of their unwillingness and/or inability to embrace Western expert knowledge, technology and management skills (i.e. market episteme).[35]

The PCI does not allow for any differentiation between countries. Take, for example, the term 'emerging market economies', which was constructed by the IFC in 1981 to encourage foreign investment in select countries in the global South. It has reduced the historically distinct cultural, social and political characteristics of entire countries to a potential investment site, or simply 'financial markets'. Yet, as Escobar suggests, this 'discursive homogenization (which entails the erasure of the complexity and diversity of Third World peoples, so a squatter in Mexico City, a Nepalese peasant, and a Tuareg nomad become equivalent to each other as poor and underdeveloped)' is necessary to exercise power over the Third World (ibid.: 53). An important consequence of discursive homogenization has been the objectification of countries rated by Wilshire through the PCI. The 'political risk factors' of the Index (i.e. political stability, transparency and productive labour standards), for instance, are presented in an unproblematic fashion as embodying the universalized understanding of how markets and states should be optimally organized, not to meet the social, physical, spiritual and mental needs of people working and living in the Third World, but instead to support the requests of foreign capitalists by constructing stable political and legal systems, so that their investments are made to feel safe and secure.

The benefits of creating a better investment climate are portrayed by the Index, and those championing entrepreneurial development more broadly, not only as a win–win situation for developing countries and foreign investors, but also as universal. According to the World Bank,

> investment climate improvements are the driving force for growth and poverty reduction. A good investment climate is one that is better for everyone in two dimensions. It benefits society as a whole, not just firms. And it expands opportunities for all firms, not just large or influential firms.
>
> (World Bank, 2004: 35)

The knowledge embedded in the prescription of desirable investment sites is further normalized by portraying the interests and goals (material gains) of foreign investors and (apolitical) markets of (homogenized) Third World countries as fundamentally the same. This portrayal effectively side-steps issues of power, struggle, class, contestation, gender and race.

Viewed against this backdrop, the SRI dimension of the PCI may be viewed as a social construct that reflects and bolsters the ultimate goal of development: expanded reproduction of capital. The 'political risk or country factors' of the PCI are not designed to address humanitarian concerns, but have been crafted, first and foremost, to assist in the establishment and reproduction of good investment climates for US institutional investors. The significance of transparent and impartial governments and legal systems vis-à-vis 'development' are not new, however. In several of its *World Development Reports*, the World Bank has stressed the importance of 'good governance' in the creation and maintenance of well-functioning markets. Corruption and lack of property rights are seen as hindering the state's ability to provide market-supporting institutions, because of the absence of effective restraints on the arbitrary behaviour of public officials (World Bank, 2002: chapter 5). In other words, certain forms of market regulation, such as those found in the developmental state model, have been rejected by foreign institutional investors.

The act of glossing over the contradictions and relations of power in global capitalism is evident in the Index's 'productive labour practices', which fall under the 'country or political risk category'. While labour codes speak directly to SRI concerns, it becomes clear on close inspection that the Index does not strive to empower workers but instead acts to appease workers' demands while remaining within the neoliberal-led development framework. The lack of regulatory or mandatory standards allows for extreme exploitation of labour, which is necessary to ensure high returns on CalPERS' investment, or at least higher returns than could be gained in the US (Taylor, 2008). Second, while organizations such as Verité provide insight into the treatment of workers in the formal sector, they ignore the informal sector. While CalPERS' neglect of the informal sector may be justified to some extent due to the difficulties involved in monitoring and measuring these notoriously illusive spaces of work, the fact remains that the PCI neither problematizes nor questions the rapid and widespread rise of the informal economy throughout the global South. According to the ILO, 'more than 80 percent of new jobs created in Latin America and Africa in recent years have been in the informal economy' (Altvater, 2002: 79). In the Philippines, for example, 82 per cent of the non-agricultural workforce, and 90 per cent of the manufacturing sector are outside the formal sector (Hutchinson, 2001: 42–70). The growth of the informal sector implies that workers are in a precarious position to exert pressures for socio-economic reform, such as legislation regarding fair labour practices. Indeed, the connection between higher profit rates in emerging markets and parallel levels of rates of exploitation are conveniently neglected by the PCI. One further point warrants discussion in terms of 'productive labour practices'. The ILO standards upon which Verité bases its assessments strive to encourage union competition and discourage centralized collective bargaining. As Teri L. Caraway argues, the ILO's understanding of freedom of association is distinctly liberal and promotes the formation of 'free' as opposed to 'powerful' trade unions (Caraway, 2006). Depending on the historical configuration of state–labour–capitalist relations, the ILO position can weaken rather than empower trade unions. This position is not surprising, however, given the dominant neoliberal position that trade unions lead to rent-seeking activities and therefore threaten good governance practices (see Chapter 5).

Conclusion

The PCI is not an innocent assessment exercise. It is an attempt to recreate the conditions for continued spatial expansion of capital accumulation. This is largely accomplished through coercive measures, such as exit strategies, as well as the construction of specific forms of knowledge that normalize the disciplinary and exploitative relations inherent in the 'new conditionality' imbued in entrepreneurial development. The result is the naturalization of the premise that Third World countries should strive to attract equity financing in their bid to achieve 'development', which has largely been understood in capitalist terms of economic growth and material prosperity. The days of the PCI seem limited, as critics decry the fact that it threatens to block access to 'burgeoning' stock markets in countries blacklisted due to poor human rights policies, weak investor protections and so forth. Regardless of the fate of the Index, critically evaluating both its neoliberal content and its social and ideological implications for global development has provided important insights into the problematic nature of the expanded meanings of the corporate governance doctrine. This discussion has also shed critical light on the fact that shareholder activism not only entails moments of resistance, but also modes of domination. The following chapter builds on this analysis by taking a closer look at the meanings, limitations and contradictions of SRI and the marketization of social justice.

7 The marketization of social justice
The case of the Sudan Divestment Campaign

SRI has quickly become a key strategy for investors to change corporate behaviour in areas of human rights, labour standards and environmental sustainability. Generally speaking, SRI refers to an investment policy that considers the social and environmental consequences of investments within the context of rigorous financial analysis (Richardson, 2008). One of the most popular forms of SRI in the US is negative screening, which involves the practice of evaluating, and eventually excluding, investment portfolios or mutual funds based on social and/or environmental criteria (Social Investment Forum, 2006). A controversial and widespread example of negative screening is the Sudan Divestment Campaign. The main objective of the boycott, which many have referred to as 'the next big movement', is to end genocidal activities perpetrated by the Sudanese government by pressuring US institutional investors to sell their shares in publicly traded corporations that are believed to help fund Khartoum's so-called 'killing machine'.[1] The Sudan boycott presents an interesting and useful case to study the relations of power and paradoxes of struggles for social justice that are framed within, and thus limited by, the parameters of profit maximization.

While some observers have been quick to dismiss SRI either as acting contrary to the fiduciary responsibilities of institutional investors or as mere window dressing, I believe there are more crucial social and political implications at stake than the dominant technical and economistic debates and analyses choose to acknowledge. A key question driving these debates, for instance, has been based on the same market ethic – profit maximization – as the corporate governance doctrine: Can social investment funds bring about social justice while delivering not only economic benefits, but also superior financial rewards? This has led to framing discussions in terms of the complementarity of, or the tension between, moral concerns (e.g. genocide) and economic concerns (e.g. risk reduction and shareholder value). In contrast, I consider the Sudan boycott and wider SRI movement to represent important features of resistance to corporate power; thus their implications for social change need to be examined critically and explained more fully. I argue that SRI initiatives, including the Sudan boycott, are framed within, and thus limited by, the bounds of the market and its sole focus on profit maximization. This has led to the embedding of struggles into, and thus the reproduction of, market rule, or what I refer to as the marketization of social justice. The latter has the effect of transforming human suffering into a cost–efficiency calculus, as opposed to fundamentally challenging the capitalist nature of corporate power and the wider investment industry.

I develop this argument in five main sections. The first section defines and details the marketization of social justice and its connection to neoliberal-led capitalism while supplying an overview of both the rise and significance of SRI, as well as the debates it has provoked. The second section attempts to demonstrate how the representations of, and official reactions to, the conflict in Sudan have reduced this complex social issue to a one-dimensional tale that can easily be inserted into, and thus dominated by, the financial code and economic laws of investment. The third section examines the Sudan conflict and the divestment campaign by situating these two features of the boycott in the wider context of neoliberal-led capitalism and thereby moving beyond the depoliticizing bounds of the market. The fourth section summarizes some of the consequences of the marketization of social justice. The final section draws some conclusions and highlights various implications for the overall argument of the book.

SRI and the marketization of social justice

Within the wider context of neoliberalism, marketization has primarily referred to the privatization of state-owned enterprises. In this sense, marketization captures the processes in which decisions about the allocation of resources have been shifted from the realm of the state to the sphere of the market. While SRI does not directly represent a privatization strategy per se, it does embody the social and political consequences of past and ongoing neoliberal forms of capitalist restructuring. Important features of neoliberal restructuring include the liberalization of trade and the deregulation of finance, both of which are aimed at providing corporations with more power to 'self-regulate' (see Chapter 3), as well as a shift in the enforcement of corporate responsibility, from the state to market actors such as shareholders. A core belief underpinning the marketization of social justice closely mirrors the basic tenet of neoliberalism that all social and political problems can be more efficiently solved in a self-regulating market than by the state, thus recreating the neoliberal assumption that states and citizens should be embedded further in the system of market rule (Harvey, 2005; Da Costa and McMichael, 2007). Market rule is not only closely intertwined with the myth of capitalist progress embodied in the Ownership Society (see Chapter 2), but also the representation of the market as an apolitical and naturally occurring space, as opposed to a construct that requires constant reproduction by powerful actors and interests in capitalist society.

The marketization of social issues and struggles within the context of SRI has served not only to further embed moments of resistance in the market, but also to fortify the dominance of neoliberalism. The emphasis on market freedoms and market ethics of the latter has led to a short-term, economistic and ahistorical understanding of the world (Gill, 1995; Harvey, 2005). Understood in the context of the broader argument developed in this book, the marketization of struggles that characterize the Sudan Divestment Campaign is symptomatic of the limits to, and disciplinary features of, the Ownership Society and the dominance of corporate governance doctrine. Both of these reflect neoliberal strategies aimed at dealing with the paradoxes and resistance inherent in the growing and uneasy dependence of corporations and financial markets on social security capital in the US (i.e. the corporate–financial nexus), as elsewhere.

I look more closely and critically at the meaning of marketization with regard to neoliberal-led capitalism and our case study below. For now, it is helpful to provide an outline of mainstream accounts of the rise and significance of SRI, as well as the debates it has provoked, particularly negative screening, which is represented in the Sudan boycott.

SRI and its discontents

SRI is not a new phenomenon. Resistance to, and dissatisfaction with, the social effects of corporations' daily operations are almost as old as corporations themselves (Kinder and Domini, 1997; Bakan, 2004). Religious investors from a variety of faiths have long shunned investments that violated their core beliefs. Quakers and Methodists, for example, frequently refused to make investments that might have benefited the slave trade, while the earliest formalized ethical investment policies avoided 'sin' stocks, or firms involved in alcohol, tobacco or gambling. There are several features that are novel with regard to modern SRI strategies, which have emerged since the 1980s. First, there is a wider scope of actors involved, ranging from social investment funds to public pension funds. Second, the amount of assets linked to SRI initiatives has been growing at a far quicker rate than traditional investments, although the latter remain the preferred type of investment. SRI assets, for instance, are believed to have ballooned from $40 billion in 1984 to $2.5 trillion in 2005 (Social Investment Forum, 2006).[2] Third, SRI has been quickly moving into mainstream investment strategies and discourse. This is evident in the so-called SRI–corporate governance nexus, which refers to the converging concerns of

> [c]orporate governance advocates and social investors over issues such as executive compensation, pay disparities, board diversity and glass ceiling issues, declassifying boards, climate risk, sustainability, proxy access and majority voting, ethics oversight, separation of CEO and chair, and general procedures for omitting resolutions.
>
> (Ibid.: 27)

Another example of this emerging SRI–corporate governance nexus is the 2006 United Nations initiative – the Principles for Responsible Investment (UNPRI) – through which institutional investors seek to ensure companies adhere to a certain level of social, environmental and corporate governance standards.[3]

Key players in the SRI movement include religious organizations, such as the ICCR, and institutional investors' organizations, such as the Investor Responsibility Research Centre (IRRC), as well as institutional investors such as public pension funds (Camejo, 2002). Many supporters of SRI have suggested that the social investment industry's spectacular growth over the past several decades has not been driven by Wall Street, but rather by consumers (Scheuth, 2002: 119). The changing agenda and strategies in the wider SRI movement are said to be the result of shifts in public opinion and political changes linked to grassroots movements (Graves *et al.*, 2001; Scheuth, 2002; Elkington, 2004). The anti-Apartheid campaigns of the 1980s, in which social investors and institutions in the US divested from companies doing business in South Africa, came to a halt with the end of Apartheid in 1994. Lessons learned from the anti-Apartheid campaign have led to analogous concerns about human rights and the need to look more closely at companies facing social, political and reputational risks associated with their international operations (see Chapter 6).

According to the Social Investment Forum, more than 80 per cent of all assets socially screened for institutional clients are managed for public pension funds or other state and local investment pools (Social Investment Forum, 2006). With more than $1.7 trillion in assets, social screening represents the largest segment of SRI activities in the US. Negative screening, the main device used in the Sudan Divestment Campaign, involves the avoidance of companies that engage in activities contrary to investors' values and moral principles (ibid.: 4). Interestingly, the question of which values and principles are chosen over others and, relatedly, whose values and principles are represented in SRI strategies is never broached in the debates

Divestment, or the selling off of company shares, represents the most extreme form of protest in the SRI universe. A fundamental assumption underpinning the decision to divest from a company is that investors are able to affect the financial fate of the targeted firms and therefore induce a change in corporate policy and/ or behaviour. The SIF, like the Sudan Divestment Campaign, suggests that social investing will have a financial impact, as investors put their money to work in ways that will build 'a better, more just, and sustainable *economy*' (Munnell and Sunden, 2005: 20, my emphasis). This position is highly contested, however.

Debating negative screens

Proponents of SRI argue that social investment not only reduces risk, but also leads to superior financial performance (Pava and Krausz, 1995; Doane, 2004). As Pedro Camejo explains, 'Social screens knock out companies that engage in discrimination or are in conflict with their local communities or workforce Elimination of these companies reduces a specific kind of risk, what we can refer to as "company-specific risk"' (Camejo, 2002: 15). The so-called 'Sudan discount' is a case in point: although only 10–15 per cent of Canadian-based Talisman Oil's overall operations were in Sudan, its stock was believed by observers to be discounted because of the controversy surrounding the Sudan operations. The Toronto-based newspaper *Globe and Mail* reported on 26 June 2000 that analysts believed the Sudan discount in Talisman's share price was in the range of $15–$25 (CDN), an effect serious enough to make the company a candidate for a hostile takeover. In response to this discounted price, it was suggested that Talisman had a financial motivation to make the image of its Sudan project acceptable to the market and to public opinion.[4]

Those opposed to SRI, by contrast, fear that the social focus of negative screens will jeopardize the economic performance of a company. In an oft-cited study conducted by Christopher C. Geczy *et al.*, the authors set out to discover the costs, if any, born by investors who choose the path of SRI. The 'Wharton study' (as it is known to some in SRI circles) draws on 46 different, non-SRI mutual funds from a universe of 894 equity mutual funds, constructing 36 portfolios of varying allocations to reflect various decision-making models (Geczy *et al.*, 2003). The study demonstrates that although the cost of social investing can range widely, most socially responsible investors in equity mutual funds pay a price for their willingness to 'do good deeds' via their investments (ibid.). According to modern portfolio theory, one of the key reasons for this underperformance is that the SRI stock universe constrains investment choice. The assumptions underlying this view are twofold: (1) that returns on all financial assets do not move in lockstep; and (2) that risk can be managed. Thus, diversification of stock ownership is necessary to offset losses with gains (ibid.).

Another critique levied against SRI is that there is no observable link between negative social screening and financial performance (Markowitz, 2008). Alicia Munnell and Annika Sunden (2005), for instance, argue that boycotting a stock is unlikely to have any impact on its price, because the demand for a firm's stock is almost perfectly elastic.[5] In other words, a relatively small change in demand for a stock – which has been shown to be the case with social investing since it represents an extremely small portion of total assets – does not meaningfully change the price of the stock or the success of the targeted investment. As long as some buyers are attracted to the stock, they can move in, purchase the stock and make money. To support their argument, Munnell and Sunden cite the 1999 study by Teoh *et al.* on how equity prices reacted to sanctions and pressures for 46 firms to divest their holdings in South Africa (ibid.). Contrary to common wisdom, the findings of Teoh *et al.* suggest that the anti-Apartheid shareholder and legislative boycotts had no negative effect on the valuation of banks or corporations operating in South Africa or on South African financial markets. If equity prices do not respond to the sanctions and pressures to divest, these authors ask, how effective is SRI in building a 'better, more just, and sustainable *economy*?' (ibid.: 20).

For us, the basic questions of inquiry do not revolve around whether or not social justice can bring about economic gains; but rather why, how and with which consequences (and for whom) social issues have become framed as problems that can only be resolved within and by the market.

Repoliticizing SRI and the processes of marketization

The SRI debates share three core assumptions that are firmly grounded in neoliberal ideology and policy (see Chapter 3). First, the discussions reproduce the common-sense assumption of standard economic theory that social issues (e.g. human rights, the environment and fair labour practices) are somehow separate from the apolitical world of financial markets. As I elaborate on more fully below, social issues do not enter the mainstream SRI discourse until they have been stripped of their 'non-economic content', i.e. 'marketized'. Briefly, the latter refers to a process, similar to the corporate governance doctrine, in which the political content (relations of power, capitalist interests and so forth) of these issues become transfigured by financial code (risk analysis, beta co-efficients, etc.) and economic laws, and thereby depoliticized (Shamir, 2008). Second, the SRI debates assume that the market is not only a natural phenomenon but also the only legitimate space in which all issues can be efficiently, democratically and rationally resolved. Third, and relatedly, owing to its belief that markets are inherently rational and self-equilibrating, the SRI debates absolve the state of any responsibility in guaranteeing welfare and security for the wider society through legal and enforceable sanctions; in effect reinforcing the assumption that voluntary self-regulation is more efficient than state-based rules. The question that arises here is: Why have social issues been framed within these neoliberal assumptions, which reduce all phenomena to the singular goal of profit maximization?

To address the above question, we need to grasp that all expressions of resistance, including SRI, must be situated and understood within their materialist context. For us, this context is represented by neoliberal restructuring strategies, such as the ongoing privatization of all facets of social life (water, entertainment, food, education, health and so forth) including old-age security in the form of pension savings. For instance, and in contrast to mainstream perspectives, the widening scope and size of SRI strategies cannot be explained solely by a shift in public opinion; but instead must be seen as resulting from state policies that have led to a situation in which hundreds of millions of people have come to rely directly on the market, as opposed to the state, to guarantee economic security in their old age (Blackburn, 2002; Langley, 2008). As noted in previous chapters, Richard Minns refers to this as the creation of 'social security capital' in which all deferred wages or salaries enter the credit system in the form of company stocks and bonds (Minns, 2001). Seen from this perspective, struggles such as those tied to the Sudan boycott contain a deep-seated paradox: in order to ensure a high return, most beneficiaries of social security capital (e.g. ethical and pension funds) are dependent on ongoing neoliberal strategies pursued by corporations – not least, highly profitable, blacklisted corporations such as PetroChina, which operates in Sudan – as well as institutional investors.

Evading the above contradiction in the analysis not only leads to the inability to identify the limits to SRI, but also acts to further embed social relations in market rule. In other words, without problematizing the market as a social construction and an integral feature of neoliberal domination (market rule), grassroots movements, such as those tied to the Sudan Divestment Campaign, remain in their depoliticized form. That is to say, the links between human rights abuses and the relations of power and paradoxes of capitalism remain concealed in the narrow economic focus of SRI. This depoliticization occurs when struggles for social justice are rearticulated *within* the bounds of neoliberalism, thereby defining the problem and the solution within the efficiency, welfare and freedom of the market. Therefore, instead of challenging neoliberal domination, SRI transfigures struggles for social justice, embedding these struggles in a competitive, pluralist and apolitical environment where the rational, objective and efficient laws of economics reign. The very act of designating, and thus reducing the complexity of, social concerns as 'non-financial issues' in the discourse of the investment industry is a case in point.

In terms of the Sudan boycott, the marketization of social justice occurs in two interrelated ways. First, the discourse of social investment reduces, redefines and redirects investors' and the general public's concern with corporate complicity in abuses against humanity to the sanitized language of risk analysis and concerns for the bottom line, where human rights are viewed as existing outside the realm of the autonomous and apolitical market. Seen from this angle, 'non-financial issues' are treated as an afterthought, or as an added feature in boosting shareholder value, i.e. 'doing good while making money'. This first expression of the marketization of social justice is evident in the above discussion of SRI. The second process involved in the marketization of social justice is the distortion and reduction of the issue at hand to the point that it is devoid of political, historical and capitalist meaning, so that it may be easily transfigured by the financial code and economic law inherent in market rule. As is evident in the next section, the representation of the Sudan conflict and discourse around the divestment campaign denies the political and historical complexity of Sudan and the conflict, as well as the role of the US government and other capitalist interests in post-colonial rule. This has resulted in the portrayal of the conflict as existing in a one-dimensional space in which the tensions between Africans and Arabs have led to human rights abuses that can be easily, painlessly (in terms of loss on potential investment returns) and quickly resolved through market mechanisms.

The marketization of the Sudan Divestment Campaign

Official representations and responses

According to mainstream discourse around the divestment campaign, the conflict in the western region of Darfur is believed to have started in 2003, when rebel groups began brutally attacking government targets. The narrative around the conflict may be summarized as follows: The government of Sudan responded to the military challenge posed by rebel movements in Darfur by arming, training and deploying Arab ethnic militias known as Janjawiid. The Janjawiid and Suda-

nese armed forces launched a campaign of ethnic cleansing and forced displacement by bombing and burning villages, killing civilians and raping women. The
first half of 2004 saw a dramatic increase in these atrocities. The conflict is
believed to have resulted in the death of over 200,000 people in the Darfur
region alone. Some were killed during armed attacks; many others died from
disease and malnutrition. Reportedly, over two million people have either fled
their homes or been displaced by the conflict.[6] The war in Darfur has largely,
and problematically, been depicted in terms of tensions between Black Africans
(Darfurians) and Arab Africans (Sudanese government and Janjawiid)
(Mamdani, 2007). The oversimplification of the conflict is discussed below. For
now, it is useful to highlight the following quote from the conservative US think
tank the Heritage Foundation,[7] as it is representative of the mainstream portrayal
of the conflict:

> [t]he situation in Sudan's western province of Darfur, currently *the world's
> worst humanitarian disaster*, continues to deteriorate. Sudan's radical Arab
> dictatorship, which has been battling a popular rebellion in Darfur since
> early 2003, has unleashed Arab militias to murder, terrorize, and forcibly
> exile the predominantly non-Arab ethnic groups of that region.
>
> (James, 2004, my emphasis)

In 2002, the US government sought to enact the Sudan Peace Act.[8] This bill was
in direct response to growing concerns and pressures on the government by a
grassroots movement comprised of a diverse set of organizations and individuals
in the US (and elsewhere). It was composed of Hollywood celebrities (Mia
Farrow and George Clooney, among others); state and federal politicians;
student, humanitarian and religious groups; and for-profit (e.g. social funds and
public pension funds) as well as non-profit organizations (e.g. Amnesty International (AI) and, most notably, the Save Darfur Coalition, which is comprised of
over 180 groups and organizations). The bill contained provisions for capital
market sanctions, 'i.e., the shares of all foreign companies operating in Sudan
would be de-listed from the NYSE and the NASDAQ' (Reeves, 2002: 169).
Although unanimously approved by the House of Representatives, the bill
remained in limbo: in part, due to the fact that capital market sanctions were
opposed by powerful business interests; and, in part, due to Sudan's changing
relationship with the US government in the immediate aftermath of 9/11, when
the Sudanese government became an ally of the Bush II administration's 'War
on Terror' (Tamm, 2004; Sidahmed and Sidahem, 2005).

In 2004, the US government declared the ongoing massacre in Darfur as genocidal. In 2005, the US Senate passed a milder version of the Sudan Peace Act:
the Darfur Accountability Act. This legislation clearly lays out sanctions and
other measures against the government of Sudan, 'including sanctions that will
affect the petroleum sector in Sudan, individual members of the government of
Sudan, and entities controlled or owned by officials of the government of Sudan
or the National Congress Party in Sudan' (Library of Congress, 2005). It should

be noted that this initiative was based upon the comprehensive trade and economic sanctions originally imposed by President Clinton in 1997 because of Sudan's alleged support for terrorism. This executive order, which in effect sought to block all US companies from doing business in Sudan, helped to transform the nature of investment in Sudan to one of portfolio holdings of foreign (public) companies – hence the importance of the divestment initiative.

In response to ongoing pressure placed on his administration due to lack of progress with respect to Sudan, President George W. Bush announced in February 2007 that the US would put further pressure on the Sudanese government in its so-called, and ill-described, 'Plan B' strategy. Plan B emerged out of frustration with what the White House perceived as a deliberate attempt by Khartoum to defy, or at least delay, the deployment of an African Union–United Nations force for as long as possible. The plan basically allows the Treasury Department 'to aggressively block US commercial bank transactions connected to the government of Sudan, including those involving oil revenues' (*Washington Post*, 2007b). Despite these attempts by the US government, many human rights activists have expressed frustration over the lack of any meaningful political dialogue and effective humanitarian intervention on the part of the US government and other international organizations, such as the United Nations Security Council (Buchwald, 2008).[9] The latter organization's actions have been constrained by the pro-Khartoum policies of powerful world leaders and the business interests of China, Russia, Pakistan and Malaysia, among others.

Rationale for divestment

In spite of the ongoing controversy surrounding genocidal activities in Darfur, the Sudanese government's revenue has increased each year since the outset of the conflict. This growth has been largely sustained by large inflows of FDI, most of which is based in the oil, energy and construction sectors, and emanates from companies situated primarily in China and India (e.g. PetroChina and Indian parastatal companies like Oil and Natural Gas Company of India and Bharat Heavy Electricals). According to the IMF, Sudan's economy grew by 12 per cent in 2006 and the government received over $2.3 billion in FDI, up nearly 50 per cent from 2004 (Sudan Divestment Task Force (SDTF), 2007). These inflows are an important source of income for the heavily debt-ridden country. There have been numerous reports documenting the connection between government revenue, especially from oil proceeds, and the Sudanese government's ability to carry out military-backed atrocities (ibid.).

Seen against the above backdrop, those who favour divestment argue that since the government relies on FDI to finance its genocidal activities in Darfur, then targeting FDI through divestment seems like a logical strategy for influencing outcomes in Sudan. This form of economic pressure, it is argued, will enhance political engagement and diplomacy – both of which have been widely perceived as ineffective thus far. History has demonstrated that the Sudanese government, which is viewed as an authoritarian regime composed of an alliance between the military and the National Congress Party (formerly the National Islamic Front), has responded to economic sanctions. Supporters of the divestment campaign point to two recent examples. First, a North American divestment campaign that began in the late 1990s to protest human rights abuses committed by the Sudanese government during its civil war with the South, and which led to the exit of Canadian-based Talisman Oil and other industrial giants such as Lundin Petroleum (a Vancouver-based mining company) and OMV (Austria's largest listed industrial corporation). These withdrawals were believed to correlate closely with Sudan's decision to enter into peace negotiations with the South that eventually ended the country's 21-year civil war (ibid.). Second, the sanctions imposed by the Clinton administration in 1997 are believed to have helped to initiate a dramatic shift in the Sudanese government's terrorism policy, including the detainment of Al Qaeda suspects, the transfer of evidence recovered in raids on suspected terrorists' homes, the expulsion of extremists and the interdiction of foreign militants moving through Sudan (ibid.; cf. Sidahmed and Sidahmed, 2005).

'Extreme SRI': the SDTF and the selective divestment model

The growing frustration with ongoing diplomatic inertia and lack of effective humanitarian intervention in Sudan, coupled with a belief in the success of past divestment practices, culminated in the formation of the SDTF in 2005. The SDTF, which is organized by a US-based, student-led group, acts as a co-ordinating body for the Sudan Divestment Campaign. While the SDTF acknowledges that shareholder engagement is, in some circumstances, a more powerful tool than divestment, it rationalizes its actions by arguing that

> extended engagement (through traditional mechanisms such as proxy voting and coalition building) often takes years – a timeframe wholly unsuited to the urgency of ongoing genocide. While the targeted divestment model still calls for engagement, it calls for that engagement to be expedited and followed by the economic 'stick' of divestment should company behaviour fail to change.
>
> (www.sudandivestment.org)

The economic stick is comprised of a 'selective divestment model', which has been designed to strike a balance between its political aims to end genocide in Darfur and the fiduciary duties of investment managers, thereby framing human rights within the bounds of the market. For instance, the Task Force believes that the divestment model is capable of 'maximizing divestment's impact on the government of Sudan while minimizing unintended harmful effects on innocent Sudanese citizens and on the health of institutional investments' (SDTF, 2007).[10] Unlike other divestment models, which advocate targeting all non-humanitarian business connections to Sudan, companies associated with agriculture, consumer goods and education are usually exempted under the targeted divestment criteria of the SDTF, since they are believed to be critical to the daily life and economic well being of the population (ibid.). According to the Calvert Group, a social investment fund that undertakes analytical work for the SDTF on a pro bono basis, the distinction between non-humanitarian business connections to companies operating in Sudan and so-called 'humanitarian' business is achieved by focusing divestment pressure on what Calvert and the SDTF understand as the 'highest offending' corporations (ibid.). In its 'Sudan Company Profile', which is updated on a quarterly basis, the SDTF reviews over 800 companies with connections to Sudan. Currently, 23 publicly held corporations fall under the 'highest offenders' category.[11] Most of these corporations are connected to the oil, mineral extraction, power and defence industries. Of the 23 worst offending companies listed in April 2008, only three were from advanced industrialized countries (Sweden, France and Finland), while the rest predominantly originated in China, Malaysia, Thailand and India. According to the report, the SDTF places a company in this category only if it generally: (1) has a business relationship with the government, a government-created project or companies affiliated with a government-created project; (2) provides little benefit to the disadvantaged populations of Sudan; and (3) has not developed a substantial business-practice policy that acknowledges and deals with the fact that the company may be inadvertently contributing to the Sudanese government's genocidal capacity' (SDTF, 2008a: 2). The divestment model permits fiduciaries to build a well-diversified portfolio without sacrificing returns or increasing risk exposure, as discussed above.[12] The SDTF's selective divestment strategy has proven to be popular among many institutional investors, especially public pension funds. Currently, over $3 billion in state assets adhere to the SDTF's targeted divestment list (*Calvert Online*, 2007).

Perceptions of success

The SDTF has enjoyed immense popularity and, to a lesser degree, success in convincing major institutional investors, municipalities and states to join the divestment campaign. As of April 2008, the following states have all adopted the SDTF model of targeted divestment: Arizona, California, Colorado, Florida, Hawaii, Indiana, Iowa, Kansas, Massachusetts, Minnesota, New Mexico, New York, North Carolina, Rhode Island, Texas and Vermont. California and nine other states have passed divestment measures, and more than 40 universities, including Stanford, the University of California and Harvard, have implemented comparable bans. According to the SDTF,

> the investment community has begun to respond to investors' demands for Sudan-free investment opportunities. A limited number of ex-Sudan investment vehicles have been developed or are being developed by asset managers such as Northern Trust, Barclays Global Investors [see discussion on Harvard University below], and State Street Global Advisors, as well as several socially responsible investing firms.

(SDTF, 2008b: 8)

The SDTF believes that its activities, as well as other shareholder- and stakeholder-led forms of protest, such as the high-profile case of Canada's Talisman Oil,[13] have helped to alter company behaviour towards Sudan. To support this position, the SDTF points to the following examples:

> A March 2006 *Forbes* magazine investigation reported that Xerox, 'is terminating [its] relationship with its Khartoum distributor in response to the situation in Darfur and spectre of divestment" while 3M has "ceased sales [in Sudan] except to UN for relief efforts." In January of 2007, Swiss power giant ABB moved to suspend its business activities in Sudan due to "political, legislative, and economic factors"– a decision in which divestment played a partial role. Weeks later, the German firm Siemens, Europe's largest electronics and electrical engineering company, followed suit, pledging to pull its operations out of Sudan "on moral and political grounds." The decision has been extensively linked to mounting pressure from investors, legislators, and activists criticizing the company's involvement in the country. Several other large multinationals with operations in Sudan [e.g. CHC Helicopter Corporation, Schlumberger, among others] have either curtailed operations or re-evaluated potentially problematic business practices in the country.
>
> (SDTF, 2007: 7)

The SDTF and its supporters have also pointed to the fact that the Sudan government reportedly spent over $1 million on an eight-page *New York Times* special advertising supplement (20 March 2006), entitled 'The Peace Dividend: Prosperity could lie ahead after years of conflict'. The supplement was aimed at attracting potential investors, as well as convincing current investors to remain in Sudan (ibid.).[14] While the SDTF has been able to politicize some corporate activity, the fact remains that the Sudanese government has not altered its position with regard to human rights abuses in Darfur. To understand the reasons for the ineffectiveness of the boycott it is necessary to go beyond the bounds of neoliberalism and its deep-seated assumption that the market, left to its own devices, will resolve social justice issues. Paying particular attention to the relations of power and contradictions within neoliberal-led capitalism, the following section explores the limits of SRI to effect meaningful social change. I attempt to repoliticize the two processes of marketization involved in the Sudan Divestment Campaign.

Deconstructing the marketization of human rights

First, drawing on a critical development lens, I attempt to deconstruct the moralistic discourse around the Sudan conflict, so that the power relations of capitalism and politics involved in the construction of social issues – in this case, genocide – may be exposed. Second, I seek to throw critical light on the neoliberal construction of the market as an unproblematic space in which social justice issues may be effectively resolved through cost–efficiency calculus and risk-management strategies, as represented in the Sudan divestment model.

Beyond the morality tale of genocide

> This is blood money.... Fear of losing money is ... not compared to the women who are being attacked today ... and the children who are being thrown into bonfires.
>
> (Mia Farrow of Dream for Darfur (www.savedarfur.org))

The limits to the divestment campaign, and SRI in general, have not been identified in mainstream literature beyond the bounds of the market. As noted above, SRI does not question the wider ideological and policy frame of market rule from which it has emerged. From this it follows that SRI strategies, such as the divestment campaign, further embed resistance struggles in the realm of the market by distorting and depoliticizing social issues. In our particular case study, this may be seen in the manner in which the divestment campaign has constructed and explained human tragedy in Sudan, that is, in moral terms devoid of any historical and political understanding of the complexity of the country. Aside from concealing relations of capitalist power and history, the moralistic discourse acts to dehumanize the conflict. The portrayal of the conflict in simple terms feeds into a quick fix, market-led response: divestment, which is a feature of the hierarchical ordering of financial concerns over social issues in SRI. To correct for this, it is necessary to repoliticize the moralistic discourse employed by the Sudan Divestment Campaign.

As with most political campaigns, the apolitical and ahistorical treatment of the conflict, especially its naming as genocide, allows for the easy packaging of the conflict as a single issue. As Mahmood Mamdani explains, casting the conflict in oversimplified terms has had its advantages in terms of creating a single issue that brings together a wide and diverse set of groups and organizations that would otherwise be adversaries on most issues of the day: the Christian Right and the Zionist lobby, humanitarian and human rights organizations, school and university-based peace movements and so forth (Mamdani, 2007). At a deeper level, the reduction of complex political and historical dimensions of the conflict to an 'Arab' versus 'African' dichotomy has led to the moralization of the violence, as well as to the depoliticization and dehumanization of struggles (Boddy, 2007), thereby making the transfiguration into economic law and financial code a smoother and easier process. As I have argued in Chapter 6, the act of denying a country its individual history, culture and politics leads to the objectification and 'othering' of complex social formations (Said, 1979). The moralistic discourse of the divestment campaign also reduces the motivations of the perpetrators to biology (race) or culture. As Mamdani observes, in the mainstream discourse, 'there is nothing messy about Darfur. It is a place without history and without politics' (Mamdani, 2007). This is evident in much of the newspaper writing on Darfur, which Mamdani rightfully accuses as having sketched a 'pornography of violence' that further depoliticizes, dehumanizes and naturalizes the conflict:

> [the media] seems fascinated by and fixated on the gory details, describing the worst of the atrocities in gruesome detail and chronicling the rise in the number of them. The implication is that the motivation of the perpetrators lies in biology (race) and, if not that, certainly culture. This voyeuristic approach accompanies a moralistic discourse whose effect is both to obscure the politics of violence and position the reader as a virtuous, not just a concerned observer.
>
> (ibid.)

David Campbell echoes the above claim by suggesting that these images also contribute to the construction and reconstruction of an 'imagined geography' in which the dichotomies of West/East, civilized/barbaric, North/South and developed/underdeveloped have assumed a central place in the depiction, and thus explanation, of the conflict (Campbell, 2007: 358). Such an imagined geography recreates the 'missionary' zeal prevalent throughout the history of colonialism, including its current economic and cultural forms, in which the West is morally obliged to civilize (or de-Islamize) the barbarians, or in the case of the Sudan 'genocide', the vilified Arabs (Boddy, 2007). As seen above, the rationale given by the SDTF for the efficacy of divestment mirrors tendencies toward missionary zeal, hints at overtones of infantilism and moral superiority, and invokes the social power of money (investment) over the weak and historically prescribed position of Sudan as a debtor country – all in the interest of compelling the 'barbaric regime' of an 'underdeveloped nation' to behave in a civilized manner.[15]

Many diplomatic representations of the conflict rehearse elements of orientalism, or misunderstanding, whether intentional or unintentional, of the plurality, diversity and hybridity not only of Sudan, but also of the entire African continent and its people. Plurality is reduced to a single entity marked by an iconography of despair, disaster and disease. Political leaders as disparate as Sudan's Vice-President and the US Deputy Secretary of State, for example, refer to the conflict as a 'tribal war', which is 'very common in Africa' (Campbell, 2007: 365). Campbell highlights the relations of power in the orientalist overtones of the discursive formation around the conflict as something akin to 'Africanism', in which the continent is homogenized, tribalized and rendered completely 'other' to its US and European counterparts (ibid.: 366). Yet, as many scholars have noted, Darfur possesses complex (messy) political and historical dimensions of insurgency and counter-insurgency that go beyond the one-sided depiction of violence perpetrated by Arabs (Prunier, 2005). As noted earlier, given the spatial constraints of this chapter it is not possible to provide a full historical account of the central and critical role of colonialism, current forms of US-led imperialism (Soederberg, 2006), and the role of oil in understanding the more recent insurgencies and counter-insurgencies currently shaping the political landscape of Sudan. Some authors, for example, trace the conflict back to the seventeenth century and the origins of the Fur state, imperial expansion, revolution and annexation by Anglo-Egyptian Sudan (Sidahmed and Sidahmed, 2005; Daly, 2007).

The divestment campaign's reliance on the label 'genocide' as a key descriptor of the violence in Sudan is uncritical and problematic. On one hand, as Gerard Prunier argues, genocide creates a brand image that warrants a 'big story' to mobilize media attention. This is especially true in the African context, where killing, due to orientalism and its attendant features of dehumanization and depoliticization, has become boring (Prunier, 2005). Relatedly, the uncritical embrace by key voices of the divestment campaign, such as 'Save Darfur', not only further supports the predominance of morality but also constructs a false sense of consensus around the label. In contrast to the US government's verdict on 23 July 2004, the United Nations has avoided labelling the conflict genocidal. The UN Commission on Darfur, for instance, was more ambiguous in its judgement. In its 2005 report, the commission found that the Sudanese government's violence was 'deliberately and indiscriminately directed against civilians. Indeed, even where rebels may have been present in villages, the impact of attacks on civilians shows that the use of military force was manifestly disproportionate to any threat posed by rebels' (Mamdani, 2007). The commission concluded that 'the Government of the Sudan has not pursued a policy of genocide ... directly or through the militias under its control'.[16]

The lack of consensus around the naming of genocide, which has been largely ignored by the divestment campaign and its supporters, amounts to more than semantics, however. It highlights the imperial power of the US government in naming one conflict genocidal and not others (Reeves, 2002; Tamm, 2004). Indeed, there appears to be a close association between the chosen subject matter of the divestment campaign around Darfur and the geo-political interests of the US government. As Mamdani points out, the violations with which the UN commission charged the Sudanese government relate not only to Darfur but also to other situations of extreme violence, such as the US occupation of Iraq, the Hema–Lendu violence in eastern Congo, and the Israeli invasion of Lebanon (Mamdani, 2007). Yet, there does not seem to be a divestment campaign in the US aimed at human rights abuses in these three cases. The relatively low-level response of US grassroots organizations and SRI campaigns to ongoing conflict in Congo is noteworthy. Statistics – the same criterion used to justify Darfur's status as the 'world's worst humanitarian crisis' – show conflict in Congo has killed millions, while hundreds of thousands have been killed in Sudan. Similar to the Darfur situation, the majority of killings in Congo, particularly in Kivu, have been undertaken by paramilitaries – many of them child soldiers – trained, organized and armed by neighbouring governments and allies of the US government (Smis and Oyatambwe, 2002).

The politics of divestment and the pursuit of profit

Identifying the limits of market-based solutions to social policy challenges requires examination of the paradoxes and power in neoliberal-led capitalism as it relates to the divestment campaign. In the face of mounting pressure from grassroots organizations such as the SDTF, the support of the federal government, states and municipalities for the divestment campaign has been motivated only superficially by moral compassion. The involvement of the state has two important consequences for the reproduction of neoliberal-led capitalism. On the one hand, its participation in naming the 'genocide' and sanctioning divestment strategies allows the US state – at all levels – to appear virtuous. On the other hand, its sanctioning of the divestment strategies naturalizes the assumption that markets are a more efficient and effective space in which to address and resolve issues of social justice. Specifically, the state has played an integral role in reproducing neoliberal domination by, first, channelling and thus depoliticizing and disciplining struggles to the realm of the market, and, second, by providing portfolio managers with enough wiggle-room to overcome the limitations set by the boycott in order to guarantee the continued expansion of capital accumulation. This is evident in the following examples involving one of the largest university endowments in the US, Harvard University, and the country's largest public pension fund, CalPERS.

At the outset, it bears noting that despite the legislative actions noted above, the US government has refused to provide investors with a comprehensive list of public companies doing business in Sudan. A proposed SEC listing of 35 public companies whose 2006 annual reports revealed business interests in Sudan was met with the same opposition as the Sudan Peace Act. On behalf of business interests, various representatives from both the Democratic and Republican parties urged the SEC to withdraw the list (*International Herald Tribune*, 2007b). Rehearsing the assumptions of neutrality and separateness from the market, and thereby reproducing the assumption that the latter is an apolitical and technical realm of economic transactions, it was deemed inappropriate for the federal government, and by extension, the SEC, to produce such a list. It was argued that such a list could introduce distortion into the market, largely because it could be construed as providing investment advice. In the words of the SEC's Deputy Director, Shelley Parratt, it is 'inappropriate for us [the SEC] to publish a list of companies whose securities might be deemed to involve terrorism-related investment risk without publishing corresponding lists for every other possible type of investment risk'.[17] Aside from signalling a separation from the market, this noncommittal position promotes vagueness about which US corporations are actually operating in Sudan and allows the state to appear progressive and responsive to grassroots movements, while financial corporations are able to continue to invest in lucrative public companies that do business in Sudan, such as PetroChina. A case in point involves Fidelity, which not only represents the largest mutual fund in the US, but also the leading investor in PetroChina. In 2005, Fidelity made it clear that it would not be guided by morals when it came to its Sudan investments: 'Fidelity portfolio managers make their investment decisions based on business and financial considerations, and take into account other issues only if they materially impact these considerations or conflict with applicable legal standards.'[18] Since no list indicating wrongdoing on the part of companies doing business in Sudan existed, Fidelity could argue that it did not violate any US laws, as 'the government should decide what foreign investments are appropriate'.[19]

Aside from the absence of an official list of public companies violating the embargo, the legislation imposed on fiduciaries is easily negotiable for those who wish to profit from corporations doing business in Sudan. Fiduciaries may channel their investments indirectly to second parties, thereby avoiding legislative restrictions and protecting their reputations, allowing them to continue profiting from highly lucrative, blacklisted corporations. PetroChina's shares, for example, traded in 2007 at 55-times earnings, versus just 13-times earnings in the case of Exxon.[20] Others have reported that share prices of PetroChina, a major firm in the Chinese economy, grew by almost 500 per cent between 2003 and 2008.[21]

In response to mounting pressure by student groups connected to the wider divestment campaign and the naming of human rights abuses in Darfur as 'genocidal' by the US government, the Harvard Corporation Committee on Shareholder Responsibility (CCSR) directed the Harvard Management Company (HMC) – the oldest corporation in the US and holder of one of the largest financial endowments of any non-profit organization in the country – to divest itself of stock held by HMC in PetroChina Company Limited (PetroChina) in April 2005.[22] A year later, HMC announced plans to divest from the Sinopec Corporation (China Petroleum and Chemical Corporation) due to the company's involvement in the crisis in Sudan.[23] It was revealed in a Harvard University newspaper (*The Crimson*), however, that Harvard's most recent federal regulatory filing with the SEC shows the university's endowment remains invested in PetroChina and Sinopec. These investments are held indirectly through the iShares China fund, which is managed by the UK bank Barclays. The iShares China fund invests according to a formula set by the *Financial Times*, the London Stock Exchange, and the Chinese news agency Xinhua. The fund allows investors to spread their assets across 25 of China's largest companies, which include Sinopec and PetroChina. Harvard also stated that it holds a further $516.2 million in shares in Barclays iShares MSCI Emerging Markets Index Fund, which represents one of Harvard's single largest investments. Harvard University is not the only corporation that has sought to appear to conform with the demands placed on it by the divestment campaign by shifting its interests in blacklisted companies from direct to indirect holdings, including holdings of other, less-visible companies whose businesses revolve around the success of blacklisted companies. There exist myriad companies within PetroChina's supply chain, as well as firms whose growth depends on PetroChina's ability to extract and process oil in Sudan, and these companies may not themselves be blacklisted. It is believed that Fidelity, which divested from PetroChina citing human rights concerns in Sudan, has also relied on a similar smoke-and-mirrors tactic.[24]

Harvard attempted to justify its actions by suggesting that the university has no direct control over the distribution of assets in its Barclays iShares funds. Furthermore, since Harvard owns the PetroChina and Sinopec shares through indexed funds, the university can only divest from the companies by selling off its entire stake in each of the two iShares entities.[25] This perspective strips HMC of any agency and thus wrongdoing. In addition, it portrays the financial market as a static, uncontested and apolitical *fait accompli.* While the SDTF has noted Harvard's continued investment in offending companies, it did not publicly confront the corporation about its choices, or the inconsistency between its rhetorical stance and investment strategies. Alternatives were available to HMC. The endowment could have requested that Barclays reweigh the index fund and then manage it in a separate account for the investor, or it could have pushed Barclays to introduce more expediently a Sudan-free passive fund.[26] Neither option was exercised.

A second case in which the lure of profitable, yet publicly tainted, investment sites could not be resisted is evident in CalPERS' attempt to hide its investments in PetroChina by way of a second party. Despite its self-made image as a responsible investor – one that has implemented a Permissible Country Index based on 'non-financial' (including political stability) and financial factors (see Chapter 6) – the CalPERS' board of directors did not initiate its strategy of 'constructive engagement' with portfolio companies doing business in Sudan until it was pressured by the California State Legislature and the wider grassroots movement of the divestment campaign. According to CalPERS, constructive engagement entails the identification of public firms that 'have a presence in Sudan, determining the impact of their business on human rights, and demanding that they respond to our concerns'.[27] Notwithstanding this position, as well as the fact that CalPERS prohibited investment in nine companies subject to legislation, including PetroChina, CalPERS firmly supported the refusal of Berkshire Hathaway Inc. (hereafter: Berkshire) to divest from PetroChina under pressure from grassroots movements that linked it to the divestment campaign. Indeed, as one of Berkshire's major shareholders, CalPERS, which owns nearly 7,500 shares worth more than $800 million, has opposed divestment. According to CalPERS spokeswoman Pat Macht, 'Shareholders should not "tell them how to invest."'[28] The irony of this position is that CalPERS has been a major force behind the shareholder activist movement in the US. The investment guru and head of Berkshire, Warren Buffett, has remained firm that both Sudan and the policies of the Chinese government are separate issues that neither he nor Berkshire could (or should) control. Nonetheless, Buffett dumped his remaining PetroChina shares in October 2007, saying the decision was undertaken not out of moral conviction, but rather on 100 per cent price considerations, as he feared PetroChina's shares were rising too far, too quickly.[29]

Taken together, the above discussion on the politics and paradoxes of divestment and the moralistic discourse of the conflict in Sudan throws critical light on the treatment of the market as an efficient, coherent, objective and apolitical space that is devoid of power, history, struggles and contradictions. Seen through this alternative lens, it becomes problematic to reduce social issues, such as human rights abuses, to the overriding concern of creating shareholder value, which is evident in the marketization of social justice of both the Sudan Divestment Campaign and the wider SRI debates.

'Giving karma, getting karma': the implications of marketization

In this final chapter, I have argued that one of the most popular cases of SRI in the US, the Sudan Divestment Campaign, is characterized by the marketization of social justice. The marketization processes, which are inherent in SRI strategies such as the Sudan boycott, serve to depoliticize struggle, while further embedding resistance to corporate power into market rule. Specifically, the act of disembedding these struggles from the relations of power and paradoxes of capitalist society, through the processes of marketization, has several consequences. First, the screening initiative not only oversimplifies the underlying causes of human rights abuses, including complex historical and political issues, but also leads to the objectification ('othering') of suffering. Second, and relatedly, once the objectification has taken place, its solution is also found in the market, i.e. divestment from companies. There are at least two issues that spring from this point. On the one hand, the marketization processes aid in normalizing the dominant understanding of social responsibility as an economic and, therefore, rational and objective act as opposed to a moral and subjective activity, which could jeopardize investment returns. On the other hand, it leads to a false sense of empowerment of grassroots movements vis-à-vis fiduciaries and corporations. In other words, it exaggerates their ability to effect change within the realm of the market simply by entering or exiting investment sites. Larger, more difficult, and more painful (economically speaking) issues linked to the campaign evade confrontation. One example is the option of boycotting Chinese exports, many of which are produced in less than 'civilized' circumstances in terms of, for example, labour standards. Third, it glosses over the politics of selection and exclusion. The marketization of social justice distorts the power and ability of the US government to construct, support and capitalize from a dominant social issue. This may, in turn, serve to divert attention away from other controversial foreign policy issues, such as the Iraq War, or the attempt by US congress to press the Chinese government to speed up currency reform and reign in its trade surplus.

Recently, AI launched a new campaign using the lure of John Lennon's music and the voices of millions of concerned individuals around the globe to halt 'the horrific human rights abuses taking place in Darfur'. According to the AI website, concerned citizens can 'Speak out, get the music and feel the instant karma!' in three easy steps:

(1) Sign the global petition and demand action from world leaders to stop the killing in Darfur, (2) Order the new double CD of John Lennon's music by some of today's best-known artists, and (3) Tell your friends and help build the movement for peace in Darfur.[30]

The Instant Karma campaign mimics the divestment boycott, especially its tendencies toward the marketization of social justice issues. Both strategies feature an approach to changing or impacting complex social issues in the global South that ignores the material effects of history and politics. The narrow, economistic framework within which SRI is debated and negotiated obscures the interests being served through the marketization of social justice struggles. Broadening the analysis by incorporating these critical perspectives exposes the interests and assumptions that underlie SRI and provides a framework through which the process of marketization can be better understood. The marketization of social justice has become an integral feature of social security capital and the wider Ownership Society. The marketization of resistance represents a double-edged sword. On the one hand, it captures moments of resistance, in the form of social investment, to the growing power of corporations over everyday life. On the other hand, it is also a central feature in retrenching the growing power of corporations over everyday life (Lefebvre, 2005).

Concluding comments: new trends in depoliticizing corporate power and ownership

> There is a growing view among investment professionals that environmental, social and corporate governance (ESG) issues can affect the performance of investment portfolios.
>
> (United Nations PRI (www.unpri.org))

The marketization of social justice is not confined to the SRI universe. Over the past several years, there has been an attempt to expand the corporate governance doctrine to include non-economic indicators such as environmental sustainability and social issues, as evidenced, for example, by the PCI (see Chapter 6). The SIF has noted that within shareholder activism there appears to be a growing convergence between traditional corporate governance advocates and social investors, or what has been referred to as the SRI–corporate governance nexus (SIF, 2006; see Chapter 6). At the global level, the UNPRI has stressed that a combination of non-economic (social and environmental) concerns must complement financial considerations in order to achieve shareholder value. In the words of the Secretary-General of the United Nations, Ban Ki-moon,

> By incorporating environmental, social and governance criteria into their investment decision-making and ownership practices, the signatories to the Principles are directly influencing companies to improve performance in these areas. This, in turn, is contributing to our efforts to promote good

corporate citizenship and to build a more stable, sustainable and inclusive global economy.

(UNPRI, 2006: 4)

The content of the SRI–corporate governance nexus reflects the same neoliberal common-sense assumptions inherent in the corporate governance doctrine, such as the naturalization of self-regulatory markets and profit maximization (see Chapters 1 and 3). Moreover, the SRI–corporate governance nexus is a product of, and thus firmly rooted in, the tension between the growing interdependency of social security capital on Corporate America and the increasing awareness of the potential power that the holders of social security capital could exercise over Corporate America in their capacity as shareowners. While the main thrust of the rise of SRI is related to growing concerns about corporate misconduct in areas of labour practices, the environment and human rights, these issues have been shifted into the apolitical terrain of the market and thus *transfigured* to become *means* to achieve financial returns by reducing the risk exposure of institutional investors. Take, for example, the Institutional Investor Network on Climate Risk, which advertises on its website: 'Global climate change is a financial issue.'[31]

The SRI–corporate governance nexus is, therefore, not a radical departure from the corporate governance doctrine and its key features of depoliticizing and marketizing conflict by reducing struggles to issues of ownership and control. Despite its altered appearance, its content remains firmly entrenched in neoliberal discipline aimed at naturalizing the concept that corporations are self-regulating, rational, economic actors that are free of political and ideological content. Put another way, the SRI–corporate governance nexus is an attempt to reformulate the *form* of the corporate governance doctrine while maintaining its neoliberal content (see Chapters 1 and 3). As the discussion and analysis of the previous chapters shows, the primary reason for the reformulation of the corporate governance doctrine is the underlying contradictions and struggles of capitalist society, upon which the doctrine is not only erected but which it is also designed to placate. This same explanation underpins the reasons for changing the *form* of other neoliberal strategies, such as the Post-Washington Consensus in the context of global development policy (Fine *et al.*, 2001) and Third Way politics in the setting of national welfare policies (Soederberg *et al.*, 2005; Taylor, 2006).

Seen against the above backdrop, the SRI–corporate governance nexus acts to reproduce neoliberal domination by changing its *form* while maintaining the same *content*. On the one hand, it seeks to co-opt struggle by distorting the complexity and heterogeneity of grassroots concerns about corporate power through the social construction of a homogenous set of values reflecting a mythical common good, which is embodied in the construct of 'Main Street America' (see Chapter 2). On the other hand, the SRI–corporate governance nexus seeks to connect these one-dimensional and fabricated societal values with corporate interests. In other words, the expanded form of the corporate governance doctrine is an attempt to reproduce the status quo, especially with regard to financial deregulation and corporate self-regulation, by addressing and co-opting contestation surrounding the growing power of Corporate America. This sentiment is captured in an article appearing at the start of the 2008 credit crisis:

> What is good for America and what is good for much of Corporate America have gotten way out of sync. Our current business culture too often emphasizes only short-term corporate profits and shareholder returns – however and wherever they are generated – and in the process, what is good for America is being pushed aside.
>
> (*Los Angeles Times*, 2008)

The approximate $1 trillion loss in value of the top 1,000 pension funds in the US since September 2008 – the worst decline in the past 30 years – will serve to widen and deepen the growing discrepancy between those individuals, classes and groups associated with the higher echelons of Corporate America and 'Main Street America' (*Pensions & Investments*, 2009).

It is perhaps a signal of the strength of neoliberal policy and ideology that despite the increased frequency, spread and depth of corporate and financial crises over the past several decades, the growing presence of corporations over most areas of social life, the asymmetrical dependency of social security capital on the corporate–financial nexus, the widening gap of socio-economic inequality, and the increasing levels of economic insecurity in the US (as elsewhere), there has been little attempt to grasp the political and ideological *content* of the corporate governance doctrine. Yet, given the central role of corporations in the destruction of all aspects of human and ecological life, it is imperative that we identify and transcend the ideologically laden and class-led nature of the corporate governance doctrine and begin to question critically who benefits and why from privileged places in the academy, policymaking circles and the media. Without a more critical and complex understanding of corporations, including the disciplinary and political implications of the mass ownership phenomenon, as inherently connected to the power and paradoxes of capitalism, resistance will continue to be depoliticized and marketized by the same dominant forces who benefit from the reproduction of the corporate governance doctrine – in all of its guises.

Notes

1 Repoliticizing corporate power and ownership in contemporary capitalism

1 A publicly listed corporation refers to a firm that has been allowed, by the government, to offer its registered securities (e.g. stocks, bonds and so forth) for purchase to the general public (cf. Braithwaite and Drahos, 2000). This sale occurs through a stock exchange, but may also occur over-the-counter. It should be noted that I use the term publicly listed or publicly traded corporation interchangeably throughout the book.

2 Although the US has ceded ground to countries such as China in recent years, it is still home to the largest number of companies with the highest market value, as determined by market capitalization, or the stock market value (i.e. share price) of a company, see *Financial Times Global 500 2008*: www.ft.com/reports/ft5002008.

3 Common stock refers to providing voting rights and entitling the holder to a share of the company's profits through dividends and/or capital appreciation. In the event of liquidation, common stockholders have rights to a company's assets only after bondholders and other debt holders, i.e. banks and preferred stockholders, have been paid out. For further information, see: www.investorwords.com. Accessed 12 April 2007.

4 Junk bonds, which were used in corporate takeovers and funding in the 1980s, refer to a high-yield corporate bond issue with a below-investment rating, i.e. high-risk investments that promise high returns.

5 The first case of shareholder activism may be traced to the Gilbert brothers, who, owning ten shares of Consolidated Gas Co. of New York, formed the first group of shareholder activists (Brancato, 1997).

2 Repoliticizing the Ownership Society and the marketization of security

1 According to its website, the mission of the Social Security Administration is 'to advance the economic security of the nation's people through compassionate and vigilant leadership in shaping and managing America's Social Security programmes'. Available at: www.ssa.gov/aboutus. Accessed 1 February 2008.

2 An exception to this claim has been the work of Robin Blackburn (2002). Blackburn's analysis regarding the state of pensions in the western world is prescient and extremely insightful. Given the broad focus of Blackburn's book, he deals briefly with the concept of the Ownership Society and therefore does not provide an in-depth analysis of its relationship to neoliberal-led restructuring of American society.

3 Of course, the privatization of old-age pensions is not confined to the US, but has been a global phenomenon of neoliberal restructuring. See, for example, World Bank (1994).

4 401(k) refers to '[a] retirement plan made available by a company to its employees, featuring tax-deferred contributions and growth. The plan may also include matching contributions by the company.' For further information, see *Moneychimp*: www.moneychimp.com/glossary/401k.htm. Accessed 18 January 2009. See also, Clark (1993) and Blackburn (2002).

5 According to polls, approximately 88 per cent of American young people believe that Social Security either is 'in trouble' today or 'will be in trouble within the next 20 years' (Tanner, 1996: 6).

6 More recently, there has been a rise in discussion surrounding the effectiveness of labour-shareholder activism in changing management behaviour. See, for example, Fung *et al.* (2001).

7 An Individual Retirement Account (IRA) is defined as a

> 'tax-deferred retirement account for an individual that permits individuals to set aside money each year, with earnings tax-deferred until withdrawals begin at age 59-and-a-half or later (or earlier, with a 10 per cent penalty). The exact amount depends on the year and the individual's age. IRAs can be established at a bank, mutual fund or brokerage. Only those who do not participate in a pension plan at work or who do participate and meet certain income guidelines can make deductible contributions to an IRA.

Available at: www.investorwords.com/2641/IRA.html. Accessed 18 January 2009.

8 Blackburn (2002) suggests that the threat of impeachment tied to the Monica Lewinsky affair at the end of 1998 also played an important part in diminishing the Clinton administration's attempt to privatize Social Security.

9 MSN Money, 2007, 'The squeeze on the middle class'. Available at: http://articles.moneycentral.msn.com/Investing/HomeMortgageSavings/MiddleClassConundrumDoYouFitIn.aspx. Accessed 14 May 2008.

3 Repoliticizing corporate governance: scandals, struggles and the Sarbanes–Oxley Act

1 Although there is emerging literature aimed at critically evaluating and contesting various facets of corporate governance theory (Scott, 1997; Engelen, 2002; Erturk *et al.* 2004; Mizruchi, 2004; Soederberg, 2004; Brennan, 2005; Overbeek *et al.*, 2007), the general tendency in the academy, media and policymaking circles has been to accept blindly the corporate governance model.

2 There are, of course, many other neoliberal policies that aided in the various corporate scandals since the 1980s, including the privatization of social welfare services, corporate welfare practices such as direct and indirect forms of subsidization, weakening the collective bargaining strength of trade unions, opening up markets in the global South to US foreign investment through SAPs, the policies of the WTO and so forth.

3 For further information, see the SEC document available at: www.sec.gov/about/laws.shtml. Accessed 3 October 2006.

4 For further information about the PCAOB, see: www.pcaobus.org. Accessed 2 November 2006.

5 It should be flagged here that despite the high level of technical knowledge required to decipher these reports, the majority of the PCAOB members are not accountants (Ribstein, 2002).

6 Options backdating refers to the practice of granting an employee stock options that are dated before the date that the company actually granted the option. The point of stock options was to provide an incentive to agents to work toward shareholder value, and therefore profit when the stock goes up. However, some executives have exploited this incentive by tinkering with the timeline of the stock options, switching

to earlier, more favourable dates, and thereby profiting from wide differentials in stock prices. In light of the Enron-like scandals, the US Congress enacted Section 409A of the Internal Revenue Code to tackle non-qualified deferred compensation by discounting backdated stock options with additional taxes and penalties at vesting or exercise. However, as witnessed by the increasing probes by the SEC since the Enron-like scandals, options backdating remains a real problem for investors and regulators.

7 In contrast to mainstream and official discourse surrounding corporate governance and the SOX, Julie Froud *et al.* (2000) astutely observe that shareholder value is a rhetorical notion, the meaning of which varies widely, being invoked as cause, consequence or justification.

8 Indeed, from the 1980s to the present, the primary impetus of growth in the US has been consumer debt. For example, household debt, including mortgage and consumer debt, skyrocketed dramatically under President Clinton's tenure to reach 97.4 per cent of disposable income (Pollin, 2003). The disciplinary nature of the freshly minted Bankruptcy and Abuse Prevention and Consumer Protection Act of 2005 is symptomatic of the ballooning debt levels in working- and middle-class households. The Act seeks to protect the interests of banks and credit card companies in the wake of an upsurge of personal bankruptcies. Interestingly, no such comparable Act exists for shareholders when corporations declare bankruptcy.

9 Recent announcements by Ford and General Motors point to another wave of massive redundancies in the car manufacture sector, which some believe to be comparable to shutting down the hourly workforce of the Chrysler Corporation in the US (*Online NewsHour*, 2006). In February 2008, General Motors announced that it would cut 70 per cent of its US workforce (74,000 workers) after it lost \$38.7 billion in 2007 (*Guardian*, 2008).

10 For an overview of the various debacles during this period and their primary causes, see: www.forbes.com/home/2002/07/25/accountingtracker.html. Accessed 15 May 2006.

11 By convention, the P/E ratio divides the market price of a firm (P) with the reported earnings (E) (Clark and Hebb, 2005: 2019).

12

Asset-backed securities are bonds that are based on underlying pools of assets. A special purpose trust or instrument is set up which takes title to the assets and the cash flows are 'passed through' to the investors in the form of an asset-backed security. The types of assets that can be 'securitized' range from residential mortgages to credit card receivables.

Excerpted from *Financial Pipeline*. For further information, see: www.finpipe.com/ assback.htm. Accessed 2 January 2006.

13 In the American 'federal system of government, for instance, the President, with the advice and consent of the Senate, appoints the officers operating in the SEC', an agency that does not face election (Ramirez, 2000).

14 For further information on the SEC's mandate, see: www.sec.gov/about/whatwedo. shtml.

15 Forward-looking statements pertain to certain sections of the Annual Report on Form 10-K. These statements

are based on management's expectations, estimates, projections and assumptions. Words such as "expects", "anticipates", "plans", "believes", "schedules", "estimates" and variations of these words and similar expressions are intended to identify forward-looking statements, which include but are not limited to projections of revenues, earnings, segment performance, cash flows, contract awards, aircraft production, deliveries and backlog stability. Forward-looking statements are made pursuant to the safe harbour provisions of the Private Securities Litigation Reform Act of 1995, as amended. These statements are not guarantees of future performance and involve certain risks and uncertainties, which are difficult to predict.

For further information, see: www.generaldynamics.com/news/forward.htm. Accessed 15 January 2006.
16 This term refers to the right to purchase a corporation's stock at a specific price. Stock options constitute the bulk of the huge pay packages of CEOs (PBS Frontline, 2002; Glassman, 2004).
17 The following website, run by the AFL-CIO, provides up-to-date trends in corporate executive pay: www.aflcio.org/corporatewatch/paywatch.

4 Deconstructing the myth of corporate democracy: the case of the equal access proposal

1 The 'Save Shareholder Rights' campaign is a joint initiative of the SIF and the ICCR in direct response to the SEC's shareholder proposals. For more information, see www.saveshareholderrights.org/issues.cfm.
2 Debates about the separation of ownership from control have been designated in terms of Marxist versus managerial approaches. As with other traditions, there are numerous and often contradictory approaches to Marxism. To avoid confusion, I make a distinction between the Marxist approaches associated with these debates as the 'class fractionalist perspective', or the American Marxist Sociology of the 1970s.
3 For a detailed discussion of the history of struggles for equal access, see 'CalPERS – Equal Access – What is it?' Available at: www.corpgov.net/news/news.html. Accessed 2 February 2008.
4 For more information, see DLA Piper, a major counsel for public and private companies. Available at: www.dlapiper.com/files/upload/CorpGov_060919.htm. Accessed 2 December 2007.
5 The Institutional Shareholder Services (ISS) is the global leader in providing corporate governance and proxy voting solutions. ISS specializes in proxy research, voting services and corporate governance advisory services to financial institutions and corporations. For more information, see: www.issproxy.com.
6 As noted earlier, the AFSCME proposal for equal access has been supported by numerous high-profile institutional investors and shareholder organizations, most notably CalPERS, NYCERS, the AFL-CIO, the CII, the ICCR, the SIF, and Responsible Wealth (a network of hundreds of affluent Americans), to name a few.
7

The SEC requires that shareholders of a company with securities registered under Section 12 of the Securities Exchange Act of 1934 receive a proxy statement before a shareholder meeting, whether an annual or special meeting. The information contained in the statement must be filed with the SEC before soliciting a shareholder vote on the election of directors and the approval of other corporate actions. Solicitations, whether by management or shareholders, must disclose all important facts about the issues on which shareholders are asked to vote.

For further information, see: ftp.sec.gov/answers/proxy.htm. Accessed 12 September 2007.
8 Proxy cards card allow shareholders to vote at the meeting, whether or not they decide to attend. By checking the appropriate boxes, signing, dating and returning the proxy card, shareholders can appoint management to represent them at the meeting and instruct management to vote their shares in accordance with their wishes, as indicated on the proxy card. If shares are held in a 'street name' in a brokerage account, the shareholder receives his or her proxy materials from the broker. A 'street name' occurs when securities are held in a broker's or other nominee's name, as opposed to

holding them in the customer's name. For further information, see: www.pgecorp. com/investors/shareholders/proxy_cards_statement.shtml. Accessed 11 September 2007.

9 Proxy contests arise when a dissident shareholder or group distributes its own proxy materials separate from management's proxy materials. Both groups then wage an active solicitation campaign to persuade shareholders to vote their respective proxy cards. The dissident's goal may be to replace the entire board, and ultimately, management, or to replace only some of the directors (a short slate).

10 While the specific features of the proposal are in place, there is still disagreement among the various shareholders and shareholder groups over certain issues, most notably the benchmark required for access to the corporate proxy to list shareholder director nominees, such as 1 per cent of the company stock held for one year, 5 per cent held for one year, 1 per cent held for two years and so forth. For specific proposals on the amendment of Rule 14a-8(i), see SEC (2002), as well as SEC (2007), 'Shareholder Proposals, Shareholders Rules', 17 CFR Part 240, 3 August 2007. Available at: www.sec.gov/rules/proposed/2007/34–56160fr.pdf. Accessed 12 September 2007.

11 See Letter from Henry A. McKinnell, Chairman, Business Roundtable, to Jonathan Katz, Secretary, Securities and Exchange Commission (22 December 2003). Available at: www.sec.gov/rules/proposed/s71903/brt122203.htm. Accessed 21 September 2007.

12 A survey by Affluent Dynamics of more than 200 highest net worth investors and professional financial advisors for FTI Consulting, an independent research firm, found that corporate boards are believed to operate in the interests of management, as opposed to shareholders. For further information, see: www.fticonsulting.com/ web/about/pressreleases/266/Corporate_Board_Seen_as_Aligned_With_Management_ Rather_Than_Shareholders_According_to_a_New_Survey_by_FTI_Consulting_and_ FD.html. Accessed 18 January 2009.

13 We pick up on these debates in our discussion of labour-led shareholder activism in Chapter 5 and SRI in Chapters 6 and 7.

14 The Competitive Enterprise Institute is a non-profit public policy organization dedicated to advancing the norms of free enterprise and limited governance in the US. For more information, see: www.cei.org.

15 The companies are AOL TimeWarner Inc., Exxon Mobil Corporation, Bank of New York Co., Eastman Kodak Co., Citigroup Inc. and Sears Roebuck & Co. For further information, see: Corpgov.net March 2003. Available at: www.corpgov.net/news/ archives 2003/March.html. Accessed 18 January 2009.

5 The limits to labour's capital and the new activism

1 Most mutual funds on the market are open-ended funds. Essentially, these funds are characterized by the fact that there are no restrictions placed on the amount of shares the fund will issue. These funds, which range from more conservative, low-risk to more aggressive (i.e. constant trading) investing strategies, also re-purchase shares when investors wish to sell. Available at: www.investopedia.com/terms/o/open-endfund.asp. Accessed 3 July 2007.

2 According to the Securities and Exchange Act, a shareholder proposal or resolution describes a recommendation or requirement that a shareholder intends to present at a meeting of the company's shareholders, which demands that the company and/or its board of directors take action. The regulations detailing the shareholder proposal process are available at the SEC's website: www.sec.gov.

3 Poison pill is a strategy undertaken by management that lowers the value of a company's stock or induces other counter-measures aimed at making the company less attractive to the potential acquirer in order to avoid a hostile take-over.

4 It is important to underline here that the labour-shareholder activism debates do not suggest that these new forms of negotiation and bargaining have replaced traditional union tactics in dealing with management, but that unions have found a complementary and potentially more effective method for achieving their goals in shareholder activism. According to Schwab and Thomas' study, unions occasionally use their shareholder power as a means to enhance traditional organizing and collective-bargaining goals (Schwab and Thomas, 1998; O'Connor, 2001).

5 Productivity growth refers to the growth of the output of goods and services per hour worked. In theory, this growth should provide the basis for the growth of living standards (Mishel *et al.*, 2007).

6 The AFL-CIO was formed in 1955. It is a voluntary federation that represents 55 national and international labour unions. The AFL-CIO represents (as of 2007) ten million working Americans and another one million non-union workers of Working America.

6 Corporate governance and entrepreneurial development: the case of CalPERS' Permissible Country Index

1 Unlike equity financing, which pertains to investment in stock markets, FDI refers to investment of foreign assets in domestic structures, equipment and organizations. Unlike equity financing, FDI is believed to be more stable and therefore beneficial, given the relative difficulty it has to move out of a host country at the first sign of financial or political trouble. See Armijo (1999).

2 Equity finance now plays a larger role than net debt flows from official multilateral creditors, such as the IMF and World Bank. For further information, see: http://econ. worldbank.org/WBSITE/EXTERNAL/EXTDEC/EXTDECPROSPECTS/EXTGDF/E XTGDF2005/0,,contentMDK:20341503~menuPK:544389~pagePK:64167689~piPK: 64167673~theSitePK:544381,00.html. Accessed 18 January 2009.

3 For further information see discussions in Chapters 2 and 4, as well as the IFC World Bank website on corporate governance: www.ifc.org/ifcext/economics.nsf/Content/ CG-Corporate_Governance_Department.

4 This figure is based on market value as of April 2009. The largest retirement plan in terms of asset size is the Federal Thrift Savings Plan ($197.3 billion). Unlike CalPERS, the Thrift Savings Plan is a DC scheme (*Pensions & Investments*, 2008c).

5 A standard definition of SRI refers to

> an investment approach that, in addition to conventional financial criteria, evaluates and selects companies based on social and ethical criteria such as legal compliance, employment practices, human rights, consumer issues, contribution to the community, and environmental issues, while seeking stable returns.
>
> (Kawamura, 2002: 14)

6 For a historical materialist study of neoliberalism and its contradictions within the context of the pioneering country, Chile, see Taylor (2006).

7 'CalPERS adds to emerging markets list', *Benefits Canada*, 20 April 2005.

8 As for April 2006, the IFC listed eight performance standards: (1) social and environmental assessment and management system; (2) labour and working conditions; (3) pollution prevention and abatement; (4) community, health, safety and security; (5) land acquisition and involuntary resettlement; (6) biodiversity conservation and sustainable natural resource management; (7) indigenous peoples; and (8) cultural heritage. For further information, see the IFC's Policy on Social and Environmental Sustainability. Available at: www.ifc.org/ifcext/enviro.nsf/AttachmentsByTitle/pol_ SocEnvSustainability2006/$FILE/SustainabilityPolicy.pdf. Accessed 3 May 2006.

9 The inclination to incorporate SRI discourse in good governance is also found in the George W. Bush administration's Millennium Challenge Account (MCA). The MCA,

which was established in 2002, is an attempt by the US government to forge a 'new compact for global development'. According to the MCA, 'Aid is most effective when it reinforces sound political, economic and social policies – which are key to encouraging the inflows of private capital and increased trade – the real engines of economic growth.' To meet this objective, the MCA draws on 16 criteria, ranging from civil liberties and political rights – both of which are defined and measured using research by Freedom House – to trade policy and inflation rates. As such, the method of screening prior to funding is quite similar to the PCI. For more information, see the MCA website: www.mca.gov, and Soederberg (2006: chapter 5).

10 Confidential interviews at CalPERS, 2 May 2005.

11 For further information, see: CalPERS, 'Corporate Governance and Core Principles and Guidelines: The United States', 6 April 2005. Available at: www.calpers-governance.org/principles/domestic/us/page01.asp. Accessed 26 May 2005.

12 See, for example, World Bank, Global Development Finance (2000).

13 Wilshire Consulting, 'Permissible Equity Markets Investment Analysis', prepared for CalPERS, April 2005, Wilshire & Associates.

14 Wilshire Consulting, 'Exposure Draft – Permissible Equity Markets Investment Analysis', prepared for CalPERS, January 2006.

15 Ibid.

16 Confidential interview with representatives from the Treasury Department of California, 6 May 2005.

17 Confidential e-mail exchange with a Senior Associate at Wilshire on 21 June 2005.

18 The sub-factors of political stability are defined by Wilshire in the following manner:

> *Civil Liberties*: The extent to which countries permit freedom of expression, association and organizational rights, rule of law and human rights, free trade unions and effective collective bargaining, personal autonomy and economic rights. *Independent Judiciary and Legal Protection*: The extent to which countries have independent judiciaries, the degree to which or the absence of irregular payments made to the judiciary, the extent to which there is a trusted legal framework that honours contracts, and delineates ownership of and protects financial assets. *Political Risk*: The extent to which there exists government stability, a high quality of socio-economic conditions, and a positive investment profile. Toward these ends this sub-factor evaluates the extent of internal and external conflict, corruption, the military and religion in politics, law and order, ethnic tensions, democratic accountability and bureaucratic quality.
>
> (Wilshire, 2005: 6)

19 For more information regarding the methodology employed in calculating 'freedom scores', see 'Methodology' at Freedom House's website: www.freedomhouse.org/template.cfm?page=35&year=2005.

20 See 'Research Services' at Verité's website: www.verite.org/research/main.html. For more detailed information regarding the methodology and findings of Verité, see 'Emerging Markets Research Project: Year-End Report', prepared for California Employees' Retirement System, December 2004. Available at: www.calpers.ca.gov/eip-docs/investments/assets/equities/international/permissible/calpers-verite-final-report-2004.pdf. Accessed 15 February 2005.

21 Although the majority of CalPERS' assets are invested on a long-term basis in US publicly traded corporations, in 2005, the fund held $3.9 billion in assets in emerging markets. See 'CalPERS adds to emerging markets list', *Benefits Canada*, 20 April 2005.

22 'CalPERS Flips and Flops in Philippines – Again', *Bloomberg News*, 22 April 2004.

23 'US pension fund quits Asian countries', *BBC World News*, 21 February 2002. Available at: http://news.bbc.co.uk/1/hi/business/1833674.stm. Accessed 14 November 2005.

24 Fiduciary responsibility describes a situation in which an individual, corporation or association (as in the case of CalPERS) holds assets for another party (public employees of the State of California), often with the legal authority and duty to make decisions regarding financial matters on behalf of the other party. According to Margaret M. Blair, public pension funds are one of the least regulated in terms of major financial institutions. However, these plans usually adhere to the same fiduciary rules as those plans regulated by the US ERISA. See Blair (1995).

25 N. Edwards, 'Pragmatism rules in Asia's ethical investing debate', Association for Sustainable and Responsible Investment in Asia, 21 February 2002. Available at: www.asria.org/pro/news&events/ethical_investing_debate.htm. Accessed 15 July 2005.

26 To put things in perspective, while broader universes of assets under professional management (i.e. non-SRI assets) are substantially greater than their SRI counterparts ($24.4 trillion as of 2005), over the 1995–2005 period, SRI assets rose more than 258 per cent, whereas non-SRI assets increased by 249 per cent over the same time. SIF, '2003 Report on Socially Responsible Investing Trends in the United States', SIF Industry Research Programme, December 2003. Available at: www.socialinvest.org/areas/research/trends/sri_trends_report_2003.pdf, and SIF, '2005 Report on Socially Responsible Investing Trends in the United States, Social Investment Forum Industry Research Programme, January 2006. Available at: www.socialinvest.org/areas/research/trends/sri_trends_report_2005.pdf. Accessed 2 February 2006.

27 'CalPERS Flips and Flops', 2004.

28 Ibid.

29 Tim Shorrock, 'CalPERS and Carlyle', *The Nation*, 1 April 2002. Available at: www.thenation.com/docprint.mhtml?i=20020401&s=shorrock2. Accessed 1 March 2007.

30 'CalPERS Ok's Selective Stock Purchases in China – Other Countries Excluded from Equity Investments', CalPERS Press Release, 18 December 2006. Available at: www.calpers.ca.gov/index.jsp?bc=/about/press/pr-2006/dec/stock-purchase-china.xml. Accessed 2 April 2007.

31 Rob Feckner acts, among his many other roles, as Association President of the California School Employees Association, and he is serving his fourteenth year on the board of directors. He also serves as an Executive Vice President of the California Labor Federation. For further information, see 'About CalPERS' at: www.calpers.ca.gov/index.jsp?bc=/about/organization/board/members/rob-feckner.xml. Accessed 3 June 2007.

32 www.calpers.ca/gov.

33 American depository receipts (ADR) refer to a negotiable certificate issued by an American bank representing a specified number of shares in a foreign stock that is traded on a US stock exchange, such as NYSE, AMEX or NASDAQ. ADRs are denominated in US dollars, with the underlying security held by a US financial institution overseas. ADRs assist in reducing administration and duty costs that would otherwise be levied on each transaction. ADRs are a convenient way to purchase shares in a foreign company while realizing any dividends and capital gains in US dollars. ADRs do not, however, eliminate the currency and economic risks for the underlying shares in another country. Global depositary receipts are very similar to ADRs and are denominated in either US dollars or euros. For further information, see: www.investopedia.com/terms/a/adr.asp. Accessed 2 September 2008.

34 CalPERS has not been using Wilshire Consulting to undertake its evaluations for the PCI since 2008.

35 Based on 191 member countries of the United Nations as of April 2006. Available at www.un.org/Overview/unmember.html.

7 The marketization of social justice: the case of the Sudan Divestment Campaign

1 The depiction of the Sudan government as a 'killing machine' is used by many human rights organizations, including the wider coalition, Save Darfur. See, for example: www.savedarfur.org/page/content/torchrelay/ny/. Accessed 20 May 2008.

2 These numbers have been contested. A. Munnell and A. Sunden argue that the size and importance of the social investment movement depend on how SRI is defined. When one applies a narrower definition to social investment activities in the US, these authors argue that the size of the funds is considerably lower than has been suggested by SRI advocates (Munnell and Sunden, 2005).

3 For further information, see: www.unpri.org.

4 'Talisman, "Human Rights" and Development Efforts, 2000–2002'. Available at: www.hrw.org/reports/2003/sudan1103/24.htm. Accessed 2 June 2008.

5 Munnell and Sunden point out that the 10 per cent figure supplied by the SIF (2005) is not only too small to affect the financial fate of targeted firms, which is the goal of negative social screening, including the Sudan divestment campaign, but also tends to overstate the importance of social investing due to inconsistencies in measurement (2005: 21).

6 See, for example, background papers on Save Darfur's website. Available at: www.savedarfur.org; Tamm (2004).

7 According to its website, the Heritage Foundation's mission 'is to formulate and promote conservative public policies based on the principles of free enterprise, limited government, individual freedom, traditional American values, and a strong national defense'. For more information, see: www.heritage.org.

8 For further information, see: www.state.gov/documents/organization/19897.pdf.

9 See also 'Darfur Activists Frustrated with US Inaction', *Human Rights Tribune*. Available at: www.humanrights-geneva.info/Darfur-Activists-Frustrated-With,1153. Accessed 1 November 2008.

10 This has led to the ability of major corporations, such as Coca-Cola, to slip under the food and medicine clause in the embargo. Coca-Cola sells its syrup to a Sudanese company, whose new $140 million dollar factory currently churns out about 100,000 bottles of soda on a daily basis (*New York Times*, 2006) we discuss more contradictions tied to the selective divestment initiative later in this chapter.

11 For a listing of the worst offending companies, see SDTF, *Sudan Company Profiles*. Washington, D.C.: SDTF. Updated 29 February 2008. Available at: www.sudandivestment.org/docs/sudan_company_profiles.pdf. Accessed 14 March 2008.

12 For example, based on analysis performed by State Street Global Advisors for Calvert, the removal of the highest offending companies from the major indices causes a negligible deviation in their market characteristics. Only one company on the list would need to be excluded from US market indices, resulting in just 3 basis points (0.03 per cent) of tracking error (a measure of the standard deviation of the difference between expected portfolio return and the index return) from the S&P 500 Index. Meanwhile, the primary MSCI indices (www.mscibarra.com/about) are affected by less than 20 basis points (0.20 per cent). This allows passive and active managers to continue to apply their strategies with little additional risk (*Calvert Online*, 2007). Link no longer available.

13 Talisman Energy of Canada held 25 per cent in the oil-producing consortium in Sudan until 2002, when, under the ambit of the Sudan Peace Act, the US government pressured the Canadian firm to sell off its shares. This was not due primarily to moral considerations, however, but rather what appears to have been economic coercion. According to its CEO at the time, Jim Buckee, 'the decision to pull-out had been made because of "US pressures" which threatened to exclude Talisman from US financial markets' (BBC News, 2003).

14 For further information about the *New York Times* advertisement, see: www.summitreports.com/sudan. Accessed 19 January 2009.

15 For further discussion of infantilism and humiliation tactics via the global financial system, see Sioh (2007).

16 It should be noted that the United Nations' position is also tactical. As Touko Piiparinen has argued, there has been a functional shift in the United Nations' strategy after Rwanda on 'how to deal with genocide'. Piiparinen notes that the UN's post-Rwandan position is that the application of 'humanitarian realism', which entails the avoidance of the term genocide, will lead to more effective forms of peace-keeping in Darfur, as the use of genocide would jeopardize the Sudanese government's co-operation with the African Union and UN operations – a factor which is vital to a successful mission. See Piiparinen (2007).

17 Conflict Securities Advisory Group, Written Testimony of Adam M. Pener, Chief Operating Officer Conflict Securities Advisory Group, Inc. Submitted to the Alaska House State Affairs Committee on 27 February 2006. Available at: www.conflictsecurities.com/about/media/penerAlaska.doc. Accessed 1 January 2008.

18 Fidelity letter of 5 October 2006. Available at: www.savedarfur.org/page/content/Fidelity_and_Berkshire_Hathaway. Accessed 14 May 2008.

19 'Buffett to face Darfur push', *Sacramento Bee*, 2 May 2007. Available at: fidelityoutofsudan.googlepages.com/pressstory. Accessed 1 April 2008.

20 'PetroChina – Ahead of the Bell', *Financial Post*, 6 November 2007. Available at: http://network.nationalpost.com/np/blogs/tradingdesk/archive/2007/11/06/petrochina-ahead-of-the-bell.aspx. Accessed 12 March 2008.

21 'Bad Council', *Chicago Maroon*, 15 April 2008. Available at: http://maroon.uchicago.edu/online_edition/article/10176. Accessed 3 May 2008.

22 'Statement by Harvard Corporation Committee on Shareholder Responsibility Regarding Stock in PetroChina Company Limited', *Harvard University Gazette*, 4 April 2005. Available at: www.hno.harvard.edu/gazette/daily/2005/04/04-sudan_release.html. Accessed 2 May 2008.

23 'Statement on Sinopec divestment', *Harvard University Gazette*, 26 March 2006. Available at: www.news.harvard.edu/gazette/daily/2006/03/23-divest.html. Accessed 2 May 2008.

24 'Bad Council'. Available at: http://maroon.uchicago.edu/online_edition/article/10176. Accessed 3 May 2008.

25 'More Sudan Stock Holdings Revealed', *The Crimson*, 8 January 2007. Available at: www.thecrimson.com/article.aspx?ref=516595. Accessed 4 May 2008.

26 University of California (UC) Sudan Divestment Task Force (2006) 'Presentation and Workshop on Targeted Investment', 27 February 2006. Available at: http://inosphere.com/sudan/home.asp. Accessed 12 January 2008.

27 CalPERS 'CalPERS Bans Investment In Nine Companies Tied To Sudan – Pension Fund Adopts Sudan Position Statement', press release, 17 May 2006. Available at: www.calpers.ca.gov/index.jsp?bc=/about/press/pr-2006/may/sudan.xml. Accessed 2 April 2008.

28 'Buffett to face Darfur push', *Sacramento Bee*, 2 May 2007. Available at: http://fidelityoutofsudan.googlepages.com/pressstory. Accessed 1 April 2008.

29 'PetroChina – Ahead of the Bell', 6 November 2007. Available at: http://network.nationalpost.com/np/blogs/tradingdesk/archive/2007/11/06/petrochina-ahead-of-the-bell.aspx. Accessed 12 March 2008.

30 For further information, see: www.amnesty.ca/instantkarma/campaign.php.

31 For further information, see: www.incr.com.

References

AFL-CIO (2007) '2007 Trends in CEO Pay'. Available at: www.aflcio.org/corporate-watch/paywatch/pay/index.cfm. Accessed 14 February 2007.

Aglietta, M. and Rebérioux, A. (2005) *Corporate Governance Adrift: A Critique of Shareholder Value*, Cheltenham: Edward Elgar.

Aitken, R. (2007) *Performing Capital: Toward a Cultural Economy of Popular and Global Finance*, New York: Palgrave.

Albo, G. (1994) '"Competitive Austerity" and the Impasse of Capitalist Employment Policy', in Panitch, L. and Miliband, R. (eds) *Socialist Register*, London: Merlin Press, pp. 144–170.

Altvater, E. (1988) 'Theoretical Deliberations on Time and Space in Post-socialist Trans-formation', *Regional Studies*, Vol. 32 (7), pp. 591–605.

Altvater, E. (2002) 'The Growth Obsession', in Panitch, L. and Leys, C. (eds) *Socialist Register*, London: Merlin Press, pp. 73–92.

American Federation of State, County and Municipal Employees (AFSCME) (1997) 'Defined Benefit versus Defined Contribution Pension Plan', *Research and Collective Bargaining of the AFSCME*, Washington, DC: AFSCME/AFL-CIO.

Armijo, L. (1999) 'Mixed Blessing: Expectations about Foreign Capital Flows and Demo-cracy in Emerging Markets', in Armijo, L. (ed.) *Financial Globalization and Demo-cracy in Emerging Markets*, New York: Palgrave Macmillan, pp. 17–50.

Arrighi, G. (1994) *The Long Twentieth Century: Money, Power, and the Origins of our Times*, London: Verso.

Augelli, E. and Murphy, C. (1988) *Quest for Supremacy and the Third World: A Gram-scian Analysis*, London: Pinter.

Babajide, W.M. (2007) 'Corporate Boards and Regulation: The Effect of the Sarbanes–Oxley Act and the Exchange Listing Requirements on Firm Value', *Journal of Corpor-ate Finance*, Vol. 13 (2–3), pp. 229–250.

Bakan, J. (2004) *The Corporation: The Pathological Pursuit of Profit and Power*, Toronto: Penguin.

Baker, D. and Fung, A. (2001) 'Collateral Damage: Do Pension Fund Investments Hurt Workers?' in Fung, A., Hebb, T. and Rogers, J. (eds) (2001) *Working Capital: The Power of Labor's Pensions*, New York: Cornell University Press, pp. 13–43.

Baran, P.A. and Sweezy, P.M. (1966) *Monopoly Capitalism: An Essay on the American Economic and Social Order*, New York: Modern Reader.

BBC News (2003) 'Talisman Pulls Out of Sudan', 10 March. Available at http://news.bbc.co.uk/2/hi/business/2835713.stm. Accessed 2 April 2008.

BBC World News (2002) 'US Pension fund Quits Asian Countries', 21 February 2002.

Available at http://news.bbc.co.uk/1/hi/business/1833674.stm. Accessed 14 November 2005.

Bebchuk, L.A. (2005) 'The Business Roundtable's Untenable Case Against Shareholder Access', Harvard Law and Economics Discussion Paper, No. 516, Cambridge, MA: Harvard Law School.

Bebchuk, L.A. (2007) 'The Myth of the Shareholder Franchise', *Virginia Law Review*, Vol. 93 (3), pp. 675–732.

Bebchuk, L.A., Grinstein, Y. and Peyer, U. (2006) 'Lucky Directors', Harvard Law and Economics Discussion paper, No. 573. Available at: http://ssrn.com/abstract=952239. Accessed 11 August 2008.

Berle, A.A. and Means, G.C. ([1932] 1991) *The Modern Corporation and Private Property*, Edison, NJ: Transaction Press.

Bieler, A., Lindberg, I. and Pillay, D. (eds) (2008) *Labour and the Challenges of Globalization: What Prospects for Transnational Solidarity*, London: Pluto.

Bivens, J.L. and Weller, C.E. (2005) 'Corporate Governance and "Job Loss" Recovery', *Review of Radical Political Economics*, Vol. 37 (3), pp. 293–301.

Blackburn, R. (2002) *Banking on Death, or, Investing in Life: The History and Future of Pensions*, London: Verso.

Blackburn, R. (2006) *Age Shock: How Finance is Failing Us*, London: Verso.

Blair, M.M. (1995) *Ownership and Control: Rethinking Corporate Governance for the Twenty-first Century*, Washington, DC: Brookings Institution.

Blair, M.M. and Stout, L. (1999) 'A Team Production Theory of Corporate Law', *Virginia Law Review*, Vol. 85, pp. 247–328.

Blasi, J.R. (1988) *Employee Ownership: Revolution or Ripoff?* Cambridge, MA: Ballinger Publishing.

Bloomberg.com (2008) 'Asia backs Sarkozy Push for Financial Market Revamp', 25 October. Accessed 21 June 2009.

Blumberg, P.I. (1975) *The Megacorporation in American Society: The Scope of Corporate Power*, Englewood Cliffs, NJ: Prentice-Hall.

Boaz, D. (2004) 'Defining an Ownership Society', The Cato Institute. Available at: www.cato.org/special/ownership_society/boaz.html. Accessed 19 January 2009.

Boddy, J. (2007) *Civilizing Women: British Crusades in Colonial Sudan*, Princeton, NJ: Princeton University Press.

Bodie, Z., Marcus, A.J. and Merton, R.C. (1988) 'Defined Benefits versus Defined Contribution Pension Plans: What are the Real Trade-offs?', in Bodie, Z., Shoven, J.B. and Wise, D.A. (eds) *Pensions in the U.S. Economy*, Chicago: University of Chicago Press, pp. 139–162.

Bogle, J.C. (2005) *The Battle for the Soul of Capitalism*, New Haven, CT: Yale University Press.

Bonefeld, W. (1995) 'Marx's Treatment of Money', in Bonefeld, W. and Holloway, J. (eds) *Global Capital, National State and the Politics of Money*, New York: St. Martin's Press.

Bourdieu, P. (1998) 'Utopia of Endless Exploitation: On the Essence of Neoliberalism', *Le Monde Diplomatique*. Available at: http://amondediplo.com/1998/12/08bourdieu. Accessed 3 March 2003.

Braithwaite, J. and Drahos, P. (2000) *Global Business Regulation*, Cambridge: Cambridge University Press.

Brancato, C.K. (1997) *Institutional Investors and Corporate Governance: Best Practices for Increasing Corporate Value*, Chicago, IL: Irwin.

Brennan, D.M. (2005) '"Fiduciary Capitalism," the "Political Model of Corporate

Governance," and the Prospect of Stakeholder Capitalism in the United States', *Review of Radical Political Economy*, Vol. 37 (1), pp. 39–62.

Brennan, D.M. (2008) 'Co-opting the Shareholder Value Movement: A Class Analytic Model of Share Repurchases', *Review of Radical Political Economy*, Vol. 40 (1), pp. 89–106.

Buchwach, A.J. (2008) 'A Commitment to Inaction: US Rhetoric and Darfur', Paper presented at the annual meeting of the MPSA Annual National Conference, Chicago, IL, 12 October. Available at: www.allacademic.com/meta/p267653_index.html. Accessed 1 December 2008.

Business Roundtable (US) (2004) 'Second Business Roundtable Comment Letter to the SEC on File No. S7–19–03 Proposed Election Contest Rules'. Available at: www.businessroundtable.org/taskforces/taskforce/document.aspx?qs=6B66BF807822B0F13DC449167F75A704791439CFC3D33B3. Accessed 13 February 2007.

BusinessWeek (2005) 'Stock Options: Old Game, New Tricks', 19 December.

BusinessWeek (2008) 'Now Wall Street Wants Your Pension, Too', 5 August.

California Public Employees' Retirement System (CalPERS) (2006) 'CalPERS Bans Investment In Nine Companies Tied To Sudan – Pension Fund Adopts Sudan Position Statement', press release. Available at: www.calpers.ca.gov/index.jsp?bc=/about/press/pr-2006/may/sudan.xml. Accessed 2 April 2008.

Calvert (Group) Online (2007) 'What Divestment Means for Investment Returns: The Impact of Constructing a "Targeted" Sudan-free Portfolio'. Available at: www.calvertgroup.com/news_newsArticle.html?article=12075&image=srinews.gif&keepleftnav=Archives. Accessed 2 January 2008.

Camejo, P. (2002) *The SRI Advantage: Why Socially Responsible Investing has Outperformed Financially*, Gabriola Island, BC: New Society Publishers.

Campbell, D. (2007) 'Geopolitics and Visuality: Sighting the Darfur Conflict', *Journal of Political Geography*, Vol. 26 (4), pp. 357–382.

Caraway, T. (2006) 'Freedom of Association: Battering Ram or Trojan Horse?' *Review of International Political Economy*, Vol. 13 (2), pp. 210–232.

Carnoy, M. and Shearer, D. (1980) *Economic Democracy: The Challenge of the 1980s*, New York: M.E. Sharpe.

Carroll, W.K. (2004) *Corporate Power in a Globalizing World*, New York: Oxford University Press.

Cato Institute (2005) 'Quick Facts', Washington, DC: Cato Institute. Available at: www.socialsecurity.org/quickfacts/index.html. Link no longer available.

Center for American Progress (2004) 'Tax Cuts Threaten Social Security', Washington, DC. Available at: www.americanprogress.org/issues/2004/02/b35099.html. Accessed 2 June 2005.

Cerny, P.G. (2008) 'Embedding Neoliberalism: The Evolution of a Hegemonic Paradigm', *The Journal of International Trade and Diplomacy*, Vol. 2 (1), pp. 1–46.

Chakrabarti, M. (2004) 'Labor and Corporate Governance: Initial Lessons from Shareholder Activism', *WorkingUSA*, Vol. 8 (1), pp. 45–69.

Chandler, A.D. (1965) *The Railroads*, New York: Harcourt Brace Janovich.

Chandler, A.D. and Tedlow, R.S. (1985) *The Coming of Managerial Capitalism: A Casebook on the History of American Economic Institutions.* Homewood, IL: Richard Irwin.

Cioffi, J.W. (2000) 'State of the Art: A Review Essay on Comparative Corporate Governance: The State of the Art and Emerging Research', *The American Journal of Comparative Law*, Vol. 48 (3), pp. 501–534.

Citizens for Tax Justice (2005a) 'Bush Tax Cuts So Far, 2001–2010', Washington, DC: Citizens for Tax Justice.

Citizens for Tax Justice (2005b) 'Year-by-Year Analysis of the Bush Tax Cuts Shows Growing Tilt to the Very Rich', Washington, DC: Citizens for Tax Justice. Available at: www.ctj.org/html/gwb0602.htm. Accessed 19 January 2009.

Clark, G.L. (1993) *Pensions and Corporate Restructuring in American Industry: A Crisis of Regulation*, Baltimore: Johns Hopkins University Press.

Clark, G.L. (2000) *Pension Fund Capitalism*, Oxford: Oxford University Press.

Clark, G.L. (2003) *European Pensions and Global Finance*, Oxford: Oxford University Press.

Clark, G.L. and Hebb, T. (2005) 'Why Should They Care? The role of Institutional Investors in the Market for Corporate Social Responsibility', *Environment and Planning A*, Vol. 37, pp. 2015–2031.

Clark, G.L. and Wójcik, D. (2007) *The Geography of Finance: Corporate Governance in the Global Marketplace*, Oxford: Oxford University Press.

Clark, G.L., Thrift, N. nd Tickell, A. (2004) 'Performing Finance: The Industry, the Media, and its Image', *Review of International Political Economy*, Vol. 11 (2), pp. 289–310.

Clark, G.L., Salo, J. and Hebb, T. (2008) 'Social and Environmental Shareholder Activism in the Public Spotlight: US Corporate Annual Meetings, Campaign Strategies, and Environmental Performance, 2001–04', *Environment and Planning A*, Vol. 40 (6), pp. 1370–1390.

Clarke, S. (1978) 'Capital, Fractions of Capital, and the State: "Neo-Marxist" Analysis of the South African State', *Capital & Class*, Vol. 5, pp. 32–77.

Clarke, T. (2000) 'Haemorrhaging Tigers: The Power of International Financial Markets and the Weaknesses of Asian Modes of Corporate Governance', *Corporate Governance: An International Review*, Vol. 8 (2), pp. 101–116.

Clawson, D. and Clawson, M.A. (1999) 'What has Happened to the US Labor Movement? Union Decline and Renewal', *Annual Review of Sociology*, Vol. 25, pp. 95–119.

Clowes, M.J. (2000) *The Money Flood: How Pension Funds Revolutionized Investing*, Hoboken, NJ: Wiley.

Competitive Enterprise Institute (2007) '"Shareholder Access" Harmful to Shareholders, Groups Say', 7 February. Available at: http://cei.org/gencon/003,05755.cfm. Accessed 15 March 2007.

Conference Board, The (2007a) 'U.S. Institutional Investors Continue to Boost Ownership of U.S. Corporations', Washington, DC: The Conference Board. Available at: www.conference-board.org/utilities/pressDetail.cfm?press_ID=3046. Accessed 2 January 2007.

The Conference Board (2007b) *The 2007 Institutional Investment Report: Trends in Institutional Investor Assets and Equity Ownership of US Corporations*, New York: The Conference Board.

CorporateCounsel.net, The (2003) 'Shareholder Access to the Ballot', 21 May. Available at: www.thecorporatecounsel.net/Audio/05_21_03_transcript.htm. Accessed 3 September 2007.

Cutler, A.C. (2003) *Private Power and Global Authority: Transnational Merchant Law in the Global Political Economy*, Cambridge: Cambridge University Press.

Cutler, A.C. (2006) 'Transnational Business Civilization: Corporations and the Privatization of Global Governance', in May, C. (ed.) *Global Corporate Power*, Boulder, CO: Lynne Rienner, pp. 199–226.

Cypher, J. (2007) 'Slicing Up at the Long Barbeque: Who Gorges, Who Serves, and Who

Gets Roasted?', *Dollars and Sense*. Available at: www.dollarsandsense.org/ archives/2007/0107cypher.html. Accessed 3 January 2008.

Da Costa, D. and McMichael, P. (2007) 'The Poverty of the Global Order', *Globalizations*, Vol. 4 (4), pp. 588–602.

Dahl, R. (1956) *A Preface to Democratic Theory*, Chicago, IL: University of Chicago Press.

Daly, M.W. (2007) *Darfur's Sorrow: A History of Destruction and Genocide*, New York: Cambridge University Press.

De Soto, H. (2000) *The Mystery of Capital: Why Capitalism Triumphs in the West and Fails Everywhere Else*, New York: Basic Books.

Dean, H. (1990) *Social Security and Social Control*, London: Routledge.

Doane, D. (2004) 'Good Intentions – Bad Outcomes? The Broken Promise of CSR Reporting', in Henriques, A. and Richardson, J. (eds) *The Triple Bottom Line: Does It All Add Up? Assessing the Sustainability of Business and CSR*, London: Earthscan, pp. 81–89.

Drucker, P.F. (1976) *The Unseen Revolution: How Pension Fund Socialism Came to America*, New York: Harper & Row.

Drucker, P.F. (1993) *Post-Capitalist Society*, Toronto: HarperCollins.

Duménil, G. and Lévy D. (2004) 'Neoliberal Income Trends: Wealth, Class and Ownership in the USA', *New Left Review*, Vol. 30, pp. 105–133.

Edwards, N. (2002) 'Pragmatism Rules in Asia's Ethical Investing Debate'. Association for Sustainable and Responsible Investment in Asia. Available at: www.asria.org/pro/ news&events/ethical_investing_debate.htm. Accessed 19 July 2007.

Elkington, J. (2004) 'Enter the Triple Bottom Line', in Henriques, A. and Richardson, J. (eds) *The Triple Bottom Line: Does it All Add Up? Assessing the Sustainability of Business and CSR*, London: Earthscan, pp. 1–16.

Elliot, L.A. and Schroth. R. J. (2002) *How Companies Lie: Why Enron is Just the Tip of the Iceberg*, New York: Crown Business.

Engelen, E. (2002) 'Corporate Governance, Property and Democracy: A Conceptual Critique of Shareholder Ideology', *Economy & Society*, Vol. 31 (3), pp. 391–413.

Entine, J. (2005) 'The Politicization of Public Investment', in J. Entine (ed.) *Pension Fund Politics: The Dangers of Socially Responsible Investing*, Washington, DC: AEI Press, pp. 1–12.

Erturk, I., Froud, J., Johal, S., Leaver, A. and Williams, K. (eds) (2008) *Financialization at Work: Key Texts and Commentary*, London: Routledge.

Erturk, I., Froud, J., Johal, S. and Williams, K. (2004) 'Corporate Governance and Disappointment', *Review of International Political Economy*, Vol. 11 (4), pp. 677–713.

Escobar, A. (1995) *Encountering Development: The Making and Unmaking of the Third World*, Princeton, NJ: Princeton University Press.

Fairfax, L.M. (2005) 'Sarbanes–Oxley, Corporate Federalism, and the Declining Significance of Federal Reforms on State Director Independence Standards', *Ohio Northern University Law Review*, Vol. 31, pp. 381–415.

Fama, E. (1970) 'Efficient Capital Markets: A Review of Theory and Empirical Work', *Journal of Finance*, Vol. 25 (2), pp. 383–417.

Fama, E. (1980) 'Agency problems and the theory of the firm', *Journal of Political Economy*, Vol. 88 (2), pp. 288–307.

Federal Register (1997) 'Part IV: The President – Executive Order 13067 – Blocking Sudanese Government Property and Prohibiting Transactions With Sudan', *Federal Register*, Vol. 62 (214), pp. 59987–59990. Available at: www.treas.gov/offices/ enforcement/ofac/legal/eo/13067.pdf. Accessed 15 March 2008.

Federal Reserve Bank of San Francisco (2003) 'Underfunding of Private Pension Plans', *FRBSF Economic Letter*, San Francisco, CA: Federal Reserve Bank of San Francisco.

Federal Reserve Board, The (2002) 'The Challenge for Corporate Governance Posed by Financial Innovation', Remarks by Governor Susan S. Bies at the Carnegie Endowment for International Peace, Washington, DC. Available at: www.federalreserve.gov/boarddocs/speeches/2002/20021001/default.htm. Accessed 23 March 2007.

Feldstein, M. (ed.) (1998) *Privatizing Social Security*, Chicago, IL: University of Chicago Press.

Financial Times (2003) 'SEC under Pressure on Board Nominations', 25 March.

Financial Times (2007) 'Shackles Severed: How the Developing World is Striving to Free Itself of Debt', 9 February.

Fine, B. (1989) *Marx's Capital*, 3rd edition, London: Macmillan.

Fine, B. (2002) *World of Consumption: The Material and Cultural Revisited*, London: Routledge.

Fine, B., Lapavistas, C. and Pincus, J. (eds) (2001) *Development Policy in the 21st Century: Beyond the Post-Washington Consensus*, London: Routledge.

Fligstein, N. (1990) *The Transformation of Corporate Control*, Cambridge, MA: Harvard University Press.

Fligstein, N. and Shin, T. (2005) *Shareholder Value and Changes in American Industries, 1984–2000*, Berkeley, CA: University of California, Department of Sociology.

Fogel, E.M. and Geier, A.M. (2007) 'Strangers in the House: Rethinking Sarbanes–Oxley and the Independent Board of Directors', *Delaware Journal of Corporate Law*, Vol. 32 (1), pp. 33–72.

Fox Business (2009) 'Is the PBGC the next in line to ask for a bail-out?' 15 January.

Friedman, A.R. and Freeman-Bosworth, L. (2001) 'The PSLRA and Obtaining Early Proof of Claims Information in Securities Class Actions', *Securities Regulation Law Journal*, Vol. 29 (3), pp. 262–274.

Friedman, M. (1962) *Capitalism and Freedom*, Chicago, IL: University of Chicago Press.

Friedman, M. (1970) 'The Social Responsibility of Business is to Increase Its Profits', *New York Times Magazine*, 13 September 1970.

Friedman, M. (2002) *Capitalism and Freedom*, Chicago, IL: University of Chicago Press.

Froud, J., Haslam, C., Johal, S. and Williams, K. (2000) 'Shareholder Value and Financialization: Consultancy Promises, Management Moves', *Economy and Society*, Vol. 29 (1), pp. 80–110.

Fung, A. and Wright, E.O. (2003) 'Thinking about Empowered Participatory Governance', in Fung, A. and Wright, E.O. (eds) *Deepening Democracy: Institutional Innovations in Empowered Participatory Governance*, London: Verso, pp. 3–44.

Fung, A., Hebb, T. and Rogers, J. (eds) (2001) *Working Capital: The Power of Labor's Pensions*, New York: Cornell University Press.

Geczy, C.C., Stambaugh, R.F. and Levin, D. (2003) [updated 2005] 'Investing in Socially Responsible Mutual Funds', Philadelphia, PA: Wharton Business School. Available at: http://papers.ssrn.com/sol3/papers.cfm?abstract_id=416380#PaperDownload. Accessed 2 March 2008.

Gereffi, G. and Korzeniewicz, M. (eds) (1993) *Commodity Chains and Global Capitalism*, New York: Praeger.

Ghilarducci, T. (1992) *Labor's Capital: The Economics and Politics of Private Pensions*, Cambridge, MA: MIT Press.

Ghilarducci, T. (2000) 'ERISA at 25: Has the Law Kept Pace with the Evolving Pension and Investment World?' Testimony of Teresa Ghilarducci to the Subcommittee on

Employer–Employee Relations, Committee on Education and the Workforce US House of Representatives, Washington, DC, pp. 1–12.

Ghilarducci, T. (2004) 'Pension Reform and the Future of Workers' Retirement', Notre Dame, IN: University of Notre Dame, Department of Economics and Policy Studies.

Ghilarducci, T. and Sun. W. (2006) 'How Defined Contribution Plans and 401(k)s Affect Employer Pension Costs: 1981–1998', *Journal of Pension Economics and Finance*, Vol. 5 (2), pp. 175–196.

Gill, S. (1995) 'Globalisation, Market Civilisation, and Disciplinary Neoliberalism', *Millennium*, Vol. 23 (3), pp. 399–423.

Glasbeek, H. (2002) *Wealth By Stealth: Corporate Crime, Corporate Law and the Perversion of Democracy*, Toronto: Between the Lines.

Glassman, J.K. (2004) 'Risking a Serious Mistake: The Role of FASB and the Role of Congress in Stock Options Accounting Policy', Testimony – Senate Committee on Governmental Affairs, Washington, DC: American Enterprise Institute.

de Goede, M. (2004) 'Repoliticizing Financial Risk', *Economy and Society*, Vol. 33 (2), pp. 197–217.

Goldstein, D. (2000) 'Hostile Takeover as Corporate Governance? Evidence from the 1980s', *Review of Political Economy*, Vol. 12 (4), pp. 381–402.

Gowan, P. (1999) *The Global Gamble: Washington's Faustian Bid for World Dominance*, London: Verso.

Graebner, W. (1980) *A History of Retirement: The Meaning and Function of an American Institution, 1885–1978*, New Haven, CT: Yale University Press.

Gramsci, A. (1992) *Selections from the Prison Notebooks*, edited by Q. Hoare and G.N. Smith, New York: International Publishers.

Graves, S.B., Waddock, S. and Rehbein, K. (2001) 'Face and Fashion in Shareholder Activism: The Landscape of Shareholder Resolutions, 1988–1998', *Business & Society Review*, Vol. 106 (4), pp. 293–314.

Greider, W. (2005a) 'The New Colossus', *The Nation* (28 February). Available at: www.thenation.com/doc/20050228/greider. Accessed 3 March 2005.

Greider, W. (2005b) 'Riding into the Sunset', *The Nation*, 27 June. Available at: www.thenation.com/doc/20050627/greider. Accessed 3 March 2005.

Guardian (2005) 'Bush Signs Bill to Curb Class-Action Suits', 19 February.

Guardian (2008) 'General Motors to axe 70 per cent of American workforce', 13 February.

Gul, F. and Tsui, J. (2004) 'Introduction and Overview', in Gul, F. and Tsui, J. (eds) *The Governance of East Asian Corporations*, Basingstoke: Palgrave Macmillan, pp. 1–26.

Hansmann, H. and Kraakman, R. (2001) 'The End of History for Corporate Law', *Georgetown Law Journal*, Vol. 89, pp. 439–468.

Harmes, A. (1998) 'Institutional Investors and the Reproduction of Neoliberalism', *Review of International Political Economy*, Vol. 5 (1), pp. 92–121.

Harmes, A. (2001) *Unseen Power: How Mutual Funds Threaten the Political and Economic Wealth of Nations*, Toronto: Stoddart.

Harvey, D. (1989) *The Urban Experience*, Baltimore: Johns Hopkins Press.

Harvey, D. (1999) *The Limits to Capital*, London: Verso.

Harvey, D. (2000) *Spaces of Hope, California Studies in Critical Human Geography*, Berkeley, CA: University of California Press.

Harvey, D. (2001) *Spaces of Capital: Towards a Critical Geography*, New York: Routledge.

Harvey, D. (2003) 'The "New" Imperialism', in Panitch, L. and Leys, C. (eds) *Socialist Register 2004: The New Imperial Challenge*, London: Merlin Press, pp. 63–87.

Harvey, D. (2005) *The New Imperialism*, Oxford: Oxford University Press.

Harvey, D. (2007) *A Brief History of Neoliberalism*, Oxford: Oxford University Press.

Hawley, J.P. and Williams, A.T. (2000) *The Rise of Fiduciary Capitalism: How Institutional Investors Can Make Corporate America More Democratic*, Philadelphia, PA: University of Pennsylvania Press.

Hawley, J.P. and Williams, A.T. (2002) 'Universal Owners and SRI', in Camejo, P. (ed.) *The SRI Advantage: Why Socially Responsible Investing has Outperformed Financially*, Gabriola Island, BC: New Society Publishers, pp. 151–172.

Hebb, T. (2001) 'Introduction: The Challenge of Labor's Capital Strategy', in Fung, A., Hebb, T. and Rogers, J. (eds) *Working Capital: The Power of Labor's Pensions*, Ithaca, NY: Cornell University Press, pp. 1–12.

Herman, E.S. (1981) *Corporate Control, Corporate Power*, Cambridge: Cambridge University Press.

Hilferding, R. ([1910] 1981) *Financial Capital: A Study of the Latest Phase of Capitalist Development*, London: Routledge & Kegan Paul.

Hirsch, J. (1986) *Das neue Gesicht des Kapitalismus: Vom Fordismus zum Post-Fordismus*, Berlin: VSA-Verlag.

Hirsch, J. (1991) 'The State Apparatus and Social Reproduction: Elements of a Theory of the Bourgeois State', in Holloway, J. and Picciottio, S. (eds) *State and Capital: A Marxist Debate*, London: Edward Arnold, pp. 57–107.

Hirsch, J. (1995) *Der nationale Wettbewerbsstaat. Staat, Demokratie und Politik im globalen Kapitalismus*, Berlin: Edition ID-Archiv.

Holloway, J. (1995) 'Capital and the National State', in Bonefeld, W. and Holloway, J. (eds) *Global Capital, National State and the Politics of Money*, New York: St. Martin's Press, pp. 116–140.

Holloway, J. and Picciotto, S. (1991) 'Capital, Crisis and the State', in Clarke, S. (ed.) *The State Debate*, New York: St. Martin's Press, pp. 109–141.

Hu, J. and Noe, T.H. (1997) 'The Insider Trading Debate', *Federal Reserve Bank of Atlanta Economic Review*, Vol. 4, pp. 34–45.

Hutchinson, J. (2001), 'Crisis and Change in the Philippines', in Rodan, G., Hewison, K. and Robinson, R. (eds) *The Political Economy of South-East Asia: Conflicts, Crises, and Change*, Melbourne: Oxford University Press, pp. 42–70.

Hymer, S. (1970) 'The Efficiency (Contradictions) of Multinational Corporations', *American Economic Review*, Vol. 60 (2), pp. 441–448.

Ingham, G. (2000) 'Class Inequality and the Social Production of Money', in Crompton, R., Devine, F., Savage, M. and Scott, J. (eds) *Renewing Class Analysis*, Oxford: Blackwell Publishers, pp. 66–86.

Institute for Policy Studies and United for a Fair Economy (2007) 'Executive Excess 2007: The Staggering Social Cost of U.S. Business Leadership', 14th Annual CEO Compensation Survey, Washington, DC: Institute for Policy Studies.

Interfaith Centre on Corporate Responsibility (ICCR) (2007) 'Due Diligence – Access to Medicines as Fiduciary Duty', *The Corporate Examiner*, Vol. 35 (8), pp. 4–8.

International Finance Corporation (2006) 'Emerging Markets Heading for Banner Year in 2006: IFC Notes Progress, Development Challenges Ahead', *IFC News*. Available at: www.ifc.org/ifcext/media.nsf/Content/Emerging_Mkts_2006. Accessed 5 January 2007.

International Herald Tribune (2007a) 'Between the Lines of Britain's class warfare', 24 April.

International Herald Tribune (2007b) 'SEC withdraws list linking companies to terrorism', 22 July.

Ireland, Paddy (1996) 'Corporate Governance, Stakeholding, and the Company: Towards a Less Degenerate Capitalism', *Journal of Law and Society*, Vol. 23 (3), pp. 287–320.

Ireland, Paddy (2001) 'Defending the Rentier: Corporate Theory and the Reprivatization of the Public Company', in Parkinson, J.E., Gamble, A. and Kelly, G. (eds) *The Political Economy of the Company*, Oxford: Hart Publishing, pp. 141–173.

Ireland, Paddy (2007) 'Property and Contract in Contemporary Corporate Theory', Law School, University of Kent, UK. Mimeo.

James, P. (2004) 'Pressure Sudan to Halt Oppression in Darfur', Executive Memorandum No. 943, Washington, DC: Heritage Foundation. Available at: www.heritage.org/ research/africa/em943.cfm. Accessed 24 March 2007.

Jensen, M. (2000) *A Theory of the Firm: Governance, Residual Claims, and Organizational Forms*, Cambridge, MA: Harvard University Press.

Jessop, B. (1991) 'Accumulation Strategies, State Forms and Hegemonic Projects', in Clarke, S. (ed.) *The State Debate*, New York: St. Martin's Press, pp. 183–203.

Kawamura, M. (2002) 'How Socially Responsible Investment (SRI) Could Redefine Corporate Excellence in the 21st Century', *NLI Research Institute*, Vol. 160, pp. 12–23.

Kinder, P.D. and Domini, A.L. (1997) 'Social Screening: Paradigms Old and New', *Journal of Investing*, Vol. 6 (4), pp. 12–20.

Kindleberger, C. (2001) *Manias, Panics and Crashes*, 4th edition, London: Palgrave.

Klein, N. (2000) *No Logo: Taking Aim at the Brand Bullies*, Toronto: Knopf.

Klein, N. (2007) *Shock Doctrine: The Rise of Disaster Capitalism*, New York: Metropolitan Books.

Kolko, G. (1964) *Wealth and Power in America: An Analysis of Social Class and Income Distribution*, New York: Frederick A. Praeger.

Korten, D. (2001) *When Corporations Rule the World*, Bloomfield, CT: Kumarian Press.

Kotz, D.M. (1978) *Bank Control of Large Corporations in the United States*, Berkley, CA: University of California Press.

Krippner, G.R. (2005) 'The Financialization of the American Economy', *Socio-Economic Review*, Vol. 3, pp. 173–208.

Krugman, P. (2005) 'Confusions about Social Security', *The Economists' Voice*, Vol. 2 (1), pp. 1–9.

Lander, G. (2004) *What is the Sarbanes–Oxley?*, New York: McGraw-Hill.

Langley, P. (2008) *The Everyday Life of Global Finance: Saving and Borrowing in Anglo-America*, Oxford: Oxford University Press.

Larner, R.J. (1970) *Management Control of the Large Corporation*, New York: Dunellen.

Lav, I.J. (2003) 'Federal Policies Contribute to the Severity of State Fiscal Crisis', Washington, DC: Centre on Budget and Policy Priorities. Available at: www.house.gov/ budget_democrats/hearings/dem_states_hrg/lav.pdf. Accessed 4 June 2005.

Lavelle, K. (2004) *The Politics of Equity Financing in Emerging Markets*, New York: Oxford University Press.

Lazonick, W. and O'Sullivan, M. (2000) 'Maximizing Shareholder Value: A New Ideology for Corporate Governance', *Economy & Society*, Vol. 29 (1), pp. 1–35.

Lefebvre, H. (1991) *The Production of Space*, Oxford: Blackwell.

Lefebvre, H. (2005) *Everyday Life in the Modern World*, New Brunswick, NJ: Transaction Publishers.

Leys, C. (1996) *The Rise and Fall of Development Theory*, Bloomington, IN: Indiana University Press.

Library of Congress, The (2005) *Darfur Accountability Act of 2005* (Introduced in

Senate), Washington, DC: Library of Congress. Available at: http://thomas.loc.gov/cgi-bin/query/z?c109:S.495. Accessed 1 January 2008.

Locke, J. (1690) *Second Treatise on Civil Government*. Available at: www.constitution. org/jl/2ndtreat.html. Accessed 12 February 2006.

Longnecker, B. (2004) 'Sarbanes–Oxley: Financial Friend or Foe?' *The Banking Law Journal*, Vol. 121 (7), pp. 606–612.

Los Angeles Times (2008) 'Renewing America's "contract with the middle class"', 1 September.

Lowenstein, R. (2005) 'The End of Pensions', *Wall Street Journal*, 30 October 2005. Available at: www.globalaging.org/pension/us/private/2005/end.htm. Accessed 20 October 2005.

Luhmann, N. (1993) *Risk: A Sociological Theory*, New York: Aldine de Gruyter.

Lundberg, F. (1937) *America's Sixty Families*, New York: Vanguard Press.

MacAvoy, P.W. and Millstein, I.M. (2004) *The Recurrent Crisis in Corporate Governance*, Stanford, CA: Stanford University Press.

MacEwen, A. (2008) 'The Greed Fallacy', *Dollars & Sense*, Vol. 277. Available at: www. dollarsandsense.org/archives/2008/0908macewan2.html. Accessed 1 December 2008.

McKinsey & Company (2002a) *Global Investor Opinion Survey on Corporate Governance*, New York: McKinsey & Company.

McKinsey & Company (2002b) *Director Opinion Survey on Corporate Governance*, New York: McKinsey & Company.

McKinsey & Company (2006) *Mapping the Global Capital Market: Second Annual Report*, New York: McKinsey & Company.

Magdoff, F. (2006) 'The Explosion of Debt and Speculation', *Monthly Review*, November, Vol. 58 (1), pp. 1–23.

Mamdani, M. (2007) 'The Politics of Naming: Genocide, Civil War, Insurgency', *London Review of Books*. Available at: www.lrb.co.uk/v29/n05/mamd01_.html. Accessed 1 April 2007.

Manning, R.D. (2000) *Credit Card Nation: The Consequences of America's Addiction to Credit*, New York: Basic Books.

Marcuse, H. (1964) *One Dimensional Man: Studies in the Ideology of Advanced Industrial Society*, Boston: Beacon Press.

Markowitz, L. (2008) 'Can Strategic Investing Transform the Corporation?', *Critical Sociology*, Vol. 34 (5), pp. 681–707.

Martin, R. (2002) *Financialization of Daily Life*, Philadelpia, PA: Temple University Press.

Marx, K. (1976) *Capital, Volume 1*, London: Penguin.

Marx, K. (1991) *Capital, Volume 3*, London: Penguin.

May, C. (ed.) (2006) *Global Corporate Power*, Boulder, CO: Lynne Rienner Publishers.

Mazzarella, W. (2003) *Shoveling Smoke: Advertising and Globalization in Contemporary India*, Durham, NC: Duke University Press.

Mekay, E. (2006) 'World Bank's New Social Standards Slippery to Enforce'. Available at: www.choike.org/nuevo_eng/informes/4003.html. Accessed 3 March 2006.

Mills, C.W. (1964) 'The Social Life of a Modern Community', in Horowitz, I. (ed.) *Power, Politics, and People: The Collected Writings of C. Wright Mills*. New York: Oxford University Press, pp. 568–576.

Minns, R. (2001) *The Cold War: Stock Markets Versus Pensions*, London: Verso.

Mishel, L., Bernstein, J. and Boushey, H. (2003) *The State of Working America, 2002/2003*, Ithaca, NY: Cornell University Press.

Mishel, L., Bernstein, J. and Allegretto, S. (2007) *The State of Working America, 2006/2007*, Ithaca, NY: Cornell University Press.

Mitchell, L.E. (2007) *The Speculation Economy: How Finance Triumphed over Industry*, San Francisco, CA: Berrett–Koehler Publishers.

Mizruchi, M.S. (1996) 'What Do Interlocks Do? An Analysis, Critique, and Assessment of Research on Interlocking Directorates', *Annual Review of Sociology*, Vol. 22, pp. 271–298.

Mizruchi, M.S. (2004) 'Berle and Means Revisited: The Governance and Power of Large U.S. Corporations', *Theory and Society*, Vol. 33, pp. 579–617.

Monks, R.A.G. (2002) 'Introduction', in Camejo, P. (ed.) *The SRI Advantage: Why Socially Responsible Investing has Outperformed Financially*, Gabriola Island, BC: New Society Publishers, pp. xiii–xix.

Monks, R.A.G. and Minow, N. (2001) *Corporate Governance*, 2nd edition, Oxford: Blackwell.

Montgomerie, J. (2008) 'Bridging the Critical Divide: Global Finance, Financialization and Contemporary Capitalism', *Contemporary Politics*, Vol. 14 (3), pp. 233–252.

Moody, K. (1988) *An Injury to All: The Decline of American Unionism*, London: Verso.

Moody, K. (1997) *Workers in a Lean World*, Verso: London.

Moody, K. (2007) *US Labor in Trouble and Transition: The Failure of Reform from Above, the Promise of Renewal from Below*, London: Verso.

Munck, R. (2005) 'Neoliberalism and Politics, and the Politics of Neoliberalism', in Saad-Filho, A. and Johnston, D. (eds) *Neoliberalism: A Critical Reader*, London: Pluto, pp. 60–69.

Munnell, A.H. and Sunden, A. (2005) 'Social Investing: Pension Plans Should Just Say "No"' in Entine, J. (ed.) *Pension Fund Politics: The Dangers of Socially Responsible Investing*, Washington, DC: The AEI Press.

New York Times (2006a) 'Universal 401(k) Accounts Would Bring the Poor into the Ownership Society', 28 December.

New York Times (2006b) 'War in Sudan? Not Where the Oil Wealth Flows', 24 October.

O'Barr, W.M. and Conley, J.M. (1992) *Fortune and Folly: The Wealth and Power of Institutional Investing*, New York: McGraw-Hill.

O'Connor, M. (2001) 'Labor's Role in the Shareholder Revolution', in Archon, F., Hebb, T. and Rogers, J. (eds) *Working Capital: The Power of Labor's Pensions*, New York: Cornell University Press, pp. 67–92.

OECD (2004) *Principles of Good Corporate Governance*, Paris: OECD. Available at: www.oecd.org/document/49/0,3343,en_2649_34813_31530865_1_1_1_1,00.htm. Accessed 11 April 2008.

OECD (2005) *Pension Markets in Focus*, Vol. 1. Available at: www.oecd.org/datao-ecd/46/2/35063476.pdf. Accessed 11 January 2006.

OECD (2007) *Pension Market in Focus*, Vol. 4, Paris: OECD.

OneWorld.net (2005) 'US: Pay Gap Widens between CEOs and Workers', 12 April.

Online NewsHour (2003) 'Ford Announces Layoffs, Closings', 23 January.

O'Sullivan, M. (2000) *Contests for Corporate Control*, Oxford: Oxford University Press.

O'Sullivan, M. (2003) 'The Political Economy of Comparative Corporate Governance', *Review of International Political Economy*, Vol. 10 (1), pp. 23–72.

Overbeek, H., Van Apeldoorn, B. and Nölke, A. (eds) (2007) *The Transnational Politics of Corporate Governance Regulation*, New York: Routledge, pp. xxi–259.

Palan, R. (2006) *The Offshore World: Sovereign Markets, Virtual Places, and Nomad Millionaires*, Ithaca, NY: Cornell University Press.

Palmer, T. (2004) *Great Thinkers on How an Ownership Society Fosters Responsibility, Liberty, Prosperity*, Washington, DC: Cato Institute.

Panitch, L. (1994) 'Globalisation and the State', in Miliband, R. and Panitch, L. (eds) *Socialist Register 1994*, London: Merlin Press, pp. 60–93.

Panitch, L. and Gindin, S. (1995) 'Superintending Global Capital', *New Left Review*, Vol. 35, pp. 101–123.

Panitch, L. and Gindin, S. (2004) *Global Capitalism and American Empire*, London: Merlin Press.

Panitch, L. and Konings, M. (2008) *American Empire and the Political Economy of Global Finance*, Houndsmills: Palgrave.

Parkinson, J.E., Gamble, A. and Kelly, G. (eds) (2001) *The Political Economy of the Company*, Oxford: Hart Publishing.

Patomäki, H. (2001) *Democratising Globalisation: The Leverage of the Tobin Tax*, London: Zed Books.

Pava, M.L. and Krausz, J. (1995) *Corporate Responsibility and Financial Performance: The Paradox of Social Cost*, Westport, CT: Greenwood.

PBS Frontline (2002) 'Bigger than Enron: Why the Largest Business Scandal in America is Just the Tip of the Iceberg – and Why Investors Should Care'. Available at: www.pbs.org/wgbh/pages/frontline/shows/regulation/etc/credits.html. Accessed 6 December 2003.

PBS Frontline (2006) 'Can You Afford to Retire?' Available at: www.pbs.org/wgbh/pages/frontline/retirement. Accessed 24 January 2007.

Pender, J. (2001) '"From 'Structural Adjustment" to "Comprehensive Development Framework": Conditionality Transformed?', *Third World Quarterly*, Vol. 22 (3), pp. 397–411.

Pensions & Investments (2007a) 'The Looming Proxy Season', 10 December.

Pensions & Investments (2007b) 'Union Funds Champs of Proxy Season', 5 February.

Pensions & Investments (2007c) 'CalPERS' Emerging Markets Policy Hit Board Seeks Review of System's Litmus Tests for Human Rights and Investor Protections', 5 March.

Pensions & Investments (2008a) 'OECD: $4 Trillion Lost by Pension Funds', 13 November.

Pensions & Investments (2008b) 'CII Urges SEC to Reject Proxy Rules', 22 February.

Pensions & Investments (2008c) 'Fed Thrift Topples CalPERS as Nation's Largest Plan', 4 February.

Pensions & Investments (2009) 'Top 1,000 Funds Drop Close to $1 Trillion', 26 January.

Peters, A. (2004) 'Sarbanes–Oxley Act of 2002, Congress' Response to Corporate Scandals: Will the New Rules Guarantee "Good" Governance and Avoid Future Scandals?' *Nova Law Review*, Vol. 28 (2), pp. 283–92.

Phillips, J. (2004) 'Pressure Sudan to Halt Oppression in Darfur', 4 October Executive Memorandum No. 943. Washington, DC: Heritage Foundation. Available at: www.heritage.org/Research/Africa/em943.cfm. Accessed 21 January 2005.

Piiparinen, T. (2006) 'Reconsidering the Silence Over the Ultimate Crime: A Functional Shift in Crisis Management from the Rwandan Genocide in Darfur', *Journal of Genocide Research*, Vol. 9 (1), pp. 71–91.

Piven, F.F. (2004) *The War at Home: The Domestic Costs of Bush's Militarism*, New York: New Press.

Piven, F.F. and Cloward, R.A. (1997) *The Breaking of the American Social Compact*, New York: The New Press.

Pollin, R. (2003) *Contours of Descent: U.S. Economic Fractures and the Landscape of Global Austerity*, London: Verso.

President's Commission to Strengthen Social Security, The (2001) 'Strengthening Social Security and Creating Personal Wealth for all Americans', Report of the President's Commission, April 2004. Available at: www.csss.gov/reports/Final_report.pdf. Accessed 5 March 2002.

Prunier, G. (2005) *Darfur*, Ithaca, NY: Cornell University Press.

Ramirez, S.A. (2000) 'Depoliticizing Financial Regulation', *William & Mary Law Review*, Vol. 41 (2). Available at: http://washburnlaw.edu/faculty/ramirez-s-fulltext/2000–41wm503.htm. Accessed 2 March 2005.

Rapoport, Michael (2003) Dow Jones Corporate Governance Newsletter, 20 February.

Reed, D. (2004) 'Corporate Governance Reforms in Developing Countries', in Reed, D. and Mukherjee, S. (eds) *Corporate Governance, Economic Reforms and Development: The Indian Experience*, New Delhi: Oxford University Press, pp. 15–27.

Reed D. and Mukherjee S. (eds) (2004) *Corporate Governance, Economic Reforms and Development: The Indian Experience*, New Delhi: Oxford University Press.

Reeves, S. (2002) 'Oil Development in Sudan', *Review of African Political Economy*, Vol. 29 (91), pp. 167–169.

Reich, R. (2007) *Supercapitalism: The Transformation of Business, Democracy, and Everyday Life*, New York: Alfred A. Knopf.

Renner, K. (1949) *The Institutions of Private Law and their Social Functions*, London: Routledge & Kegan Paul.

Ribstein, L.E. (2002) 'Market vs. Regulatory Responses to Corporate Fraud: A Critique of the Sarbanes–Oxley Act of 2002', *Illinois Law and Economic Working Papers Series*, Champaign, IL: University of Illinois College of Law, pp. 1–74.

Richardson, B.J. (2008) *Socially Responsible Investment Law: Regulating the Unseen Polluters*, New York: Oxford University Press.

Rifkin, J. and Barber, R. (1978) *The North Will Rise Again: Pensions, Politics and Power in the 1980s*, Boston, MA: Beacon Press.

Rist, G. (2002) *The History of Development: From Western Origins to Global Faith*, London: Zed Books.

Rochester, A. (1936) *Rulers of America a Study of Finance Capital*, New York: International Publishers.

Ruggie (2004) 'Reconstituting the Global Public Domain – Issues, Actors, and Practices', *European Journal of International Relations*, Vol. 10 (4), pp. 499–531.

Rupert, M. (1997) 'Globalization and the Reconstruction of Common Sense in the US', in Gill, S. and Mittelman, J. (eds) *Innovation and Transformation in International Studies*, Cambridge: Cambridge University Press, pp. 41–59.

Saad-Filho, A. and Johnston, D. (eds) (2005) *Neoliberalism: A Critical Reader*, London: Pluto Press.

Said, E. (1979) *Orientalism*, New York: Vintage Books.

Sale, H.A. (1998) 'Heightened Pleading and Discovery Stays: An Analysis of the Effect of the PSLRA's Internal Standard of '33 and '34 Act Claims', *Washington University Law Quarterly*, Vol. 76, pp. 537–595.

SAPRI Report, The (2004) *Structural Adjustment – The Policy Roots of Economic Crisis, Poverty and Inequality*, New York: Zed Books.

Save Shareholder Rights (2007) 'Social Investment Forum Talking Points on SEC Proposals'. Available at: www.saveshareholderrights.org/issues.cfm. Accessed 3 October 2007.

Scheuth, S.J. (2002) 'Socially Responsible Investing in the United States', in Camejo, P. (ed.) *The SRI Advantage: Why Socially Responsible Investing has Outperformed Financially,* Gabriola Island, BC: New Society Publishers, pp. 115–122.

Schwab, S.J. and Thomas, R.S. (1998) 'Realigning Corporate Governance: Shareholder Activism by Labor Unions', *Michigan Law Review*, Vol. 96, pp. 1018–1094.

Scott, J. (1997) *Corporate Business and Capitalist Classes*, Oxford: Oxford University Press.

Securities and Exchange Commission (SEC) (2002) 'Request for Rulemaking to Amend Rule 14a-8(i) to Allow Shareholder Proposals to Elect Directors', New York: SEC. Available at: www.sec.gov/rules/petitions/petn4–461.htm. Accessed 2 February 2008.

Securities and Exchange Commission (SEC) (2007a) 'Shareholder Proposals Relating to the Election of Directors'. Available at: www.sec.gov/rules/final/finalarchive/finalarchive2007.shtml. Accessed 20 May 2008.

Securities and Exchange Commission (SEC) (2007b) 'Speech by SEC Chairman: Opening Remarks at the SEC Open Meeting'. Available at: www.sec.gov/news/speech/2007/spch072507cc.htm. Accessed 4 March 2007.

Shamir, R. (2008) 'The Age of Responsiblization: A Market-Embedded Morality', *Economy and Society*, Vol. 37 (1), pp. 1–19.

Shiller, R. (2006) *Irrational Exuberance*, 2nd edition, New York: Doubleday.

Shleifer, A. and Vishny, R.W. (1997) 'A Survey of Corporate Governance', *The Journal of Finance*, Vol. 52 (2), pp. 737–783.

Sidahmed, A.S. and Sidahmed, A. (2005) *Sudan*, London: Routledge.

Sioh, M.K.L. (2007) 'Pricing Race, Circulating Anxieties, and the Fate of Malaya's Currency Reserves at Independence', *Cultural Critique*, Vol. 65, pp. 115–139.

Sklair, L. (2001) *The Transnational Capitalist Class*, Oxford: Blackwell.

Sklar, H. (2005) 'Is this your Ownership Society?', *Tribune News Service*. Available at: www.commondreams.org/views05/0225–28.htm. Accessed 19 January 2009.

Skyes, A. (2000) *Capitalism for Tomorrow: Reuniting Ownership and Control*, Oxford: Capstone Publishing.

Smis, S. and Oyatambwe, W. (2002) 'Complex Political Emergencies, the International Community and the Congo Conflict', *Review of African Political Economy*, Vol. 29 (93/94), pp. 411–430.

Smith, A. ([1776] 1904) *An Inquiry into the Nature and Causes of the Wealth of Nations*, London: Methuen & Co.

Social Investment Forum (2006) '2005 Report on Socially Responsible Investment Trends in the United States – 10 year review', Washington, DC: Social Investment Forum.

Social Investment Forum (2007a) '2007 Report on Socially Responsible Investing Trends in the United States', Washington, DC: Social Investment Forum.

Social Investment Forum (2007b) 'Socially Responsible Investors Applaud SEC Decision not to Curtail Shareholder Resolutions, But Strongly Oppose Curbs on Director Nomination Process', 28 November.

SocialFunds.com (2003) 'The Key to Director Independence: Equal Access to Corporate Board Elections'. Available at: www.socialfunds.com/news/article.cgi/1079.html. Accessed 3 September 2007.

Soederberg, S. (2004) *The Politics of the New International Financial Architecture: Reimposing Neoliberal Domination on the Global South*, London: Zed Books.

Soederberg, S. (2006) *Global Governance in Question: Empire, Class, and the New Common Sense in Managing Globalization*, London: Pluto.

Soederberg, S., Menz, G. and Cerny, P.G. (eds) (2005) *Internalizing Globalization: The Rise of Neoliberalism and the Erosion of National Models of Capitalism*, London: Palgrave.

Stiglitz, J. (2002) *Globalization and Its Discontents*, New York: W.W. Norton & Company.

Stiglitz, J. (2006) *Making Globalization Work*, New York: Norton.

Stopford, J., Strange, S. and Henley, J.S. (1991) *Rival States, Rival Firms: Competition for World Market Shares*, Cambridge: Cambridge University Press.

Strahota, R.D. (2002) 'The Effects of the Sarbanes–Oxley Act on Directors' Responsibilities and Liabilities', Prepared for Third OECD South-Eastern Europe Corporate Governance Roundtable in Zagreb, Croatia.

Sudan Divestment Task Force (SDTF) (2007) 'Arguments for the Efficacy of Targeted Divestment from Sudan', Washington, DC: Sudan Divestment Task Force.

Sudan Divestment Task Force (SDTF) (2008a) 'Sudan Company Profiles', Washington, DC: SDTF. Available at: www.sudandivestment.org/docs/sudan_company_profiles. pdf. Accessed 14 March 2008.

Sudan Divestment Task Force (SDTF) (2008b) 'The State of Sudan Divestment: An Overview of States, Cities, Universities, Companies, and Private Pensions Currently Working on Sudan Divestment', Washington, DC: SDTF. Available at: www.sudandivestment.org/position.asp#state. Accessed 15 March 2008.

Swedberg, R. (2003) *Principles of Economic Sociology*, Princeton, NJ: Princeton University Press.

Sweeney, J.J. (2002) 'Labour Day Address', Washington, DC: AFL-CIO. Available at: www.aflcio.org/mediacenter/prsptm/sp09012002.cfm. Accessed 17 February 2004.

Tamm, I.J. (2004) 'Dangerous Appetites: Human Rights Activism and Conflict Commodities', *Human Rights Quarterly*, Vol. 26, pp. 687–704.

Tanner, M. (1996) 'Public Opinion and Social Security Privatization', Washington, DC: Cato Institute.

Taylor, M. (2006) *From Pinochet to the Third Way: Neoliberalism and Social Transformation in Chile*, London: Pluto Press.

Taylor, M. (ed.) (2008) *Global Economy Contested – Power and Conflict across the International Division of Labour*, London: Routledge.

Teivainen, T. (2002) *Enter Economism, Exit Politics: Experts, Economic Policy and the Political*, London: Zed.

Thompson, E.P. (1991) *The Making of the English Working Class*, London: Penguin.

Tkac, P. (2006) 'One Proxy at a Time: Pursuing Social Change through Shareholder Proposals', *Economic Review – Federal Reserve Bank of Atlanta*, third quarter, pp. 1–20.

Toporowski, J. (2000) *The End of Finance: The Theory of Capital Market Inflation, Financial Derivatives and Pension Fund Capitalism*, London: Routledge.

Tosi, H.L., Werner, S., Katz, J.P. and Gomez-Mejia, L.R. (2000) 'How Much Does Performance Matter? A Meta-analysis of CEO Pay Studies', *Journal of Management*, Vol. 26 (2), pp. 301–339.

Tracey, A.M. and Fiorelli, P. (2004) 'Nothing Concentrates the Mind Like the Prospect of a Hanging: The Criminalization of the Sarbanes–Oxley Act', *Northern Illinois University Law Review*, Vol. 25 (1), pp. 125–150.

University of California (UC) Sudan Divestment Task Force (2006) 'Presentation and Workshop on Targeted Investment'. Available at: http://inosphere.com/sudan/home. asp. Accessed 12 January 2008.

U.S. Chamber of Commerce (2006) 'Shareholder Activism: The Good, the Bad, and the Ugly', Remarks By Thomas J. Donohue, President and CEO, U.S. Chamber of Commerce at Equities Magazine Conference, Yale Club, New York. Available at: www.uschamber.com/press/speeches/2006/060421_shareholders_activism.htm. Accessed 3 February 2007.

Useem, M. (1984) *Large Corporations and the Rise of Business Political Activity in the U.S. and U.K,* New York: Oxford University Press.

Useem, M. (1993) *Executive Defense: Shareholder Power and Corporate Reorganization,* Cambridge, MA: Harvard University Press.

Van Apeldoorn, B. and Horn, L. (2007) 'The Marketisation of European Corporate Control: A Critical Political Economy Perspective', *New Political Economy,* Vol. 12 (2), pp. 211–235.

Van den Berghe, L. and De Ridder, L. (1999) *International Standardisation of Good Corporate Governance,* Boston: Kluwer Academic Publishers.

VanDerhei, J.L. (2002) 'The Role of Company Stock in 410(k) Plans', *Risk Management & Insurance Review,* Vol. 5 (1), pp. 1–20.

Veblen, Thorstein ([1923] 1996) *Absentee Ownership: Business and Enterprise in Recent Times – The Case of America,* Piscataway, NJ: Transaction.

Vives, X. (2000) *Corporate Governance: Theoretical and Empirical Perspectives,* Cambridge: Cambridge University Press.

Vogel, D. (1978) *Lobbying the Corporation: Citizen Challenges to Business Authority,* New York: Basic Books.

Weber, H. (2004) 'The "New Economy" and Social Risk: Banking on the Poor?' *Review of International Political Economy,* Vol. 11 (2), pp. 356–386.

Wei, S. and Milkiewicz, H. (2003) 'A Case of "Enronitis"? Opaque Self-Dealing and the Global Financial Effect', Policy Brief No. 118 Washington, DC: Brookings Institution.

Weismann, M.M. (2004) 'Corporate Transparency or Congressional Window-Dressing? The Case Against Sarbanes–Oxley as a Means to Avoid Another Corporate Debacle: The Failed Attempt to Revive Meaningful Regulatory Oversight', *Stanford Journal of Law, Business & Finance,* Vol. 10 (1), pp. 98–137.

Weller, C.E. (2004) 'Bush's "Few and Rich Owners"-ship Society', Centre for American Progress Action Fund. Available at: www.americanprogressaction.org/issues/2004/few_rich.html. Accessed 3 March 2006.

Weller, C.E. and White, D. (2001) 'The New Kid on the Block: Unions are Playing their Institutional Investor Card', *Social Policy,* Vol. 31 (3), pp. 46–52.

Westbrook, D.A. (2004) 'Telling All: The Sarbanes–Oxley Act and the Ideal of Transparency', *Michigan State Law Review,* Vol. 2, pp. 441–462.

White House (2002) 'Remarks by the President at Signing of H.R. 3763, the Sarbanes-Oxley Act of 2002', Washington, DC: White House. Available at: www.whitehouse.gov/news/releases/2002/07/20020730–1.html. Accessed 14 June 2006.

White House (2004) 'Fact Sheet: America's Ownership Society: Expanding Opportunities'. Speech Delivered by President George W. Bush. Available at: www.whitehouse.gov/news/releases/2004/08/20040809–9.html. Accessed 15 August 2005.

White House (2005a) 'State of the Union Address', Washington, DC: White House. Available at: www.whitehouse.gov/news/releases/2005/02/20050202–11.html. Accessed 16 March 2006.

White House (2005b) 'Strengthening Social Security for Future Generations: Presidential Action'. Available at: www.whitehouse.gov/infocus/social-security. Accessed 17 March 2007.

Wilshire Consulting (2005) 'Permissible Equity Markets Investment Analysis', prepared for the California Public Employees' Retirement System, Wilshire & Associates.

Wilshire Consulting (2006) 'Exposure Draft – Permissible Equity Markets Investment Analysis', prepared for the California Public Employees' Retirement System, Wilshire & Associates.

Wolfensohn, J. (1999) 'A Proposal for a Comprehensive Development Framework', to the Board, Management, and Staff of the World Bank Group from President James D. Wolfensohn on 21 January 1999, Washington, DC: World Bank.

Wolff, E.N. (2006) 'The Retirement Wealth of the Baby Boom Generation', Department of Economics, New York University: Mimeo. Available at: www.carnegie-rochester. rochester.edu/April06-pdfs/wolff2006.pdf. Accessed 5 February 2007.

World Bank (1994) *Averting the Old Age Crisis: Policies to Protect the Old and Promote Growth*, Oxford: Oxford University Press.

World Bank (2002) *World Development Report 2002: Building Institutions for Markets*, New York: Oxford University Press.

World Bank (2004) *World Development Report 2004: A Better Investment Climate for Everyone*, New York: Oxford University Press.

World Bank (2005) 'Global Development Report: Mobilizing Finance and Managing Vulnerability'. Available at: http://econ.worldbank.org/WBSITE/EXTERNAL/EXTDEC/ EXTDECPROSPECTS/EXTGDF/EXTGDF2005/0,,contentMDK:20341503~menuPK :544389~pagePK:64167689~piPK:64167673~theSitePK:544381,00.html. Accessed 4 January 2006.

World Bank (2006), *World Development Report 2006: Equity and Development*, New York: Oxford University Press.

World Bank (2007) *Global Development Finance 2007: The Globalization of Corporate Finance in Developing Countries*, New York: Oxford University Press.

World Bank (2008) *Global Development Finance 2008: The Role of International Banking*, New York: Oxford University Press.

Zeitlin, M. (1974) 'Corporate Ownership and Control: The Large Corporation and the Capitalist Class', *The American Journal of Sociology*, Vol. 79 (5), pp. 1073–1119.

Zeitlin, M. (1989) *The Large Corporation and Contemporary Classes*, New Brunswick, NJ: Rutgers University Press.

Zhuang, J., Edwards, D., Webb, D. and Capulong, M. (eds) (2000) *Corporate Governance and Finance in East Asia: A Study of Indonesia, Republic of Korea, Malaysia, Philippines, and Thailand*, Manila: Asian Development Bank.

Zingales, L. (1998) 'Corporate Governance', in Newman, P. (ed.) *The New Palgrave Edition of Economics and the Law*, London: Stockton Press, pp. 497–502.

Index

9/11 events 33
401(k) plans 26, 31, 34–5, 36, 40, 41, 90

AARP (American Association of Retired Persons) 29, 32
ABB (Swiss power company) 149
ABS (asset-backed securities) 58–9
access: in social security 42–3
accountability 11, 48, 53, 55, 71, 98
activist funds 84
ADRs (American depository receipts) 167n34
AFL-CIO (American Federation of Labor and Congress of Industrialized Organizations) 29, 32, 63, 97
Africa 136
'Africanism' 151
AFSCME (American Federation of State, County, and Municipal Employees) 31–2, 68, 70, 84
agency theory 4, 5, 48, 52, 69
agent–principle relations 5, 55
AI (Amnesty International) 145, 156–7
AIG (American International Group Inc.) 50, 68
Albo, Greg 102
Altvater, Elmar 56–7
American Association of Retired Persons (AARP) see AARP
American depository receipts (ADRs) see ADRs
American Enterprise Institute 26
American Federation of Labor and Congress of Industrialized Organizations (AFL-CIO) see AFL-CIO
American Federation of State, County, and Municipal Employees (AFSCME) see AFSCME

American International Group Inc. (AIG) see AIG
American Marxist Sociology 163n2
Amnesty International (AI) see AI
Angelides, Phil 121
Anglo-American model 4, 8, 48, 112, 118–19, 128, 132, 133
anti-Apartheid campaigns 141, 142
anti-market activists 84
anti-value activism 72–3, 85, 99, 103
Apple Inc. 63
arbitrage capitalism 56–7, 58, 61, 109
Arkansas Teachers' pension scheme 58
Arthur Andersen 33
asset-backed securities (ABS) see ABS

backdating scandals 50, 63, 97
Bakan, Joel 7, 14
ballot systems 68–9, 70–1, 84
Ban Ki-moon 157–8
Bankers Trust 34
banking institutions 78
bankruptcies 11, 35, 45
Barber, Randy 30, 95
Barclays Bank 84
Barclays Global Investors 29, 67, 73, 81, 148
Barclays iShares MSCI Emerging Markets Index Fund 154
Bebchuck, Lucian Arye 71, 73
benchmarking strategies 111
Berkshire Hathaway Inc. 66–7, 73, 81, 84, 155
Berle, Adolf 9, 74–5
Berle–Means thesis 74–6, 77
Better Investment Climate for Everyone, A 115–16
Bharat Heavy Electricals 146
Bivens, L. Josh 96